Publisher
buybook
Radićeva 4, Sarajevo
Telephone:+387 33 716-450, 716-451
Zelenih beretki 8, Sarajevo
            +387 33 712-010, 712-011
E-mail: fabrikaknjiga@buybook.ba
           www.buybook.ba

For Publisher
Goran Samardžić
Damir Uzunović

Authors
Tim Clancy
Willem van Eekelen

Contributing author
John Snyder

Design
Nedim Meco

Printed in Croatia by Zrinski

CIP - Katalogizacija u publikaciji
Nacionalna i univerzitetska biblioteka
Bosne i Hercegovine, Sarajevo

338.483 (497.6) (036)

CLANCY, Tim
    Central and north Bosnia : a guided journey
through Central and north Bosnia / Tim Clancy,
Willem van Eekelen. - Sarajevo : Buybook, 2005. -
171 str. : ilustr. ; 22 cm

ISBN 9958-630-61-3
1. Eekelen, Willem van
COBISS.BH-ID 13953542

Text copyright ©2005 Tim Clancy & Willem van Eekelen
Photographs copyright ©2005 Tim Clancy, Samir Arnautović,
Brank Media d.o.o., JICA Study Team & Tuzla Canton Tourism Association
All rights reserved. No part of this publication may be reproduced, stored in a
retrieval system, or transmitted in any form, electronic, mechanical, photocopying,
recording or otherwise without prior consent of the publishers

A GUIDED JOURNEY THROUGH

CENTRAL & NORTH BOSNIA

Tim Clancy
Willem van Eekelen

buybook
Sarajevo, 2006

A guide to Central & North Bosnia

To Sanja who, uniquely, always sees
things as they are.

THE SERIES

As Bosnia and Herzegovina emerges as one of the newest and most exciting tourist destinations in Europe, there is a growing need for detailed and thorough information on this country. In response to this demand **buybook** publishing company now offers a series of new books that cover the cultural, historical, natural and culinary heritage of Bosnia and Herzegovina. Four books are on the shelves already:
- Sarajevo and the surrounding areas
- Herzegovina
- Central and North Bosnia
- Forgotten Beauty – Hiking to BiH's highest peaks

More titles are to follow.

The first part of the regional guides is a general introduction to Bosnia and Herzegovina. This section is the same for each of the guides and provides you with the standard information needed to enjoy a journey in any part of the country. The second part of each guide is a comprehensive and region-specific travel companion, covering hotels, restaurants, café's and clubs, transport, travel agencies and a wide range of activities for all types of visitor. Each guide also has an eco-tourism section highlighting the natural beauties, flora and fauna, wildlife photography, fly-fishing, and more. The guides cover all major destinations, but also a great many places that are off the beaten track. In many cases, you will need a detailed map to find these hidden treasures.

Welcome to the brighter side of Bosnia and Herzegovina – enjoy your trip!!

CONTENTS

Acknowledgements 11

THE COUNTRY

Background Information 13
Facts and Figures 13
Geography 14
Climate 17
Flora and Fauna 17
People 20
Demographics 20
Language 21
Economy 22
Religion 24
Culture 25
History 30

Practical Information 45
When to visit 45
Entering Bosnia and Herzegovina 45
Diplomatic missions 46
Getting there and away 49
Tourist information 55
Maps 56
Health 56
Safety 57
What to take 59
Media 60
Communications 61
Money 63
Budgeting 64
Accommodation 65
Eating 66
Drinking 68
Public holidays 70
Shopping 70
Interacting with local people 71

CENTRAL BOSNIA 75
Zenica 76
Vareš 79, Olovo 79
Kraljeva Sutjeska 80
Bobovac 81
Visoko 83
Kreševo 83
Fojnica 84
Vranica Mountain 85
Travnik 86
Vlašić Mountain 92, Bugojno 94
Jajce 95
Šipovo 97, Mrkonjić grad 98
Pliva River Region 98
Introduction to the Pliva River Region 99,
Fishing 100, Kayaking and boating 106,
Herb and mushroom collection 107,
Wildlife viewing, birding and photo safaris 109

CENTRAL WEST BOSNIA 113
Livno 113
Tomislavgrad 114
Blidinje Nature Park 115
Kupres 116

NORTH BOSNIA 119

NORTHWEST BOSNIA: BOSANSKA KRAJINA 121
Banja Luka 122
Around town 129
Prijedor 130
Kozara National Park 131, Eco-Centre Loncari 131
Bihać 131
Una river 133, Krupa 136, Cazin 137,
Velika Kladuša 138, Drvar 138, Sanski Most 139

NORTHEAST BOSNIA 141
Tuzla 142
Kladanj 147
Bijeljina 147
Brčko 148
Gradačac 148
Srebrenik 149
Doboj 149
Gračanica 150, Teslić 150, Tešanj 151,
Maglaj 152, Zavidovići 152
Nature Park Tajan 153
Zvornik 155
Srebrenica 156

APPENDIX	**LANGUAGE 161**
APPENDIX	**MORE INFORMATION 165**
	INDEX 168

ACKNOWLEDGEMENTS

We're happy to say that there are many people to thank. Where to start? Let's go full circle... this project started in 2001, during our hike in one of Europe's last primeval forests in Sutjeska National Park. Two things struck us: this was the most beautiful place we had ever seen, and there wasn't a soul in sight. Tourists, apparently, didn't know about this country's beauty.

Three years later, in the spring of 2004, Paddy Ashdown and three representatives from Bosnia and Herzegovina traveled around Europe to shed some light on this hidden little treasure called Bosnia and Herzegovina. This generated, perhaps for the first time, large scale interest in the 'lighter side' of this country. To turn interest into visits, people need information – henceforth, our chance to write this booklet!

The creation of this series had many contributors. The Japan International Cooperation Agency allowed us to use their wonderful research, which greatly enhanced the eco-tourism section of this series. John Snyder did some of the best research on wildlife habitats, fly-fishing, fish species identification and the entire eco-tourism package to date. The European Youth Group, with its great corps of volunteers, did great research on Sarajevo and Banja Luka. Boris Rebac, Barbara-Anne Krijgsman and many people at the various tourism associations suggested valuable additions. Jim Marshall did many fine-tunings to the text and his tremendous knowledge of the conflict will certainly help the reader understand a bit better what happened here. Others wrote texts as well – as is indicated in the text. Thanks to Trudi Bolten and Hans van Eekelen too: they edited the first part of this booklet.

Azra Skajlo at Green Visions showed once again how patient she can be after we repeatedly placed tasks on her desk to check and double-check phone numbers, addresses and whatever else was needed. Thanks Azra. The same thanks go to Suad Salkić, who spent many evenings verifying and adding all sorts of things.

Brank Media were very generous and allowed us to use some of their amazing photographs. The Dutch Embassy kindly covered much of the costs of producing this series. For that to happen, Hans de Vries did his bit of proposal writing – and came to love the country so much that he is now married to Sabina. Thanks Hans, and congratulations!

CENTRAL & NORTH BOSNIA

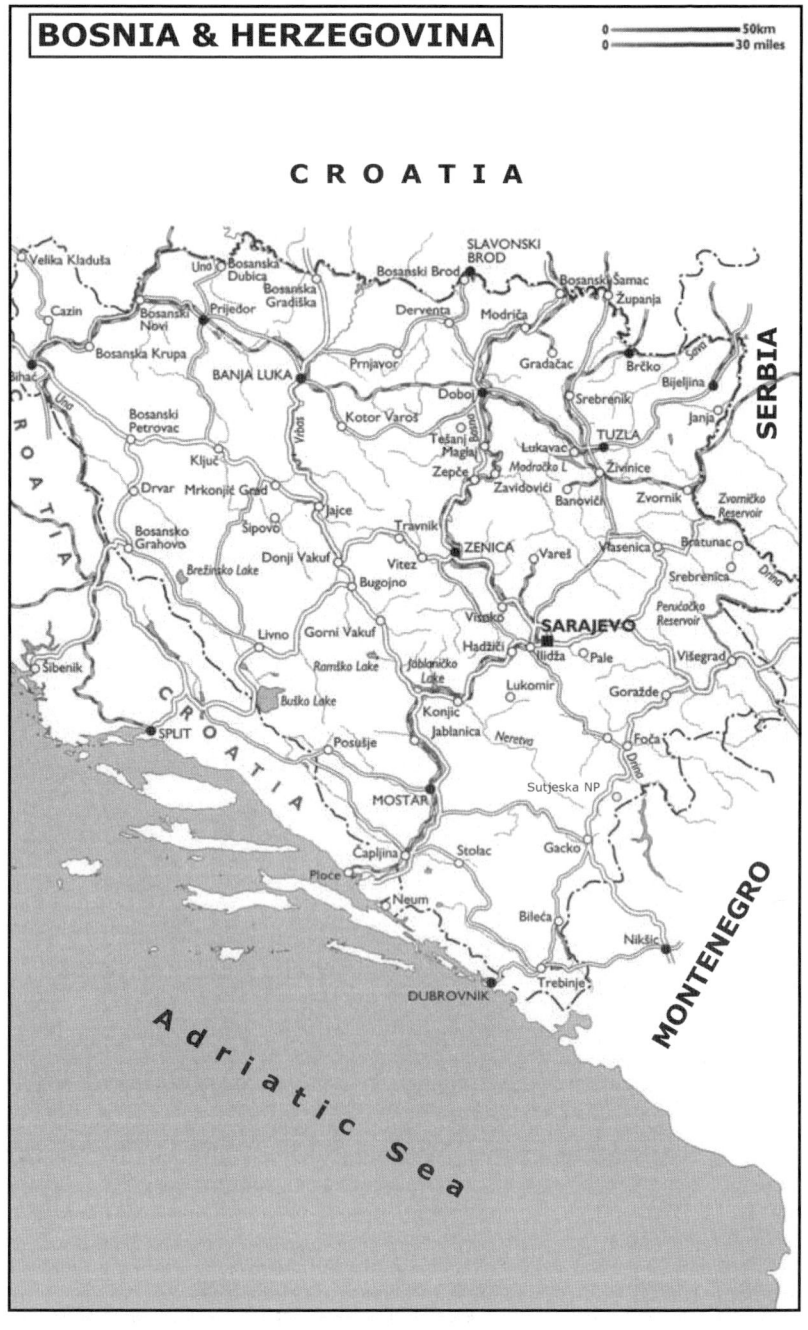

THE COUNTRY

BACKGROUND INFORMATION

Facts & Figures

Location: Southeast Europe, bordering Croatia (932 km), Serbia (312 km) and Montenegro (215 km)
Land area: 51,129 km²
Status: Republic
Languages: Bosnian, Croatian, Serbian
Population: probably around 3.8 million
Religions: Muslim (44%), Orthodox Christian (32%), Roman Christian (17%), Others (7%)
Capital: Sarajevo, with a population of around 400,000
Other major cities and towns in the country: Banja Luka, Tuzla, Zenica, Mostar, Bihać
Administrative division: The country is divided into two entities: the Federation of Bosnia and Herzegovina, and the Republika Srpska. The Federation of Bosnia and Herzegovina is subdivided into ten cantons.
Time: CET (GMT + 1 hour)
Currency: Convertible Mark (KM or BAM)
International telephone code: +387

Bosnia and Herzegovina is a long name for a country that measures just over 50,000 km². Bosnia covers the north and centre of the country. Its name is probably derived from 'bosana', an old Indo-European word meaning water, and refers to the country's many rivers, streams and springs. The southern region of ancient Hum, ruled by Herceg Stjepan (Duke Stjepan), was later named Herzegovina after the region was conquered by the invading Ottomans. Together, these two areas form a triangular country in the middle of what used to be Yugoslavia. It is a mountainous country that borders on Croatia and Serbia & Montenegro, two other former Yugoslav republics. It is here that eastern and western civilizations met, often clashed but also enriched and reinforced each other.

GEOGRAPHY

The trip from Sarajevo to Mostar is a two-hour drive. Halfway, a tunnel links Bosnia to Herzegovina. On the one side of this tunnel there is lush vegetation on gently rolling hills. On the other side there are the high, rugged mountains of the Dinaric Alps. This mountain range is the natural boundary of the Mediterranean and continental Alpine climates. The warm Adriatic temperatures clash with the harsher Alpine ones, producing one of the most diverse eco-systems in Europe. A bit further towards Mostar, these mountains are gone again and you are in a fertile flatland. That is Bosnia and Herzegovina: three worlds in a two hour drive. Had I been in a different bus when writing this section, I would have started it with moonlands, waterfalls, piping hot spring water steaming up to the road, snow (in May), fierce rivers, thick medieval forests and green mountain lakes.

Land

Much of Bosnia and Herzegovina is mountainous. The long chain of the Southern Alps – the Dinaric Alps - stretches from northwest Croatia through the heart of Bosnia and Herzegovina and into Montenegro, and finishes in the Prokletija Mountains on the Albanian border. Herzegovina hosts the highest and wildest of this mountain range, which for centuries provided the population protection from Roman invaders, and which slowed the Ottoman conquest of Bosnia.

Other parts of the country – even the other mountainous parts - look very different from the rugged Alpines. The central belt of Bosnia has both rocky mountains and green, rolling hills covered with conifer forests and lined with countless freshwater streams and rivers. Some northern areas are part of the long and agriculturally rich plains that extend from Hungary, through Slavonia and Croatia into the fertile fields of the Sava and Drina River valleys. Part of the northwest of the country is all karst topography, with deep limestone caves and underground rivers. These limestone fields are connected to the low limestone valleys of the south. Together, they form the single largest karst field in the world.

Waterfalls

1. Bukovi na Uni ili Veliki slap
2. Štrbački buk
3. Vodopad Plive
4. Vodopad Skakavac
5. Vodopad Skakavci
6. Kravice
7. Provalija

THE COUNTRY

Mountains

1. Maglić, 2396m
2. Volujak, 2336m
3. Velika Ljubušnja, 2238m
4. Čvrsnica, 2226m
5. Vranica, 2110m
6. Prenj, 2103m
7. Treskavica, 2086m
8. Vran, 2074m
9. Bjelašnica, 2067m
10. Lelija, 2032m
11. Zelengora, 2014m
12. Cincar, 2006m

Mountains in Bosnia and Herzegovina

The Dinaric mountains

From the high central ranges, the Dinaric Alps cut east towards Visočica, Bjelašnica, and Treskavica Mountains. This area has some very deep canyons. Many of the highland settlements here date back to medieval times. Moving further east, bordering Montenegro, are Bosnia and Herzegovina's highest peaks. Protected in Sutjeska National Park, Maglić Mountain (2,386m) towers above the surrounding natural fortresses of Zelengora Mountain, Volujak, Lelija and the Mesozoic walls of Lebršnik Mountain. The young limestone mountains of the Dinaric system can be found in the middle part of the county. Together, these three sub-areas are good for ten peaks above the 2000 metre mark.

Vran	2074m
Čvrsnica	2226m
Čabulja	1789m
Velež	1969m
Prenj	2103m
Bjelašnica	2067m
Visočica	1974m
Crvanj	1921m
Treskavica	2086m
Lelija	2032m
Zelengora	2014m
Ljubišna	2242m
Volujak	2336m
Maglić	2396m (highest peak in the country)

Then, there is the mountain range that forms the natural connection between Herzegovina and Bosnia.

Ivan	950m
Makljen	1123m
Kupreška vrata	1324m
Čemerno	1293m

And lastly, to the north, next to the river Sava and the low basin of the Bosna River, lies the flat valley of Posavina, surrounded by a long stretch of low mountains. These mountains are not high, but they are impressive as they rise like lonely islands out of the valley.

Majevica	916m
Motajnica	652m
Vučjak	368m
Prosara	363m
Kozara	977m

Water

Bosnia and Herzegovina is a country full of water. Much of that water flows under the ground. You can hear it, but you can't always see it. Some underground water exits in the form of submarine springs in the Adriatic Sea. Other water gushes from mountain sides, in springs that come hot and cold and in all shapes and intensities. Many springs appear as a gentle stream, but in Blagaj it's a whole river that gushes out of the mountain. Most water is crystal clear, but some water carries such a density of minerals that the water is colored.

Some water feeds into lakes. The Deransko-Svitavsko Lakes are part of Hutovo blato, a large bird reserve in the south of the country. Boračko Lake and Blidinje Lake are equally beautiful and maintain their own eco-systems. Perhaps even more spectacular are the glacial lakes in the mountain regions of Prenj, Čvrsnica, Satora, Vranica, Treskavica, Crvanj and Volujak.

The country's biggest lake - Buško Lake – is manmade. With an average size of 55km^2, this lake was formed by regulating the waters of the Livanjsko and Duvanjsko valleys, destroying, as artificial lakes often do, unique eco-systems in the process. The most popular tourist lakes are artificial as well: the lakes of Jablanica and Modrac, both formed by hydro-electric dams.

CLIMATE

In Bosnia and Herzegovina, Mediterranean and Alpine influences meet and create a mosaic of climate types within a relatively small area. The south enjoys warm, sunny and dry weather, with very mild winters. In the more continental areas the weather is similar to that of central Europe – hot summers, cool springs and autumns, and cold winters with considerable snowfall. The Mediterranean and continental climates meet in the middle, creating eco-systems that cannot be found anywhere else.

The mountains create a climate of their own. The Alpine climate rules the mountain terrains of the high Dinarics above 1700 meters. The winters there are extremely cold, with temperatures well below zero for more than six months of the year. Snow covers the terrain until summer and the winds often reach hurricane strength.

FLORA AND FAUNA

Bosnia and Herzegovina faces the challenge of preserving its natural wealth, and it is not well prepared. Less than one percent of Bosnia and Herzegovina's land surface is protected – compared to the European average of seven percent – and the country risks losing much of its pristine wilderness and forests to uncontrolled development, clear cutting, and exploitation of its abundant fresh water supply.

Flora

Beech, oak, evergreen, chestnut, spruce and dozens of other types of trees form thick forests that cover over a third of the country. Conversely, black pines often stand alone. Shaped like skinny mushrooms, they do not require earth and grow on rocks, sometimes all alone on otherwise barren mountainsides.

Many of the country's forests are absolutely spectacular, but none matches the rough beauty of Perućica forest. This primeval forest dates back over 20,000 years. It lays in a valley, hidden below Maglić Mountain, the country's highest peak. Here, massive beech trees are complemented by the high black pines that grow on the rock faces that surround the valley. A hike through the heart of these woodlands is an unforgettable and awe-inspiring experience.

The climates suit a surprising variety of plants and trees. The country's central and eastern forests are very similar to those found in northern and central Europe. Herzegovina and western Bosnia, which are covered by large areas of karst, are characterized by vegetation typical of the coastal and mountainous regions of the Mediterranean.

Unsurprisingly, the country's two large floral regions intersect along the same lines, and have a richness that only tropical and sub-tropical regions can match. Very favorable conditions have preserved species from the times of diluvia glaciations right up to the present. Together, the Euro-Siberian and Mediterranean floral regions are home to over 3,700 species of flowering plants, including hundreds of endemic species (species that are unique to the region). If you like flowers, come in spring. You will see them, in their thousands, in all shapes, sizes and colors, and absolutely everywhere.

Fauna

Bosnia and Herzegovina was once home to one of the largest bear populations in the world and had thriving wolf, deer, wild boar and wild goat communities. These populations suffered severely from the war. Throughout the conflict many frontlines were in the high mountain regions. This exposed bear, wild goat, wild boar and wolf populations to heavy gun and artillery fire, and to being hunted for food by soldiers. Many have been killed, or fled to quieter forests in neighboring countries.

Despite their diminished numbers it is not uncommon to see a bear, or occasionally a wolf, in Sutjeska National Park in eastern Bosnia. Most wild goats live in Herzegovina's Neretva Valley, but some are found in Sutjeska National Park and on the southern slopes of Bjelašnica and Visočica Mountains as well. Wild boars have even made a real comeback and are experiencing population overgrowth. They are usually found in lush, conifer areas in the medium sized mountain ranges but can be occasionally be spotted in Herzegovina as well. In addition, there are foxes, otters, pine martens, bobcats, deer, porcupines, many types of snakes and a variety of other little creatures in the country's large stretches of untouched wilderness.

There is a plethora of birds as well. Hutovo blato is the largest bird migration centre in southeast Europe. In these marshy wetlands in southern Herzegovina you can find 240 types of birds, many of them on a migration path between Europe and North Africa. Heron, Greek partridge, coot, owls, pheasants, and wild duck permanently make their home in this tiny oasis. The Brdača Reserve in the north of the country is also a haven for many types of birds and is in the process of attaining protection status. But you don't have to come to parks to see rare birds. The high mountains have always been home to eagles, hawks and falcons and it is not uncommon to see them on a walk or hike almost anywhere in the country. Driving on the main highway from Bihać towards Bosanski Petrovac you are almost guaranteed to spot large hawks perched on the old electricity cables lining the road.

> **Illegal hunting**
>
> In talks about the tourism potential of Bosnia and Herzegovina, people in the business regularly list their hunting grounds as attraction number one. Hunters should come to Bosnia and Herzegovina, they say, and shoot bear. This is illegal, but apparently hunting regulation is so poorly enforced that some people feel they can ignore it completely. That is most unfortunate, as bear and other populations have been depleted as a consequence of illegal hunting, mines, and a mass exodus during the war years.

Fish are abundant in Bosnia and Herzegovina. Most of the fresh water rivers are teeming with trout. Carp, grayling, and bass are found throughout the country. These fish are of some economic importance: the first organized tour group that returned to Bosnia and Herzegovina after the war was here for fly-fishing, and this type of tourism is bound to increase, creating employment in otherwise rather peripheral parts of the country.

THE COUNTRY

PEOPLE

The geography and climate of Bosnia and Herzegovina have had a profound influence on the country's people. A rugged and creative mountain culture has emerged from this region, connecting man and nature in ways rarely seen in modern times. Every second mountain walk will pass by an ancient village that preserves 'old world' Europe. Here, modern medicines and exotic spices will never replace the medicinal herbs that have long been used to cure illnesses, heal wounds, improve circulation and spice up meals.

In the open valleys between these mountains sprawl Mostar, Jablanica, Konjic, Sarajevo, Foča and many other towns. They are all very old. Some of them – Mostar, Travnik – once grew at strategic places along trade routes. Others – Srebrenica, Tuzla – were founded on the wealth of minerals. Gold, silver, salt, and copper have all been mined here since Roman times.

In the south, the rivers and Mediterranean climate offer ideal conditions for agricultural settlements, and the Neretva River Valley and the Neretva Delta have been inhabited since the Paleolithic Age. These areas produce fruits such as figs, oranges, mandarins, and pomegranates, and have had a winemaking tradition since Roman times. In the north, water has been equally valuable. Jointly, the Una, Sana and Vrbas Rivers have long protected the area against invaders. The fertile valleys these rivers created are sacred to their inhabitants, and guests will find these rivers spoken of as members of the family.

DEMOGRAPHICS

According to the last population census there were 4,354,911 inhabitants in Bosnia and Herzegovina in 1991. Due to war-related death and migration, that number is lower now. Policy makers estimate that the country's population is now around 3.8 million people and steadily growing, and that over one million Bosnians now live abroad. The ethnic composition remains similar to the pre-war percentages: Bosniacs (Muslims) 44%, Serbs (Christian Orthodox) 32%, and Croats (Catholics) 17%. The remaining 7% of the population is composed of Yugoslavs, Albanians, Gypsies, Jews, and several other minority groups.

If ever a new census were to be held, I would be intrigued to know the population's division by sex. Wherever I look, I see more women than men. Is that true, or could it be my flawed perspective? The war probably had its impact. But isn't the male-dominated fighting compensated by the female-dominated outward migration? I don't know. A few friends told me that women have always outnumbered men in some of the country's main towns and cities.

LANGUAGE

> ### The politics of language
>
> Americans speak English; Austrians speak German; and until not long ago the southern Slavs spoke Serbo-Croatian. The political fractions that occurred in the early 1990's brought along with it the politics of language as well. Bosnian, Croatian and Serbian barely differ at all, but are nonetheless considered three different languages. It is a political choice, not a linguistic reality, as the border police illustrated when I said the exact same sentence four times when driving from Sarajevo to Belgrade via Croatia:
>
> Exiting Bosnia and Herzegovina: 'Hey, where did you learn to speak Bosnian?'
>
> Entering Croatia: 'Hey, where did you learn to speak Croatian?'
>
> Exiting Croatia: 'Hey, where did you learn to speak Croatian?'
>
> Entering Serbia and Montenegro: 'Hey, where did you learn to speak Serbian?'

The pre-war language of former Yugoslavia was Serbo-Croat. This term is virtually extinct now. Nowadays, there are three 'official' languages spoken in Bosnia and Herzegovina: Bosnian, Croatian, and Serbian. Local people attach great importance to the name of the language. For practical purposes, these languages are one and the same. The differences are similar to those between American and British English.

Bosnian/Croatian/Serbian is a Slavic language. Many words are similar in Czech or Slovakian, even Polish and Ukrainian. The language is distinctly different from but part of the same family as Russian. Illustrating the common Ottoman past, there are many Ottoman words that Bosnia and Herzegovina shares with the Egyptian dialect of Arabic.

In the Federation only the Latin alphabet is used, but in the Republika Srpska, the other of the two entities of Bosnia and Herzegovina, many signs are in Cyrillic. This includes road signs. If you are unable to decipher that script you might find it difficult to know exactly where you are.

In the cities it is not uncommon to find English-speaking people. Because of the large refugee and migrant population that lived in Germany during the war there are many German speakers as well. In the rural areas neither language is spoken among the adults, but there may well be children able to chat with you in English. Some useful words and phrases can be found in the language section of the Appendix.

Sign Language

Although isolated by a large mountain range, Bosnia and Herzegovina possesses many Mediterranean characteristics. Body and hand language is one of them. If a non-English speaking person is having trouble communicating with you, be prepared for him or her using other means to get the message across. People here don't behave like British or Americans and just speak louder – they *move*. So:

- If a Bosnian makes a waving motion (sort of like 'come here') in the vicinity of his or her mouth: would you like to eat?
- If a local takes a hitchhiker's thumb and bobs it towards his or her mouth: would you like a drink?
- If one pinches the forefinger and thumb together, with the pinky finger out and gently bobs the hand: let's go for a coffee.
- If the right arm shoots up above the shoulder: either 'forget it' or 'screw you'...your call.
- If the right arm sweeps across the front of the chest like hitting a ball or something: 'don't worry about it'...'so what'
- A thumbs up does not mean you are great or that things are OK – it means one, the number one.
- The neck disappearing into the shoulders and both hands shrugging in front means 'it wasn't me' or 'how do I know?'
- The index and pointer finger, tapped against the lips: can you spare a cigarette?

ECONOMY

Imagine this. There is a place that goes through a devastating war. Before the war, the place was a relatively poor and underdeveloped part of a country with a centrally planned economy. After the war, the place is an independent nation in the midst of an intensely competitive free market world economy. Before the war, there used to be import protection and there were secure trade links with the wealthier republics of the country it then belonged to. In times of hardship, these wealthier republics cushioned the blows by providing some economic support. After the war, this now independent nation is bound by free trade agreements with the rest of the world. Even without any further impediments, businesses would find it almost impossible to compete successfully in this whole new setting. This place, obviously, is Bosnia and Herzegovina, and unfortunately there *are* further impediments.

Before the war, Bosnia and Herzegovina concentrated on the production of basic goods (wood, agricultural produce, iron bars) and intermediate products (parts of cars, parts of shoes, parts of furniture). Other regions of former Yugoslavia bought these intermediate products and used them to make final consumer products. Because of the war, these buyers had to find new suppliers. After the war, these buyers will only come back to their pre-war suppliers if these suppliers offer the best and cheapest products available on the world market. With factories in shambles, infrastructure destroyed and workers displaced or killed, producing the best and cheapest products is not an easy task.

The war came to an end with a peace agreement that dictates a horrifyingly complex government structure. A company has to deal with several layers of government, each of which has complicated and sometimes non-sensible legislation. A simple change of business address, for example, requires procedures at the level of the municipality, canton, entity, and state. New companies face complex pre-war anti-private sector legislation and a government that provides problems rather than support in return for tax money. The only companies that benefit from the government – in the form of subsidies – are the public companies of the past. Without government support, very few of them would stay in business. In many cases, they have become uncompetitive dinosaurs, using outdated equipment and led by people chosen for their political affiliation rather than their technical expertise.

Imagine all this. It is a miracle that Bosnia and Herzegovina has some sort of functioning economy at all.

Ever since the Dayton Peace Accords were signed at the end of 1995, Bosnia and Herzegovina has been in a long, slow and painful process of economic recovery. The reform process has been slow for a number of reasons. First, there is no tested recipe for the economic revitalisation of a place that left the world economy as part of a centrally planned country and re-emerged as a war-torn independent country in a competitive free-market economy. It is simply not known what such a country should do to adapt. Second, pro-business legislation causes harm in the short run. People will lose their jobs and this is a particularly bad time to lose one's job. For obvious reasons, politicians and people will resist such legislation. Third, the focus in the immediate post-war years has been on political consolidation, not economic development. Fourth, there are very few seasoned economists available. Even the international organizations often resort to recruiting junior anthropologists to tackle issues that require senior and specialized economists. And lastly: corrupt government officials and a thriving mafia have not been helpful.

And yet, not all is bad. The currency is strong, inflation is low, the country is not heavily indebted, and much of the infrastructure has by now been reconstructed. In addition, some bad indicators do not reflect reality. At roughly 40 percent, the official unemployment rate indicates a non-functioning economy. In reality, many people registered as unemployed work in the informal sector. Similarly, the people who moved abroad have proven to be exceptionally loyal to the people they left behind. In all likelihood, they will continue to send money in the years to come. Most economists do not consider remittances a healthy economic foundation and point out that these remittances allow for the continuation of an import-based economy. True, but there is a difference between the long-term perspective and the short-term needs: the fact is that, as in other unstable (post) war parts of the world – Lebanon, the Palestinian Territories - this cash inflow does keep things afloat in times of hardship.

The next few years will be crucial. Will Bosnia and Herzegovina be able to come closer to Europe? Will the country manage to cut back its bureaucracy, privatise its public companies, and attract investments? Will logging, agriculture, steel, mining, services, textiles and building materials be the economic pillars of the future, or will new sectors arise? Will the country manage to utilise more fully its potential in agriculture (with a competitive advantage in organic farming), eco-tourism, hydro-electric power (many large dams function at only a quarter of their full potential), and wood-processing? Will the country perhaps regain its role as a producer of intermediate goods, once again supplying factories in the surrounding countries? When I look at many of the politicians, I am not very hopeful. But when I visit trade fairs and see an ever-increasing number of young companies that successfully identified market niches, I tend to think that Bosnia and Herzegovina has a bright future to look forward to.

RELIGION

In this country it is hard to find a town that doesn't have both churches and mosques. This illustrates that, indeed, Bosnia and Herzegovina is at the crossroad of eastern and western civilizations. Despite the wars, the area of Bosnia and Herzegovina has survived for over five centuries as a very multi-religious part of the world.

The medieval Bosnian church is a good starting point for understanding contemporary Bosnia and Herzegovina. Inheriting the fierce self-reliant attitude from the indigenous Illyrian clans, the newly arrived Slavic tribes adopted their own form of Christianity. While most of Europe and the Balkans were under the influence of either of the two major Christian belief systems, geographically isolated Bosnia and Herzegovina celebrated a Christian god with many elements of paganism, and without the structure and hierarchy of the organized churches. Both Catholicism and Orthodoxy vied for power in the region, but the Bosnian Church was able to maintain its unique belief system for centuries.

The arrival of the Ottomans had a more substantial religious influence on the history of Bosnia and Herzegovina than the Orthodox and Catholic submission attempts of the previous period. The first Muslims came to the region in the mid-fifteenth century, and over the next one hundred and fifty years Bosnia saw a large portion of its population convert to Islam. In the sixteenth century a fourth group entered the region. Many of the Sephardic Jews that had been expelled from Spain in 1492 resettled in Sarajevo, Mostar, Travnik and other major Bosnian cities.

In Tito's Yugoslavia, most people strayed from their religious beliefs. Religious practice was allowed but frowned upon, secularism was encouraged and the religious leaders were chosen by the communist party. For a number of reasons, the breakdown of Yugoslavia has caused a significant rise in the sense of religious belonging. First, people felt more at ease practicing their religions after the collapse of a country that was, essentially, proudly atheist. Second, a war and the suffering it causes often brings religion to the forefront. Third, this particular war was fought on ethnic lines and made many people more aware of their ethnic and thus religious identity. Fourth, and unfortunately, some of the religious revival can be attributed to nationalist agendas that use religion to inspire hatred.

Notwithstanding all the political rhetoric, the three main religious groups have influenced each other in the course of the five centuries in which they lived together. Consequently, and although many nationalists would deny it, Islam, Orthodoxy and Catholicism in Bosnia and Herzegovina are quite different from Islam, Orthodoxy and Catholicism anywhere else. Believers of each group often have more in common with their fellow-Bosnians than with their fellow-believers in other countries.

CULTURE

Some museums are good, but the exhibits of even the best ones do not match the power of the cultural manifestations that you will find everywhere in everyday life. Many of these cultural manifestations have this little twist that makes them unique to Bosnia and Herzegovina. Mosques around the world shy away from depicting living things, but the multicolored mosque in Travnik has elaborate flower scenes painted on the outside. The tombstones that line the countryside show roughly carved people with very large hands – something I have not seen anywhere else in the world. Many houses have no paintings at all, but many others have paintings covering their walls three rows high. Order a plate of meat or fish for a group of people and you will get an artfully composed and humorous mountain of niceties.

In Bosnia and Herzegovina, concepts are pursued until the very end. You see it in literature, where themes are considered from every possible side before the story goes on. You see it in the eye for detail when people dress up. You see it in the composition and variety of a mixed grill. You see it in the copper market in Ferhadija, where anything made of metal – trays, coffee sets, and even bullets and mortars - can be turned into a piece of art.

On the other hand, simplicity is treasured. A Turkish table, an Egyptian tray or a Palestinian dress are all about complexity and detail. Not an inch of material is left uncarved, uncut, unembroidered. Bosnia and Herzegovina shares the same Ottoman heritage, but its tables, trays and attires look decidedly different. They focus on beauty, not complexity. No-Man's Land, the Oscar-winning movie about the war, illustrates that this ability to transmit no-frill messages is still very much alive. The entire war is reduced to three men in a trench.

Art

There are very few cave paintings in Europe older than 14,000 years. The carvings in the Badanj Caves in southern Herzegovina are among them. Closely followed by pottery and artfully sculpted figures (on display at the National Museum in Sarajevo), they are the oldest art yet discovered in Bosnia and Herzegovina.

More refined art forms were taken from the Greeks and the Romans. In the Hellenistic and Roman eras, the Daorsi tribe - ahead of the other tribes - sometimes sided with and was influenced by both. The Daorsi left Hellenistic town remnants and moulds from jewelers' workshops. They introduced the symbols of early Christianity to the region, and left behind beautiful basilicas and mosaics.

These Paleolithic, Neolithic, Hellenistic and Roman remains are interesting, but do not yet show Bosnia and Herzegovina's unique face. That face appears in the medieval times. A new script appears – bosančica – and there are the symbols and art forms of the Bosnian church. Perhaps the most inspiring of these are the engraved tombstones, stećci in Bosnian, that still dot the countryside. These stećci, with pagan and Christian symbols of earth, moon, family, animals, dance and crosses, form a permanent reminder of the early Slavs' creativity.

Four centuries of Ottoman rule had a profound impact on the region. The many Ottoman bridges, mosques, markets, houses, libraries, dervish convents, streets and trading route resting places still give the country a decidedly oriental feel. Many of these Ottoman treasures are outside or can be visited. In the same period, the Christians painted the frescoes, icons and paintings that can be seen in the country's many monasteries. The orthodox monasteries of Paprača, Lomnica, Dobričevo, Žitomislići and Trijebanj and the Catholic monasteries of Kraljeva Sutjeska, Fojnica, Kreševo, Olovo, Gorica and Toliša are all well worth a visit.

Contemporary art has been influenced by all that preceded it. The Ottoman heritage lives forth in the work of the copper, gold, silver and leather crafts, and in the paintings of Safet Zec (famous for his delicate paintings of the oriental feel of a European Bosnia) and Mersad Berber (who portrays Muslim life in works such as Chronicle About Sarajevo). Other painters such as Gabriel Jurkić and Karlo Mijić and the abstract work of Affan Ramić depict the natural wonders of the Bosnian landscape, demonstrating the intimate ties between man and nature.

The war shines through in much of the most recent work of artists around the country. Artists display expressions of resistance, hope and peace. Sculpture, paintings, graffiti and graphic design all portray the new generation's struggle to heal the wounds of the past and rid the collective consciousness of the lunacy of the war.

Film

Bosnia and Herzegovina has produced some of the finest films to come out of the former Yugoslavia. Even Emir Kusturica, the great filmmaker from Serbia, was born and raised here. The modern film scene has taken off with the production of Danis Tanović's No-Man's Land (Ničija zemlja), this country's first-ever Oscar winning movie. In this brilliant tragic comedy, a few opposing soldiers, stuck in an abandoned trench between frontlines, represent the entire war. All is lost. In the end, the last man is left to die, unseen by the media, while an incompetent international representative walks away claiming a successful operation. In the back you hear a Bosnian bedtime song. Go to sleep. All is well.

Other striking movies, mostly about the war, include Perfect Circle (Savršeni krug) by Ademir Kenović, Fuse (Gori vatra) by Pjer Žalica, Re-Make by Dino Mustafić, and Summer in the Golden Valley (Ljeto u zlatnoj dolini), the 2004 winner of the Rotterdam Film Festival Tiger award. One of the latest Bosnian film productions is "Kod amidže Idriza", written by Namik Kabil and directed by Pjer Žalica. The film is a magnificent depiction of the peculiar and pronounced details of a Muslim family from Sarajevo. The attention to detail – particularly Bosnian cuisine and the inability of males to express their emotions - makes it a slow film, but one you don't want to end. If true insight into the heart of a typical Sarajevo family interests you, go see this film.

Literature

Ever since Ottoman times, Bosnia and Herzegovina has been a country of books. Muslim scholars, Serbian priests and Franciscan monks all contributed to Bosnia and Herzegovina's literary tradition.

Throughout the centuries, what shone through most writings was a strong sense of patriotism, the spirit of self-reliance, and the moral issues related to the political and social abuses suffered by all three peoples.

The most important pre-20th century authors

Mustafa Ejubović	Islamic scholarly thought.
Ahmed Sudi	Islamic scholarly thought.
Fevzi Mostarac	Wrote the famous Bulbulistan in 18th-century Persian.
Mula Mustafa Bašeskija	Wrote a diary of life in Sarajevo in the last half of the 1700s. He wrote it in a unique Turkish dialect that was only spoken in Sarajevo.
Hasan Kaimija	A poet who gained popularity as a defender of common folk.
Fra Matija Divković	Wrote the first published book in bosančica in Bosnia and Herzegovina in 1611 (printed in Venice).
Brother Filip Lastrić	The best-known historian of the Bosna Srebrena province. He wrote books that preserved the heritage of the old Bosnian State.
Nicifor Dučić	An orthodox monk who published nine volumes of historical works.
Joanikije Pamučina	Portrayed folklore and history in the Glorious Martyrdom of the Virgin Hristina Rajković.
Gavro Vučković Krajišnik	Wrote Slavery in Freedom or Mirror of Justice in Bosnia and The Bloody Book of Brother Ante Knežević. Both books were banned by the Ottoman government.
Vaso Pelagić	This was the greatest of the 19th-century Bosnian Serb writers. He stood out not only for his literary skill but also as one of the sharpest thinkers and political figures of his time.
Ivan Franjo Jukić	This Franciscan from Banja Luka personified the freedom struggle and wrote great works in many genres reflecting the emancipation movement that dominated 19th-century life in Bosnia and Herzegovina.

In the early twentieth century, many newspapers were established and Bosnian writers were fully exposed to European thought for the first time. After more than four centuries of Ottoman and Austrian rule, a struggle for national identity dominated the literature of this period. It was this struggle that had polarizing effects on the future of Bosnia. On the one hand it paved the way for the union of the southern Slavs. On the other hand it created ethnic rifts amongst the Slavs through the intensity of the nationalist voices which emerged. Ivo Andrić began his writing career in this period.

Alongside the nationalist fervor was the liberal movement of writers in The Comrades Book. This left-wing movement, with a passion for the social issues of the time, produced famous writers such as Novak Šimić, Hasan Kikić and Mak Dizdar. They were catalysts for the cultural revolution of the second half of the 20th century.

The greatest writers in Bosnia's history emerged post World War II in socialist Yugoslavia. Ivo Andrić continued his literary domination in the Bridge over the Drina, Travnik Chronicles and The Damned Yard. In 1961 he was awarded the Nobel Prize for Literature. Soon after, Mak Dizdar and Meša Selimović published two of Bosnia's most famous pieces: Stone Sleeper and Death and the Derviš. In the late sixties yet more masterpieces were published: Nedžad Ibrišimović's Ugursuz, Vitomir Lukić's Album, Skender Kulenović's first book of sonnets, and Branko Ćopić's book of stories The Blue Mallow Garden.

In post-war Bosnia the leading literary thinkers are Aleksandar Hemon, Nenad Veličković, Faruk Šehić, Dario Džamonja, Dževad Karahasan and Marko Vešović. Philosopher and writer Ivan Lovrenović offers one of the most insightful and objective viewpoints in Bosnian intellectual circles. For moving war accounts, read Miljenko Jergović's Sarajevo Marlboro and Zlata Maglajlić's Zlata's Diary. There are many others. They are now scattered across the globe, but their themes and inspiration tend to remain close to home.

The books of many of the writers mentioned here have been translated into English. Some of these books are available at the few bookshops in the country that have a sizeable English language selection.

Music

There are countries where a group of people who spend the evening together enjoy themselves talking or dancing. In Bosnia and Herzegovina, people tend to sing. For an outsider, it is a joy to watch. After an hour or so, somebody starts a 'sevdalinka', and the tone of the evening has been set: there is no more talking from that moment onwards. Instead, songs come and go, with or without instruments, for hours and hours. In just one voice, everybody sings the same nostalgic folk songs about life before the war. And everybody seems to know them all.

Most of this folk music traces its origins to Ottoman times and combines oriental elements with the popular heritage of Bosnia and Herzegovina. Most of these songs are songs of love and tragedy. They helped to get through turbulent times.

The sounds of the highlanders are equally fascinating. The music of the Dinaric shepherds has echoed through the mountain valleys for centuries. This type of mountain yodel is called ojkanje and is a mixed melody of male and female 'oi' sounds. Highlanders have always celebrated in open fields with the 'gluho kolo' or deaf dance. The villages' young bachelors and girls gather for a large circle dance accompanied by song. This ceremony continues through the night. It is often the setting for courting.

Then there is the ganga, a deep, non-instrumental, chant-like music most often sung by Croat men in Herzegovina. There is the Serbian gusle, a type of banjo, that accompanies century-old stories. There are the šargija instruments of the northwest of the country, and there is the Persian saz that most commonly accompanies traditional music in the cities. It's all unique to this region, and it's all equally tantalizing.

There is contemporary music as well. Famous groups from the old Yugoslavia are still held in high regard and their songs still crowd the airwaves. Groups like Bijelo dugme, Zabranjeno pušenje, Indexi and Crvena jabuka represent the climax of Yugoslav 1980s rock. Yesterday's and today's most famous pop stars are probably Dino Merlin and Kemal Monteno. With very different musical styles, they both enjoy huge popularity with young and old.

Sarajevo is the centre of Bosnia and Herzegovina's modern music scene but there are great bands from Mostar, Tuzla and Banja Luka as well. Mostar Sevdah Reunion is a magnificent band with a smooth mix of jazz, blues and a touch of tradition. Jazz bands and clubs have become increasingly popular and every November Sarajevo hosts a great International Jazz Festival. Digital music has hit the scene with Adi Lukovac i Ornamenti and others. But the tradition of rock and alternative music never died, and groups like Knock-Out, Kiks, Tifa, Sikter, and Protest still attract big crowds and play at venues throughout the country. Skroz and Dubioza kolektiv are the most popular new emerging bands.

Classical music, by Keziah Conrad

Sarajevans often pride themselves on sophisticated cultural tastes, including an appreciation for high-quality classical music. This music represents civilization, a link with the wider Western world—but more than that, it signifies beauty, passion, life, hope in the face of the darkest night. Many outsiders are familiar with the story of Vedran Smailović, a cellist in the Sarajevo Philharmonic Orchestra, who defiantly played on the streets and in ruined buildings while bombs and bullets rained down. Musicians have been a crucial part of the restoration of Sarajevo, giving voice to suffering, offering healing through beauty, taking part in projects that cross borders and lead toward reconciliation.

Three institutions are prominent in Sarajevo's classical music scene: the National Theater (with its Philharmonic Orchestra, Opera and Ballet), the Music Academy of Sarajevo University, and "JU Sarajevo Art", which coordinates performances of artists from Bosnia and Herzegovina and beyond. Sarajevo's National Theater opened in 1921, and since that time has been the scene of thousands of theatrical and musical performances. In 2004, musical events produced by the National Theater have included Mozart's *Requiem*, Orff's *Carmina Burana*, Beethoven's 5th Symphony, Verdi's *Nabucco*, Horozić's *Hasanaginica*, and a world premiere of Čavlović's opera *The Women of Srebrenica*. Sarajevo

Art organizes the annual summer festival Baščaršian Nights and an ongoing program of performances by local and international artists.

A range of amateur choirs and cultural societies perform regularly around the country. Several of these, such as Pontanima Interreligious Choir and the women's ensembles Gaudeamus and Allegra, have earned international recognition for their musicianship. Other groups include the choirs of the Cathedral, the Orthodox Church, and the Islamic *medresa* (school of theology).

Classical music in Bosnia and Herzegovina faces severe underfunding and a demoralizing lack of resources that has forced many prominent musicians to leave—but many others have stayed and are still working with passion and talent. Visiting artists and audience members often observe that musicians from this country have an electric energy and striking depth of feeling that is not easy to find elsewhere. Perhaps this is the product of artistry honed by suffering; a living vibrancy that arises out of intimate experience with death.

HISTORY

The history of the region of the former Yugoslavia has, for many, been a bewildering subject. Perhaps the most important thing to keep in mind while trying to fit the pieces of the Bosnian puzzle into a coherent context, is that the nationalist sentiments that were born at the end of the nineteenth century and are alive today, do not reflect the life and sentiments of the tiny, isolated communities of this country from the seventh to thirteenth centuries. The 'mental baggage' that is carried today by Serbs, Croats or Muslims can simply not be applied to a population which previously held no affiliation to a national or ethnic identity. The Orthodox from eastern Herzegovina did not wave a Serbian flag, the Catholics from Bosna srebrena did not have dreams of coming under Zagreb's rule, and the converted Muslim community had no aspirations to create a European Mecca in the heart of Bosnia. It is largely unknown whether the original Slav settlers, well into the Middle Ages, even referred to themselves at all as Serbs or Croats. All too often history is the story of kings and queens, conquerors and defenders, and provides little if any understanding of the life of the ordinary people. The early Slav tribes never engaged in bitter debates or wars over their Serbian or Croatian belonging; they lived in peace with each other, spoke the same language and worshipped the same god. Outside influences often divided communities but the impetus for such divisions never came from within.

In the historical context of Bosnia and Herzegovina much is still argued over, both domestically and internationally. What no one can debate, however, is today's rightful claim of all the peoples of Bosnia and Herzegovina to call this their home. Serbs, Croats and Bosniacs (the term used for Bosnian Muslims, identifying nationality and not religion) can confidently say that their homeland is Bosnia and Herzegovina and that they have been here for many, many generations. Claiming rightful ownership of one group over another from a historical perspective, with all its complexities, is simply an impossibility.

Ancient History

The territory of Bosnia and Herzegovina is profusely scattered with remnants of human life that spans the period from the Paleolithic age to the emergence of the Illyrian clan alliances.

Research into the Stone Age indicates that the northern parts of Bosnia and Herzegovina near the Bosna, Ukrina and Usora rivers were the most developed at that time. The leap from Neanderthal man in the middle Paleolithic, to the homo sapiens of the Late Paleolithic is signified by the first cave drawing of that period, found in Badanj Cave near Stolac in Herzegovina. This rare sample is dated at 12,000BC and there have been similar finds in only three other locations: Spain, France and Italy. The end of the Paleolithic Age saw tremendous climatic change, changes so drastic that much of human life disappeared from this area until about 4,000BC.

After this long, dark Mesolithic period a rich Neolithic culture developed in the third millennium BC. Conditions were ideal for the formation of settlements that developed a new kind of social organization and enjoyed over a millennium of continuity. Many of the fine pottery and arts and crafts of this age are on display in the National Museum in Sarajevo. This highly skilled culture signified a golden age where spiritual life was matched by creative talent. The ancient settlement of Butmir, presently a suburb south of Sarajevo at the base of Igman Mountain, can alone testify to the craftsmanship achieved in that territory by Neolithic man. This unique Neolithic culture disappeared from Bosnia and Herzegovina without a trace somewhere between the third and second millennia BC.

A great metamorphosis swept across the Balkans in a movement that began with the arrival of nomadic tribes from the Black Sea steppes. With their arrival to the Balkans came a new Copper Age. This Aeneolithic period saw a parallel development of stone and metal. The use of metal became increasingly valuable for weapon making, as well-armed tribes from west Pannonia expanded south and southeast towards the end of the second millennium. Wars became more frequent, and Bosnia became very popular for the sanctuary its deep valleys, thick forests and rugged mountains provided.

Illyrians

The first few centuries of the first millennium BC in Bosnia and Herzegovina, as throughout the entire western Balkan Peninsula, saw the gradual creation of a broad ethnic and cultural foundation. From the tribes belonging to the Iron Age culture emerged an ethnic group that history has collectively named the Illyrians.

The Illyrian tribes settled across a large swathe of the western Balkans from the Adriatic Coast in the west to the river Morava in the east, and from present day Albania in the south to the Istrian Peninsula in what today is northwest Croatia. These loosely bound tribes began to form new territorial and economic ties in the middle of the first millennium BC. This process appears to have been the most profound amongst the southern Illyrian tribes, including those tribes of present day Bosnia and Herzegovina.

The Celtic migration inland and the Greek colonies established on the Adriatic Coast in the 4th Century BC, marked a new and painful chapter in Illyrian history. These events brought about significant cultural and spiritual change. It also increased the desire of the Roman Empire to expand and conquer these areas.

The Romans attacked in 229BC, first capturing the islands and crushing the Illyrian navy. In 168BC the famous Illyrian king Gentius was defeated and this gave the Romans a stronghold on Illyrian soil. The inland tribes of Illyria, however, put up a ferocious fight and it took a century and a half of the Romans' best commanders and military forces to defeat the defiant clans. Finally, from 35-33BC, under the direct command of Emperor Octavian, the Roman army launched a major attack that, after the Emperor himself was seriously wounded from a guerilla attack, forced the surrender of the Dalmati clan. The coastal clans were by and large conquered by the overwhelming size of the Roman army.

In the last 'battle royal' for the inland territories held by the Illyrian tribes in what is the heart of present day Bosnia, the clan alliances staged what is known as the *Batonian Uprising*. Two namesakes of large Illyrian tribes united to fend off the invaders. Panicked by the rumors that there were '800,000 insurgents, including 200,000 elite warriors and 9,000 horsemen', Emperor Augustus sent two of his top commanders, Tiberius and Germanicus, to subdue and conquer the fierce and stubborn Illyrians. The fighting went on for years, with both sides exchanging defeats and victories. The last Illyrian stronghold to fall was the citadel at Vranduk near the central Bosnian city of Zenica. According to Roman records, when the Illyrian leader Batan surrendered, the Illyrian women, holding their children, threw themselves into the fire to avoid being captured and enslaved. The Romans incorporated the two Illyrian provinces of Pannonia and Dalmatia into their empire. Some extremely isolated remnants of Illyrian tribes probably survived and eventually assimilated with the Slavs when they arrived in the 7th century.

There are still a few archeological sites that mark the Illyrian civilization in Bosnia and Herzegovina. Many of the Illyrian fortifications were expanded upon by the Romans and later by the Bosnian aristocracy and the Ottomans. New research, however, has uncovered a fascinating aspect of Illyria. At Vranduk in central Bosnia, Blagaj near the Buna River in Herzegovina and on the Cyclopean walls at Osanići near Stolac, finds have indicated that the culture of antiquity came long before the Romans, most likely in Hellenistic form. Osanići was home to the Daorsi tribe and recent archeological findings point to a third century BC link to a northerly extension of the great Hellenistic civilization.

Much of Illyrian culture will forever remain a mystery but one cannot deny the spiritual and cultural impact it has had, even almost two millennia after their disappearance.

Ancient Illyricum

With the fall of the Illyrian clan alliances to the Romans, the territory of present day Bosnia and Herzegovina became part of the vast Roman Empire.

The early period of Roman occupation was peaceful and stable. There were, of course, some tribes who rejected Roman rule but for the most part the efficient Romans quickly set aim at taming Illyricum to cater to the Empire's needs. A Roman administration was established and the task of building roads, mining for iron, gold, lead and rock and mobilizing a large labor force and military were the first priorities. The Illyrians were actively recruited into the Roman army.

The most populated areas continued to be the Empire's regional centers. By the third century AC Illyricum had flourished into a proper Roman province. Its people had equal standing within the Empire and could even aspire to political office. Although Christianity was introduced and largely accepted, elements of Illyrium pagan beliefs were maintained and passed on.

With the disintegration of the western Empire in the fifth century much of the Illyrian lands fell into the hands of the Ostrogoths. The Illyrians again enjoyed a period of relative peace and stability but by the mid-6th century the eastern Empire was able to regain most of the Illyrian lands. As the Roman Empire declined new attacks occurred on the northern frontiers, this time from the Avars and Slavs.

After several centuries of drastic social change in Europe a mélange of cultures made their mark on present day Bosnia and Herzegovina. Basilicas from the late Roman period can be found as their use was continued by the new settlements of Slavs. Remains can be found in Čapljina, Blagaj and Ljubuški in Herzegovina; Breza, Zenica, Travnik and Kiseljak in central Bosnia; and Banja Luka and Mrkonjić Grad in the northwest of the country.

The Slavs

With the fall of the western Empire the new era in Bosnia and Herzegovina was largely dominated by the Slavs. From the sixth century onwards sizeable Slav migration flows came from the east. The Avars gradually retreated to Pannonia but the Slavs remained in their new homeland. It is this ethnic group that most of present day Bosnia and Herzegovina's ethnic make-up is based upon.

Historical evidence of the first centuries of Slav settlements in the area of Bosnia and Herzegovina is practically non-existent. The first recorded evidence of Bosnia and Herzegovina under the Slavs dates from the tenth century. Several centuries later a Byzantine writer stated that 'Bosnia is not a vassal state but is independent, the people lead their own life and rule themselves.'

Graveyards have become the most important source of information about the culture of this time. Archeological digs in older necropolises have unearthed locally made jewellery and weapons from the Slav period. A unique aspect of this time was the development of skilled work with stone. This art would later surface in what is seen today as a national trademark of Bosnia and Herzegovina – the *stećak* (plural *stećci*). These medieval tombstones were elaborately carved with drawings depicting Christian and pagan beliefs. *Stećci* date from the eleventh to the thirteenth centuries and can be found today at dozens of locations all over Bosnia and Herzegovina. These tombstones are unique to this part of the world.

Medieval Bosnia

The early Middle Ages placed the southern Slavs in a very precarious position – wedged between the two great cultural bodies of eastern and western Christianity. Both Byzantium and Rome set out to influence the political and religious structure of this crossroads region. The geographical position of the southern Slavs became an important factor in the eleventh century split between the Orthodox and Catholic churches. Both churches asserted their influences and left a permanent mark on the region's cultural history.

The spiritual culture that developed in medieval Bosnia was very similar to that of its Illyrian predecessors. There was a large degree of cultural resistance and fierce independence that resulted in a creative mold of Christianity. In a relatively inaccessible and isolated area emerged what was to be a unique form of Christianity in medieval Europe – the Bosnian church. Whilst still influenced by the great divide and spread of Orthodoxy and Catholicism the Bosnian church, along with its own alphabet – *bosančica* (similar to both Glagolithic and Cyrillic) - flourished in the medieval Bosnian state. In an era that saw Europe dominated by religious exclusiveness, Bosnia was able to maintain a high level of secularism in all spheres of life.

Cultural development in medieval Bosnia

Written records don't show how the ordinary persons lived, what lifestyle they enjoyed, and what cultural heritage developed in medieval Bosnia. What we do know is that many unique forms of language, art, literature, and worship evolved in Bosnia during the Middle Ages.

The key to Bosnia's wealth was its copper, silver, lead, gold and other natural resources. Copper and silver were mined at Kreševo and Fojnica in central Bosnia; lead was mined in Olovo to the northeast of Sarajevo; and gold, silver and lead in were mined in Zvornik on the River Drina. The most significant and productive area in all of Bosnia and Herzegovina was the silver mine at Srebrenica. A large working class developed around this industry, some of which can still be found today.

During the Middle Ages Bosnia became a very important trading route. Merchants from both east and west moved and traded their goods through or in Bosnian territory. Trading towns and routes sprung up or rejuvenated in Visoko, Jajce, Travnik, Goražde and Livno. Many locals became involved in trade, particularly with Ragusa (Dubrovnik). Bosnia and Dubrovnik today still share close cultural ties.

A unique alphabet evolved in medieval Bosnia. Cyrillic and Glagolithic had been introduced in the tenth century and a special form of Cyrillic developed during the middle-ages. Glagolithic and Cyrillic were used simultaneously for some time, both copying texts and manuscripts from each other. The use of these two alphabets slowly merged into one - Bosnian Cyrillic or *bosančica*. It became the most commonly used alphabet in later medieval times.

Whereas most literature in medieval Europe came from clergy and monasteries, Bosnian writings were remarkably secular. The most famous of these is the Kulin Charter of 1189, written to the people of Dubrovnik. This was the first official act written in the national language of the Slavic south. Many documents show that it was not only the nobility but merchants and craftsmen who reached a relatively high level of literacy. There are, however, also many religious documents from this time. Examples include the Cyrillic *Miroslav Missal*, produced by the Duke of Hum in the 12th century, the *Divoš Tihoradić Gospel* from the 14th century and the *Čajniče Gospel* which is the only medieval codex still in existence in Bosnia today. These manuscripts used a wealth of human and animal miniatures all drawn in a unique south Slav style. The Franciscan monastery in Kraljeva

Sutjeska possesses some of the earliest written works and the first bible, complete with the *bosančica* alphabet. They can be viewed in the museum and library in this small town in central Bosnia.

Art took many forms in medieval Bosnia. Silver, gold, bronze and copper were used, particularly in the 14th and 15th centuries, for jewellery making, costumes, coins, bowls, and other artifacts. Many of the designs resemble Romanesque-Gothic styles, some with an eastern mystical flavor. The most important art of medieval Bosnia, though, was the stonework of the *stećci* (gravestones). These unique gravestones from Bosnia and Hum are not found anywhere else in Europe.

In different styles, these *stećci* portray crosses, swords, symbols of purity, and anthropomorphic symbols (dance, traditional attire, sacred symbols, deer, horses). The Bosnian Cyrillic script showed its most artistic face on these *stećci*. But the most remarkable trait of the *stećci* is their poetic and philosophical power. They stand apart from any known conventional European burial rites. They are found mostly in Bosnia and Herzegovina but there are also *stećci* in Dalmatia, the Croatian hinterland, western Serbia and Montenegro – all within the boundaries of the former Bosnian State. This art form continued into Ottoman times and well into the 16th century, with some of the later *stećci* including Islamic symbols.

Bosnia and Herzegovina is a living gallery of the stone art of the middle-ages. Over 60,000 *stećci* tombstones are dotted throughout the country with the largest necropolis at Radimlja near the Herzegovinian town of Stolac. Mak Dizdar, the most famous of Bosnian poets, wrote frequently of the *stećci* and their meaning in *Kameni spavač*, the *Stone Sleeper*. Whether or not his interpretations of the *stećci* are right, they remain a national symbol of Bosnia and Herzegovina.

It should be well noted that most of medieval European history does not see it fit to mention much of the contributions of women during this time. The mainly male dominant and patriarchal depiction of this era is to say the least unfair – as women have always made significant contributions in art, agriculture, family life, and even male dominated politics. The authors do not wish to exclude women by any means but have simply been unable to unearth their major contributions of this time. What we do know is that women in the region of Bosnia and Herzegovina at this time were not persecuted as witches as were their counterparts in much of western Europe.

Ottoman rule

In the summer of 1463 the Ottoman army, after years of penetration into Bosnian territory, captured the Bosnian banate and the region around Sarajevo. These lands would be in more or less firm Ottoman control for the next four centuries. Many of the gains in the northern half of Bosnia, however, were reversed by King Mathias of Hungary. He established a northern banate under Hungarian rule and named the Bosnian 'ban' King of Bosnia. The kingdom slowly dwindled as Ottoman incursions wore down the resistance, and by the 1520s the kingdom's capital, Jajce, came under constant siege until it fell in 1528.

Herzegovina also succeeded in repelling the Ottomans for some time after 1463. Herceg Stjepan Vukčić held most of Herzegovina for the next two years, until another swarming invasion sent him into exile in Novi (later named Herceg-Novi in his honor), Montenegro. His son Vlatko attempted to enlist the help of the Hungarians and Venetians but internal strife with local noblemen and neighboring Ragusa enabled the Ottomans to take a strong hold by the 1470s, and in 1482 the last fortress in Herzegovina was overrun.

The Ottomans conquered territories, particularly in the north towards Europe, not to convert the inhabitants, but for the land, for acquiring new conscripts for further Ottoman gains, and for the taxes the Empire could impose to wage these wars. Besides conquering Bosnia and Herzegovina, Mehmed II destroyed the Venetian army in Greece, began making incursions into Moldavia and Hungary, and was on the verge of launching a full scale invasion of Italy when he died in 1481. His successor, Bayezit II, continued consolidating Ottoman gains. Suleyman the Magnificent's rule from 1520-1566 managed to reduce Hungary to the status of a vassal territory and the Ottomans came inches away from capturing Vienna. The 1533 peace treaty with Austria established a long and static confrontation line between the Hapsburg and Ottoman Empires. Each side spent years building up their respective frontier zones, thus assuring that Bosnia's borders did not see heavy military activity until the Sultan waged war on the Hapsburgs in 1566. Military campaigns continued from 1593 to 1606. The Ottoman presence in Bosnia was a military enterprise from where major offensives against the Hapsburgs were launched.

In the course of 150 years, more and more of Bosnia's inhabitants converted to Islam. The Islamicization of the Bosnian population is possibly the most distinctive and maybe the most important event in its history. There was, and still is, a lot of controversy surrounding this issue, with most arguments being based on myth and folklore. Although one will still find today bitter 'memories' of 'forced' conversion, the process as a whole did not largely come by force or through war.

While the evidence available does not prove that there was a policy of forced conversions, this is not to say that there was no persecution and oppression of Christians. The Orthodox Church, falling under the jurisdiction of the Ottoman Empire, was an accepted institution. The Catholic Church, the church of the enemy Austrians, was treated with a heavier hand. In the geographical territory of Bosnia at the time of the Ottoman conquest, there were few Orthodox communities. They grew in size during the Ottoman occupation. Conversely, there were an estimated 35 Franciscan monasteries in Bosnia and Herzegovina before the invasion, but by the mid-1600s only ten remained.

The religious practices of both the Bosnian Christians and Muslims point to a mystical convergence of the two faiths. Even today, Christians and Muslims share the same superstitions in the power of amulets, with many Muslims having them blessed by Franciscan monks. Many holy days and festivals were celebrated by both religious communities. 'Muslim' ceremonies were often conducted in Christian churches and masses were held in front of the Virgin Mary to cure or ward off illness. There are records of Christians calling for Muslim dervishes to read verses from the Qu'ran to cure or bless them. It is quite clear that a synthesis of diverging beliefs occurred in Bosnia and Herzegovina, where 'all sects meet on a common basis of secular superstition.'

Most of Bosnia and Herzegovina's present day cities and towns were created during the Ottoman period. A focus on building towns and constructing roads and bridges to connect these towns brought the whole country, for the first time, into an urbanized sphere. Never before had any central administration effectively embarked on a vision of building a country. Islamic art and culture added a remarkable aspect to life in Bosnia and Herzegovina. Unlike the often brutal feudal systems seen elsewhere in Europe at that time, the Ottoman Empire allowed the Orthodox Church and the new Jewish community to enjoy growth and prosperity.

A small community of Sephardic Jews who had been expelled from Spain in 1492 settled in Sarajevo, Travnik and Mostar, and was tolerated by the Ottomans. Jewish merchants quickly established themselves in the textile and silk trades. This tradition would stand until the destruction of the Jewish community in the Second World War. They were skilled metal workers and it is believed that the Anatolian Jews greatly advanced Ottoman weaponry. For this priceless gift it is said that the Jews were given their own mahala in Sarajevo near the central market. Several synagogues and a hram were built. From an early stage after their arrival, the Jews of Bosnia and Herzegovina played an important role in the cultural and religious life of the cities where they settled.

The decline of the Ottoman Empire

A major Ottoman defeat at the hands of the Austrians in 1683 signaled a drastic decline in the Empire. In 1697 Eugene of Savoy advanced on Bosnia and reached Sarajevo. Sarajevo was put to the torch and most of the town went up in flames. When he retreated many Catholics left with his army for fear of reprisals. This decimated the Catholic population and only three Franciscan monasteries remained open. The frontier lands in the Krajina were in constant conflict, and unrest in eastern Herzegovina along the Montenegrin border became commonplace.

At the turn of the nineteenth century Napoleon and France defeated Austria and took over Venetia, Istria and Dalmatia. Austria again declared war on France in 1809 and by 1813 Austria ruled those areas again. The biggest threat, however, was no longer the Austrians but the powerful rebellions to the east in Serbia. Large-scale revolts took place in which Slav Muslims were massacred. The Ottomans granted Serbia a greater amount of autonomy in 1815. By the end of the Napoleonic wars it became clear to Istanbul that the Empire was so weak that it would collapse without aggressive reform. Now fighting battles on all fronts it was too difficult for the Ottomans to reestablish control of Bosnia. Bosnia's local governors and military leaders looked for more autonomy and began making demands to the Ottoman authorities. Many local militias offered the Ottomans military assistance but with strict demands on self-rule and insisting that taxes levied by the Empire be waived. Christians and Muslims alike were seeking sweeping reforms within the Empire. A final blow was struck in a massive revolt that lasted three years from 1875 to 1878. This revolt effectively ended Ottoman rule in Bosnia and Herzegovina. Russia had declared war on the Ottoman Empire in 1877, and the earlier plans of the Austrians and Russians would soon become reality. By October 20, 1878 the total occupation of Bosnia and Herzegovina was complete. A new era under Austro-Hungarian rule began.

Austro-Hungarian rule

The Congress of Berlin redrew the map of the Balkans and approved the Austro-Hungarian occupation of Bosnia and Herzegovina in 1878, and the

Austro-Hungarians wasted no time in establishing their rule.

By holding the territory of Bosnia and Herzegovina, Austro-Hungary acquired great economic and market potential. More importantly, it enabled the empire to effectively establish an opposition to Russian influence in the Balkans. They were able to keep a close watch on Serbia and could begin 'experimenting' on an even greater ambition – expansion to the east. These factors shaped Austro-Hungarian policy in Bosnia and Herzegovina. Austro-Hungarian rule allowed the feudal system, however backwards and outdated, to continue and govern everyday life. Meanwhile, progressive and modern measures in certain spheres of life were rapidly embarked upon.

The most visible changes under Austro-Hungarian occupation were the introduction of European styles of architecture, cuisine, behavior, and dress, and the population reshuffle. Lacking confidence in the native inhabitants, foreign officials, mainly Slav, assumed the administrative duties of governing the state. Large numbers of peasants from the Empire's other territories were brought into Bosnia and Herzegovina's already overwhelmingly peasant population. Muslims from Bosnia and Herzegovina emigrated south and east on a massive scale as the Empire implemented a policy of rebalancing the country's religious make-up.

Within the framework of a new colonial policy, widespread and rapid social change and national diversification occurred. These changes fueled national and political antagonisms so powerful that even the mighty Austro-Hungarian Empire could not keep them at bay. It was not so much an organized agenda of political affiliation but rather a spontaneous expression, largely by youth, of a revolutionary spirit. Nationalist agendas did arise in the beginning of the 20th century but the general resistance was more at a class level than at a national one. Acts of terrorism began when Bosnia and Herzegovina was officially annexed in 1908. In 1910, there was a failed assassination attempt on Emperor Franz Joseph. In the same year the governor of Bosnia and Herzegovina, general Marijan Varešanin, was shot, and in June 1914 a young Serbian nationalist by the name of Gavrilo Princip shot dead Prince Ferdinand and his pregnant wife on a bridge in Sarajevo. This event not only sparked the end of Austro-Hungarian rule in Bosnia and Herzegovina, but also led to the large political fallouts between the great powers that preceded the first battles of World War I.

Austro-Hungary's declaration of war on Serbia on July 28, 1914 carved deep wounds and strengthened aged alliances amongst the world powers. Bosnians and Herzegovinians were sent to fight against the regime that repressed them.

The Kingdom of Serbs, Croats, and Slovenes and the First Yugoslavia

Towards the end of WWI the Austro-Hungarians attempted to 'rearrange' the status of Bosnia and Herzegovina. The governor of Bosnia and Herzegovina, Baron Sarkotić, suggested to the Emperor that the country join with Croatia or be granted special autonomy under the Hungarian crown. As the war efforts continued to falter towards the end of 1918, the idea of Bosnia and Herzegovina remaining under Austro-Hungarian rule was completely abandoned and talks of the creation of a Yugoslav state began. The leader of the Bosnian Muslims, Mehmed Spaho, had the task of uniting the divided loyalties of the Muslim populations. Although some disparities still existed amongst the Muslims he declared the Muslims of Bosnia and Herzegovina were in favor of a Yugoslav state. National Councils were formed, first in Zagreb and then in Bosnia and Herzegovina, renouncing the rule of the Hapsburgs in countries formerly under Austro-Hungarian authority. Days later, Croatia, Bosnia and Herzegovina and Slovenia joined with the Kingdom of Serbia to form the Kingdom of Serbs, Croats, and Slovenes. Within this new kingdom, Croatia, as well as the Bosnian Muslims and Bosnian Croats, sought some sort of regional self-governance. The Kingdom of Serbia, supported by the Bosnian Serbs, did not feel for that and established a centralist style rule from Belgrade.

Resistance against the Serb domination mounted, and in 1932 the leader of the Croatian party, Vlatko Maček, issued a 'Resolution' calling for a return to democracy and the end of Serbian hegemony. The Slovenian and Bosnian leaders followed suit with similar statements and all three were subsequently arrested. Their arrests did not go down well, and in 1934 King Aleksandar was assassinated. A year later his successor, Prince Paul, ordered new elections. The resulting loose new alliance lasted a shaky four years and ended when a Serbian minister asserted to parliament in a speech that the 'Serb policies will always be the policies of this house and this government.' Later that evening five key ministers resigned and the government imploded.

Hitler had by now begun advancing on Czechoslovakia, and his devout admirer Ante Pavelić in Italy was pushing for the break-up of Yugoslavia. It was apparent that there was a desperate need for the Serbs to bring the Croats back on board and to find a solution the Croats would accept. Cvetković and Maček met and began discussing the restructuring of the national territories, which would include giving Croatia some political power of its own. The new solution carved-up Bosnia giving some parts to Croatia and leaving other parts to be devoured by Serbia. The Bosnian Muslim leader Spaho died during these negotiations and his successor Džafer Kulenović sought the creation of a separate banate for Bosnia. His requests were ignored as much of the banates not absorbed into the new Croatia banates had a majority Serb population who wanted to maintain close ties with the remaining banates dominated by Serbia.

These debates continued until the pressure asserted from the German Reich became too much to bear for the Yugoslav government. With Hitler on their border and the Italians already in Greece, Prince Paul realized the impossibility of protection from Great Britain and signed the Axis pact in Vienna on March 25, 1941. When the Yugoslav delegation returned, the Prince was ousted in a bloodless coup and a new government of national unity was formed. The new government tried to continue a conciliatory policy towards Germany but ten days later massive bombing raids on Belgrade began, and Yugoslavia was invaded by German, Bulgarian, Hungarian and Italian forces. The 'resistance' lasted eleven days, after which the Yugoslav army surrendered to the German High Command.

The Second World War

After the defeat of the Yugoslav army, Yugoslavia was divided between the Axis powers. Its territories became important for communication and supplies of natural resources and labor to fight the Allied powers. The Axis powers were focused on defeating the Allied forces and were not prepared for the war against the Yugoslav resistance movements, and the two civil wars that ensued.

Before the end of the blitzkrieg the Germans had proclaimed a new 'Independent State of Croatia' (known as NDH), which also engulfed all of Bosnia and Herzegovina. Croatian extremists conducted a war largely against the Serb populations in Croatia and Bosnia and Herzegovina. There was also war between the two main resistance groups – the *četnici*, who were Serbs loyal to the monarchy, and the communist partisans that enlisted Serbs, Muslims and Croats.

Under the leadership of Josip Broz, or Tito, the partisans envisioned a communist victory over the Germans and a social revolution that would create a post-war communist state. Tito was a Stalin loyalist whose revolutionary ideology attracted a population that was weary and worn by nationalist agendas.

Two of the most crucial battles of WWII in Yugoslavia took place in Bosnia and Herzegovina. In the early months of 1943 the most epic battle for the partisans began – the Battle of the Neretva. A surprise counter offensive was launched by the partisans in the direction of Herzegovina and Montenegro. In retreat from battles in the Krajina region the partisans reached the Neretva River with 4,000 wounded and many more villagers who had joined the partisans in fleeing from German attacks. With over 20,000 *četnik* troops on one side and Axis forces on the other, Tito sabotaged the bridge at Jablanica, leading the enemy to believe the partisans had changed course. He ordered the bridge to be destroyed and improvised a wooden footbridge. All the wounded were brought across and the footbridge destroyed, thus deceiving the German forces. The partisans now faced the *četnik* army, and in a fierce battle the *četniks* were wiped out. Tito and the partisans were able to secure a safe passage to Montenegro. The remains of the bridge can still be seen today in Jablanica and there is a full account of the battle at the museum in that town.

By May the Germans had begun preparations for the largest campaign of the war. Over 100,000 troops, backed by air power, surrounded the outnumbered partisans in the mountainous region near the River Sutjeska in eastern Bosnia. The Partisans attempted to break through to the eastern border with Montenegro and over 7,000 partisans lost their lives. Today Sutjeska is a National Park that pays tribute to the downed partisans.

Tito's Yugoslavia

Depending on who you talk to, Tito was either a monstrous communist dictator or a peacekeeping socialist visionary. The truth probably lies somewhere in the middle. At the end of WWII, Yugoslavia, like much of Europe, was a mess. Tito quickly introduced Stalinist methodology in running his new communist republic. His logic was that in order to plant the seeds of socialist ideology, nationalist sentiments must be uprooted and weeded out at all costs. This resulted in the death of what some estimate to be 250,000 Croats, Muslims and Serbs. The Department for the Protection of the People, Tito's secret police, arrested and often severely punished anyone who opposed 'brotherhood and unity', and in fact anyone they *thought* might threaten the new fragile state. The Croats were especially targeted, some having supported the ustaša and been followers of Ante Pavelić.

The Franciscan clergy in Herzegovina were also singled out, having been suspected of supporting the *ustaša* against the Partisans. Many churches were destroyed and monasteries shut down. Serbian *Četniks* were also seriously persecuted and many either left the country or retreated to isolated mountain areas. The Muslims were also served harsh punishments; executions of the Muslim intellectual elite were commonplace in the early years after the war. The courts of Islamic sacred law were suppressed, teaching of children in mosques became a criminal offense, women were forbidden to wear the veil and many Muslim cultural societies were forced to close.

In 1948 Stalin expelled Yugoslavia from the Cominform. At this time Tito quickly changed his platform from being a stark Stalinist to being a more open minded, independent and liberal socialist. By the mid-fifties, religious life in Yugoslavia improved, with new laws that allowed freedom of religion, although the state was mandated with directing and controlling these institutions.

Whereas the first half of the new Yugoslavia was built around establishing authority, rebuilding, and weeding out opposition, Yugoslavia in the 1960s and beyond brought about a kind of national renaissance. It is from this point on that people speak of the glorious days of Tito - when everyone had a job and there was free education. There were no homeless and people were free to travel around the world.

Massive changes to the infrastructure, particularly road systems, opened much of the impenetrable Bosnia and Herzegovina for the first time. The National Roads Launch of 1968 aimed at connecting every town in the country with asphalt roads. Almost a thousand schools and libraries were built. The library program was co-funded by Nobel Laureate Ivo Andrić. He donated half of his prize money for this project. Schools in rural areas and small villages were established as were small medical clinics or 'ambulanta.' The university system was expanded from Sarajevo to Banja Luka, Tuzla, Mostar, Zenica, and other major cities in Bosnia and Herzegovina.

Tito established and maintained good relations with both the United States and the Soviet Union and Yugoslavia received financial aid from both of them in a typical cold war 'tug-o-war.' New incentives by the communist party for 'self-management' within the republics gave the population a sense of pride and independence. For the average person in Bosnia and Herzegovina, life was good. People had jobs, relatively comfortable lifestyles and were free to travel and work abroad.

After Tito

After the death of Tito in 1980, Bosnia and Herzegovina continued to enjoy relative prosperity. The deepening crisis in Kosovo in the early eighties, however, gave further fuel to the Serbian nationalist cause. Dobrica Ćosić, a Serbian nationalist Communist, complained that 'one could witness among the Serbian people a re-ignition of the old historic goal and national idea – the unification of the Serbian people into a single state.' This statement led to his expulsion from the Central Committee. Ćosić also fiercely opposed the granting of national status to the Bosnian Muslims. Anti-Muslim, and for nationalist propaganda purposes, anti-Islamic, sentiment was fuel for the fire of Serbian nationalism.

By the mid-1980s, the economic situation in Yugoslavia began to deteriorate. Without the strong leadership of Tito, poor economic times gave further rise to nationalism. In 1987 inflation rose 120% and by the next year that rate had doubled. In the last few years of the eighties strikes and protests became commonplace. In 1989 strikes against the local party leaders in Vojvodina and Montenegro set the stage for the new leader of the Serbian Communists – Slobodan Milošević.

Milošević clearly had an agenda of transformation in Serbia and he quickly replaced party leaders with his own supporters. In March 1989, at Milošević's request, the Serbian Assembly passed a constitutional amendment that abolished the autonomy of Kosovo and Vojvodina. This was met by massive strikes in Kosovo that were violently dealt with by the Serbian security forces. In a general atmosphere of discontent among the masses, due to the worsening economic times, political finger pointing stirred a nationalist fury that few could have imagined. The Serbs could now either dominate Yugoslavia or break it up. Even at this point, however, few Bosnians saw the rise of nationalism or the deepening economic woes as a sign of war or disintegration. Life, for the most part, carried on as normal.

The break-up of Yugoslavia

The symbolic turning point in the collapse of Yugoslavia came in the summer of 1989 at Kosovo polje. Hundreds of thousands of Serbs gathered at this ancient battle-field to pay respects to Prince Lazar, who had been slain at this place in 1389 in battle against the Ottomans. In the weeks leading up to the ceremony the bones of the Prince toured Serbia, stirring the pot of unsettled scores in the minds of many Serbs. Milošević addressed those assembled saying that 'we are again engaged in battles and quarrels. They are not yet armed battles, but this cannot be ruled out yet.' His words clearly stuck a resounding chord and were met with thundering applause. Through careful nationalist rhetoric Milošević secured half of the eight votes in the federal government. He controlled Serbia, Montenegro, Kosovo and Vojvodina. In his eyes that left only the challenge of getting Macedonia on board to gain a majority and further implement constitutional change in favor of Serbian dominance.

With the fall of the Berlin wall came the unification of East and West Germany and the almost overnight collapse of the Soviet Union. Faced now with a struggling economy and the shift from a planned to a market economy, there were demands by the republics for more freedom and sovereignty from the federal government. The Serbian government attempted to block any movement toward the break-up of Yugoslavia. Talk of independence increased in Slovenia and Croatia in 1990, and at the 14th Congress of the League of Communists of Yugoslavia, President Slobodan Milošević issued a warning that republics seeking independence would face border changes on the assumption that anywhere a Serb lived was part of Serbia. This only fueled Croatian nationalism which had become more radical in the late eighties. As Milošević's power base expanded, the 'dream' of an independent Croatia became increasingly appealing to many Croats.

In Bosnia and Herzegovina, the Serbian propaganda machine shifted its focus from the *ustaša* hordes to the Islamic fundamentalist threat. In reality, Bosnia's Muslim population, especially after almost 50 years of socialism, was mainly secular and pro-Europe. Holding a 44% minority in the country they feared that both Serbian and Croatian lust to take Bosnia and Herzegovina would leave them nation-less.

As was done in Slovenia and Croatia, a referendum for independence was held in Bosnia and Herzegovina in March 1992. The Bosnian Croats and Muslims voted in favor, whilst a majority of the Serbian population boycotted the vote. With sixty-five per cent of Bosnia's population voting in favor, Bosnia and Herzegovina declared independence notwithstanding Serbian threats. The day the results were announced Serb paramilitary forces set up barricades and sniper posts near the parliament building in Sarajevo. Suddenly, the heavy artillery and tanks that had already surrounded Sarajevo and several other cities before the independence vote, were a very real threat.

On April 6, 1992 the European Union and the United Nations recognized Bosnia and Herzegovina as an independent state. On the same day the Yugoslav National Army and Serbian paramilitaries attacked Sarajevo. Tens of thousands of Sarajevans of all nationalities took to the streets to protest in front of the barricades. As the crowd peacefully marched toward the barricade a sniper from the hillside fired into the crowd, killing a woman from Sarajevo and a Muslim woman who had fled the fighting in Dubrovnik. This sparked the beginning of what would be a long and brutal campaign against Bosnia's non-Serb populations.

In less than a year Yugoslavia saw three of its six republics secede. Macedonia followed suit and a UN preventive force was sent to intersect any pending ambitions Serbia had on Macedonia. Serbia and Montenegro, together with the provinces of Vojvodina and Kosovo, were now all that remained of Yugoslavia

The conflict

There have been so many books written about this subject that the authors have decided to let the reader, if they so choose, to further research the conflict. For the sake of sparing this book from the dark days of the early 1990's we will skip the details of the war that flashed on our screens from 1992 to 1995. Although this issue is still a topic of heavy debate here it is clear that Bosnia and Herzegovina experienced the worst genocide on European soil since WWII. Addressing the truths of the war is a necessary process for healing – both by victim and aggressor, but we feel that this is not the place for this. In short, we have moved on from those days and hope our readers will too and fully experience the beauty of Bosnia and Herzegovina today.

What one rarely learns or reads about of conflicts such as this one is the 'other side of the coin.' A spirit of resistance and survival thrived during these times. Communities mobilized to help one another. An untapped strength and creativity was expressed through the war theatre in Sarajevo that put on plays for the duration the siege. The newspaper *Oslobođenje*, meaning Freedom, did not miss a single day of print despite the lack of paper and supplies. Cultural life did not die during these times, it flourished in the most defiant form of non-violent resistance. Bosnians walked through the hail of gunfire to have coffee with a friend and held a Miss Sarajevo beauty pageant in a basement during one of the worst periods of the war. The attempts to erase all material traces of Bosnia's Muslim and Islamic culture may have partially succeeded in the torching of libraries and razing of mosques, but the spirit of a multi-ethnic community never died. Hundreds of thousands of Bosnians – Muslim, Serb and Croat – lost their lives, some in the most horrific ways imaginable. And although in some circles the madness of ethnic purity still exists you will find that in most places in Bosnia today people are determined to live a normal life again, and to live together...as they always have.

Post-war Bosnia and Herzegovina

Difficult times and a long rehabilitation process followed the signing of the Dayton Peace Accords. Although progress and reform has come slow in the eyes of the local inhabitants, great strides have been made in the normalization of life in Bosnia and Herzegovina. In the early years after Dayton the peace was monitored and enforced by a large NATO presence. Sarajevo became the headquarters of the multi-national peacekeeping force and the Brits, Americans and French commanded their respective jurisdictions in the rest of the country with smaller NATO countries under their command. More importantly, electricity, food, and water returned to the beleaguered population. Shops were once again filled with European products and a massive reconstruction program began on a scale not seen since the Marshall Plan.

Freedom of movement between the entities was improved with the introduction of standardized car license plates. Registration plates after the war clearly stated which entity one was from, which often led to harassment and/or random violence. The return of refugees was a slower process and one that is still ongoing. Large numbers of refugees and displaced persons have returned to their rightful homes, but many remain in third countries or internally displaced within Bosnia and Herzegovina.

Government reform was and still is a painful process. The nationalist parties that led the country into war still ruled in the immediate years after Dayton. The new constitution stipulates the full equal rights and representation of all three peoples of Bosnia and Herzegovina, giving even minority groups an unprecedented voice in government. The presidency is not a one-person position but rather a three-person consortium with rotating powers to the Serb, Croat, and Bosniac delegates. The circus of establishing an equally balanced government was no less than a poorly constructed jigsaw puzzle. Ministry positions were given to political parties regardless of the background or competency of the individuals involved. Appointees stuck hard to party lines instead of nation building. Corruption was rampant and became an inherent part of the system, and has proved very difficult to uproot. This did little to improve the power of a centralized government, nor help begin the process of reconciliation.

Bosnia and Herzegovina was assigned an internationally mandated governing body to oversee the rebuilding process, called the Office of the High Representative (OHR). Most Bosnians viewed the NATO forces as peaceful and necessary occupiers and have a similar opinion of the OHR. The powers of the OHR are broad and sweeping, so much so that in essence they play an ad hoc protectorate role. Free and fair elections were implemented by the Office for Security and Cooperation in Europe (OSCE). The elections in 2002 were the first elections to be fully implemented by the local government. Previously elected officials were only able to serve two-year terms that were often counter productive to time consuming reform. The elections of 2002 were the first four-year term mandates in post Dayton Bosnia and Herzegovina. The OHR has embarked on an aggressive campaign to eliminate corruption and bureaucratic overspending. Steps to attract foreign investment have finally been implemented. European standards are being pushed on taxes, environment and transparency.

What this means for the ordinary person here is hope for a stable future. The short-term reality however is a rather corrupt system that lacks a coherent vision of building a united country. Great strides have been made but life in Bosnia and Herzegovina still faces rough economic times, with war criminals still not brought to justice, and many people left to deal on a daily basis with the scars of war. This may not seem so evident to the visitor. The quest for a normal life has in many places created a lively atmosphere. Café's are always full of smiling faces, people walk the streets wearing the finest of European fashions, and the warm hospitality you're sure to find everywhere will certainly make you ask 'Why did this happen here? This is really a great place.' Bosnians ask themselves this question every day.

PRACTICAL INFORMATION

WHEN TO VISIT

For the two co-authors of this book it's very difficult to say when the best time to visit would be - we both live in Bosnia now and we love it all year round. Summer and Spring are the obvious warm seasons with plenty of fun and sun to be had. But winter skiing and the autumn colours are equally nice. People are always out and about in this country - it's certainly one of the most social places we've come across - and you'll never miss the local crowds. You've got the best of both worlds here, Alpine and Mediterranean - enjoy them both, any time of year!

In spring, the country is at its best. So green, so many flowers. The days are pleasantly warm and the evenings are refreshingly cool. In summer time, it is nice and warm in Sarajevo, but sometimes a little too hot (30+ °C) in Mediterranean Herzegovina. Prices for accommodation are generally a little higher in July and August.

If you come to Bosnia and Herzegovina only once, and you are not into winter sports, spring and summer are the best times. But if you come to the country regularly, or if you are into wet walks, autumn is not to be missed. October and November are good months to avoid the crowds and enjoy the barrage of orange, red and yellow leaves that paint the forests. These months see both rainy and cool, sunny days.

Bosnia in general and the mountainous regions in particular have very cold winters and high snow precipitation. If you are a skier, the best time for a visit is from January to March. Olympic skiing on the Bjelašnica, Igman and Jahorina mountains is perfect in these three months. In this period, people from the region flock to these areas. If you plan on coming and you want a hotel close to the ski lifts, it is best to make reservations. And make sure to buy snow chains: the road clearance teams are getting better but the roads in winter are still not quite as good as they would be in other parts of the world.

ENTERING BOSNIA AND HERZEGOVINA

With the right papers, entering Bosnia and Herzegovina is easy. Procedures at both the borders and the airport are standardized and uncomplicated. Only during the holiday season, when the people living in the Diaspora flock into the country, do border crossings sometimes take a bit of time.

Bosnia and Herzegovina can only be entered with a valid passport. EU, American and Canadian citizens do not require a visa to enter the country. Most other people do need a visa, and getting one is difficult. Visas are issued by the country's diplomatic missions. Visas for private travel require an application form and a letter of intent from somebody who resides in Bosnia and Herzegovina. Business visas require an application form, an invitation from an in-country business partner and a letter of intent from the Bosnia and Herzegovina Trade Office. Visa applicants from certain countries should also provide evidence of possession of cash assets, as well as HIV test results.

Fees for visas issued by diplomatic/consular offices:

Single entry-exit visas and transit visas	31.00 KM
Multiple entry-exit visas for periods up to 90 days	57.00 KM
Multiple entry-exit visa for periods over 90 days	72.00 KM

Officially, people who enter the country on a visa need to register themselves with the police within 24 hours after their arrival in the country. Any violation of this regulation could officially entail a financial penalty or even deportation. In reality, I have frequently received visitors who required a visa to enter, I never registered any of them and none of them ever ran into any type of problem as a consequence. Similarly, you might be asked to fill in a card upon arrival in Sarajevo Airport – but at the time of writing this card was no longer being distributed.

If you enter Bosnia and Herzegovina by car, you will have to buy vehicle insurance at the border. It is an uncomplicated and fairly inexpensive affair. You do not need this insurance if you have a green card that covers Bosnia and Herzegovina (something that is not normally the case).

Both local alcoholic beverages and cigarettes are relatively cheap in Bosnia and Herzegovina, and the only money you could save would be on brand-name alcohol. You are allowed to import 200 cigarettes and 2 liters of liquor.

DIPLOMATIC MISSIONS

Bosnia and Herzegovina embassies overseas

Australia:	5 Beale Crescent, Deakin, ACT 2600 Canberra; tel: +61 2 6232 4646; fax: +61 2 6232 55 54
Austria:	Tivoligasse 54, A-1120 Wien; tel: +43 1 810 1252; fax: +43 1 811 8569
Belgium:	Rue Tenbosch 34, 1000 Bruxelles; tel: +32 2 644 2008; fax: +32 2 644 1698
Canada:	130 Albert St, Suite 805, Ottawa, Ontario K1P 5G4; tel: +1 613 236 0028; fax: +1 613 236 1139
Croatia:	Torbarova 9, Zagreb 10000; tel: +385 1 468 3761; fax: +385 1 468 3764

THE COUNTRY

Denmark:	Nytory 3, 1450 Copenhagen K; tel: +45 33 33 80 40; fax: +45 33 33 80 17
France:	174 rue de Courcelles, 75017 Paris; tel: +33 1 42 67 34 22; fax: +33 1 40 53 85 22
Germany:	Ibsenstrasse 14, D-10439 Berlin; tel: +49 30 814 712 10; fax: +49 30 814 712 11
Greece:	Hatzikosta 3, 11521 Atena; tel: +30 210 64 11 375; fax: +30 210 64 23 154
Hungary:	Pasareti śt 48, 1026 Budapest; tel: +36 1 212 0106; fax: +36 1 212 0109
Italy:	Via Fabio Filzi 19, Milano; tel: +39 02 669 82 707; fax: +39 02 669 81 467

The Netherlands: Bezuidenhoutseweg 223, 2594 AL, The Hague; tel: +31 70 35 88 505; fax: +31 70 35 84 367

Norway: Bygday Alle 10, 0262 Oslo; tel: +47 22 54 09 63; fax: +47 22 55 27 50

Serbia and Montenegro: Milana Tankošića 8, 11 000 Belgrade; tel: +381 11 329 1277

Slovenia: Kalarjeva 26, 1000 Ljubljana; tel: +386 1 432 4042; fax: +386 1 432 2230

Spain: Calle Lagasca 24.2, Izda, 28001 Madrid; tel: +349 1 575 08 70; fax: +349 1 435 50 56

Switzerland: Jungfraustrasse 1, CH-3005 Bern; tel: +41 31 351 1051; fax: +41 31 351 1079

Sweden: Birger Jarisgaten 55/3, 11145 Stockholm; tel: +468 44 00 540; +468 24 98 30

Turkey: Turan Emeksiz Sokak 3, Park Siteler 9/3, Gaziomanpasa, Ankara; tel: +90 312 427 3602; fax: +90 312 427 3604

United Kingdom: 5-7 Lexan Gardens, London W8 5JJ; tel: +44 20 7373 0867; fax: +44 20 7373 0871

United States of America: 2109 E St NW, Washington DC 20037; tel: +1 202 337 1500; fax: +1 202 337 1502

Foreign embassies in Bosnia and Herzegovina

The country code is +387. All embassies are in Sarajevo. The postcode for Sarajevo is 71000.

Austria:	Džidžikovac 7; tel: 033 668 337; fax: 033 668 339
Bulgaria:	Soukbunar 15; tel: 033 668 191; fax: 033 668 182
Canada:	Grbavička 4/2; tel: 033 222 033, 033 447 901; fax: 033 222 004
China:	Braće Begić 17; 033 215 102; fax: 033 215 108
Croatia:	Mehmeda Spahe 16; tel: 033 444 330/1; fax: 033 472 434; Consular Section: Skenderija 17; 033 442 591; fax: 033 650 328

CENTRAL & NORTH BOSNIA

Czech Republic: Franjevačka 19; tel: 033 447 525, 033 446 966; fax: 033 447 526
Denmark: Splitska 9; tel: 033 665 901; fax: 033 665 902
Egypt: Nurudina Gackića 58; tel: 033 666 498; fax: 033 666 499
France: Mehmed-bega Kapetanovića Ljubušaka 18; tel: 033 668 149, 033 668 151; fax: 033 212 186
Germany: Mejtaš-Buka 11-13; tel: 033 275 000, 033 275 080; fax: 033 652 978, 033 443 176
Greece: Obala Maka Dizdara 1; tel: 033 213 439; fax: 033 203 512
Hungary: Hasana Bibera 53; tel: 033 205 302; fax: 033 268 930; Consular Section: Safet-bega Bašagića 58a
Iran: Obala Maka Dizdara 6; tel: 033 650 210; fax: 033 663 910
Italy: Čekaluša 39; tel: 033 203 959; fax: 033 659 368
Japan: Mula Mustafe Bašeskije 2; tel: 033 209 580; fax: 033 209 583
Libya: Tahtali sokak 17; tel: 033 200 621; fax: 033 663 620
Macedonia: Emerika Bluma 23; tel: 033 269 402, 033 206 004; fax: 033 206 004
Malaysia: Trnovska 6; tel: 033 201 578; fax: 033 667 713
Malta: Mula Mustafe Bašeskije 12; tel: 033 668 632; fax: 033 668 632
Netherlands: Grbavička 4, I sprat; tel: 033 223 404, 033 223 410; fax: 033 223 413
Norway: Ferhadija 20; tel: 033 254 000; fax: 033 666 505
Pakistan: Emerika Bluma 17; tel: 033 211 836; fax: 033 211 837
Palestine: Čemerlina 4; tel: 033 272 700/1; fax: 033 238 677
Poland: Dola 13; tel: 033 201 142; fax: 033 233 796
Portugal: Čobanija 12; tel: 033 200 835; fax: 033 443 117
Romania: Tahtali sokak 13-15; tel: 033 207 447; fax: 033 668 940
Russia: Urijan Dedina 93-95; tel: 033 668 147; fax: 033 668 148
Saudi Arabia: Koševo 44; tel: 033 211 861; fax: 033 212 204
Slovenia: Bentbaša 7; tel: 033 271 260; fax: 033 271 270
Spain: Čekaluša 16; tel: 033 278 560; fax: 033 278 582
Serbia and Montenegro: Obala Maka Dizdara 3a; tel: 033 260 080; fax: 033 221 469
Sweden: Ferhadija 20; tel: 033 276 030; fax: 033 276 060
Switzerland: Josipa Štadlera 15; tel: 033 275 850; fax: 033 665 246
Turkey: Hamdije Kreševljakovića 5; tel: 033 445 260; fax: 033 443 190

United Kingdom: Tina Ujevića 8; tel: 033 282 200;
fax: 033 666 131;
Consular Section: Petrakijina 11; tel: 033 208 229;
fax: 033 204 780
United States of America: Alipašina 43; tel: 033 445 700;
fax: 033 659 722
Vatican: Pehlivanuša 9; tel: 033 207 847; fax: 033 207 863

In Mostar

Office of United States of America: Mostarskog bataljona bb;
tel: 036 580 580
Consulate of Republic Croatia: Zagrebačka 8; tel: 036 316 630
General Consulate of Republic Turkey: Mala Tepa 24;
tel: 036 551 209

In Banja Luka

Austria: Jovana Dučića 52; tel: 051 311 144
Croatia: Milana Karanovića 1; tel: 051 304 258
Germany and France: DR.M.Stojanovića 1; tel: 051 303 925
United Kingdom: Simeuna Đaka 8; tel: 051 216 843
United States of America: Jovana Dučića 5; tel: 051 221 590

GETTING THERE AND AWAY

Bosnia and Herzegovina has a well-connected capital. It is easily accessible by air, bus, or train. The airport is only 20 minutes away from the city centre and has direct flights to many European capitals and thus indirect flights to everywhere else. Many local and international bus lines depart from the centre of town. The train schedule is less extensive, but does offer a few really good trips in comfortable trains at very modest prices.

By air

The state-of-the-art Sarajevo airport (033 289 100) is located at the base of Mount Igman. In winter, this is probably the worst possible location for an airport in Sarajevo and surroundings. In the cold months, early-morning flights are regularly cancelled as the entire area is often covered with heavy fog until late morning or later. In all other seasons, this airport is a pleasure to arrive at and depart from.

The airport is 12 km from the town centre. There are no shuttle buses and no bus routes in the vicinity of the airport. At various rates, the major hotels - and some of the smaller ones - offer airport pick-ups and drop-offs. Otherwise, taxis will take you to town for either the meter fee or a fixed amount of 20 KM.

You can change money at the airport exchange desk, rent a car from one of the car rental boots located in the arrival hall, and, in case you need to contact your hotel, buy a phone card at the post office. If your luggage did not arrive, you have to register the missing suitcases at the lost and found office, located next to the coffee shop in the arrival hall.

As Bosnia and Herzegovina is neither a main destination nor a major hub, flights to Sarajevo are relatively costly. The most affordable tickets used to come from the official airline of Bosnia and Herzegovina - Air Bosna – but this airline recently went bankrupt. Depending on the season, a return ticket from London will cost between £200 and £400. From most Euro countries a ticket will costs between 250 and 450 Euro, and from New York it will be between $700 and a little over $1,000. At the time of writing, ten international carriers have regular flights to and from Sarajevo:

Adria Airways: Ferhadija 23/II; tel: 033 289 245 (airport), 033 232 125/6; fax: 033 233 692

Avio Express Airlines: Zelenih beretki 22; tel: 033 653 179; fax: 033 208 334

Austrian Airlines: Maršala Tita 54; tel: 033 474 445 (airport), 033 474 446/7; fax: 033 470 526

Croatia Airlines: Kranjčevićeva 4/1a; tel: 033 258 600 (airport), 033 666 123; fax: 033 463 158

Lufthansa: Alipašina bb; tel: 033 474 445 (airport), 033 278 590/1/2

Turkish Airlines: Kulovića 5; tel: 033 289 249 (airport), 033 666 092; 033 212 938

Malev: Kurta Schorka 36; tel: 033 289 246 (airport), 033 473 200/1; fax: 033 467 105

JAT: Zelenih beretki 6; tel: 033 259 750 (airport), 033 259 750/1; fax: 033 223 083

Sometimes, it is cheaper to buy your tickets from a travel agency. The cheapest and most reliable ticket agent in Sarajevo is Kompas Travel in the city centre (Maršala Tita 8; tel: 033 208 014; fax: 033 208 015; email: kompas@kompas-sarajevo.com; web: www.kompas-sarajevo.com). A comprehensive overview of all other travel agencies is available at the Sarajevo Old Town Tourist Information Office.

There are international airports in Mostar, Tuzla and Banja Luka as well.

By ferry

Bosnia and Herzegovina has only one tiny strip of coast at Neum and there are no ferries that dock there. With seasonal schedules, ferries do come from Italy (Ancona and Bari) to the ports of Split and Dubrovnik. If you are traveling by car, these ferries may save you traffic jams along the Croatian coast. If you do not have your own means of transport, you will find the transfer to the bus stations at the port (in Split) or close to it (in Dubrovnik) easy and hassle-free. If you are a ferry person, check the ferry companies websites: SEM (www.sem-marina.hr), Jadrolinija (www.jadrolinija.hr) and Adriatica Navigazione (www.adriatica.it).

By rail

Buses drive fast, use curvy roads and confine you to your chair from beginning to end. Getting around by train is a little slower, but much more comfortable. In Bosnia and Herzegovina, trains are punctual, low-cost, and sometimes fairly luxurious, with couches that can be turned into beds, and cabins that are very often completely empty.

Before the war the rail network connected most Bosnian cities. This has changed dramatically. There are now only three routes that originate in Sarajevo: the Sarajevo-Zenica-Banja Luka-Zagreb route takes about ten hours from start to finish; the northern route to Budapest goes via Tuzla; and the southern route towards the Adriatic coast is Konjic-Jablanica-Mostar-Čapljina-Ploče (Ploče is in Croatia). This last route goes through the Neretva Canyon and is particularly scenic. Even on these three routes, trains do not go quite as frequently as the buses do.

Daily trains to and from Sarajevo

	To	From	cost (KM)	duration
Budapest	20.20	18.30	92/180	13 hours
Ploče	06.20/18.40	05.00/13.30	18/29	5 hours
Zagreb	09.49	09.00	45/74	9 hours

Recently, Bosnia and Herzegovina joined the Eurorail system. Perhaps that will fill up these sadly empty trains a bit more.

By bus

The bus system of Bosnia and Herzegovina functions well. Centrotrans and a range of smaller bus companies have reliable bus routes to and from all towns and many villages. Every city and town has a bus station with the daily departure and arrival times posted in local language on the station's wall. Ask the people behind the counters if the schedule is not clear to you: they are not likely to speak English (though in Sarajevo they often do) but will point you in the right direction. Asking a person who is standing around waiting is also a good way of double-checking that you are getting on the right bus. People are very willing to help.

Bus travel is reasonably priced and a one-way ticket to the furthest in-country destination from Sarajevo will not cost more than 30 KM. At the smaller stations, you pay when you get on the bus. At the main bus stations, you are meant to buy your ticket at the ticket booth, but even there you can normally get it on the bus as well. Usually there is an extra charge of 1 or 2 KM for each sizeable bag you carry with you. Bus stations do not have lockers or temporary luggage storage places.

Longer trips have breaks, the frequency and duration of which depending on whether or not the driver smokes. In addition, bus drivers may have special deals with restaurants en route. If so, the breaks will be longer to encourage you to eat and drink.

You might want to check out the bus before you get on. Most buses are comfortable and clean but there is the occasional company that has ratty buses with broken seats, windows that don't open, no air conditioning and a driver who smokes the entire length of the journey.

Useful terms

place of departure	mjesto odlaska
destination	destinacija
day of trip	dan vožnje (Pon-Mon, Uto-Tue, Sri-Wed, Čet-Thu, Pet-Fri, Sub-Sat, Ned-Sun)
time of departure	vrijeme odlaska
search	pretraga
departure	odlazak
arrival	dolazak
duration	trajanje
price	cijena

Centrotrans is a Eurolines member and runs regular buses from many European destinations to Sarajevo. Bus schedules, on-line reservations and main European office addresses can be found on the Centrotrans website: www.centrotrans.com. At the time of writing, the Centrotrans schedule is as follows:

From	Days	Single (KM/Euros)	Return (KM/Euros)
Amsterdam	Wed, Sat	250/127	370/188
Antwerp	Wed	230/114	330/165
Berlin	Sat	225/115	325/115
Dortmund	Mon, Tue, Thu, Fri, Sat	239/122	358/183
Dubrovnik	every day	40/20.50	60/ 30.5
Hamburg	Fri	239/122	358/183
Ljubljana	Mon, Wed, Fri	70/36	120/ 61
Makarska	every day	27/14	38/ 19.5
Munich	every day	102/52	141/ 72
Pula	Mon, Wed, Fri, Sat	80/41	130/ 66.5
Rotterdam	Sun, Thu	240/122	340/174
Stuttgart	Sun	156/80	235/120
Split	every day	30/15.50	45/ 23
Vienna	every day	72/37	115/ 59
Zagreb	every day	50/25.50	80 / 41

THE COUNTRY

By car

If you are in a hurry to get from A to B, Bosnia and Herzegovina is not the ideal place to be. There are no real highways and there is not much scope for high-speed driving as roads tend to wind through river valleys and up- and downhill. However, if you are not in any particular hurry, driving from town to town in Bosnia and Herzegovina is as pleasant as driving gets. There is lots of beautiful scenery, the roads tend to be quiet, and there are plenty of quality places to stop for a drink or a meal. Strangely, some of the country's best restaurants are right next to a major road. There is little chance of running out of petrol in the middle of nowhere as there are many petrol stations pretty much everywhere. Equally comforting is the number of garages. For relatively little money and almost always right away, the 'automehaničar' will make repairs and the 'vulkanizer' will fix your flat tire.

Driving in Bosnia and Herzegovina is nice, but some warnings are in order:

- The first few times you go through them, the tunnels of Bosnia and Herzegovina are unnerving. They are unlit and entering them on a sunny day is blinding. Your eyes will need a few seconds to adjust to the pitch black. You cannot just assume that straight driving will be safe as tunnels may curve and may have pot-holes and water dripping from the ceiling. Most tunnels have a sign indicating the length of the tunnel to prepare you for what is in store. Don't forget to take off your sunglasses before entering! I forgot it once and will never forget the experience.
- Take a good map with you. Road signs in some areas are frequent and accurate but they may suddenly be gone altogether.
- Road signs in the Republika Srpska are mostly in Cyrillic. There is a Cyrillic alphabet section in the back of this book.
- First-hand and second-hand spare parts for German-made cars are widely available. For other cars, spare parts may be a little more difficult to find.
- People might tell you that fuel is best bought in the Federation, as some stations in the Republika Srpska have a reputation for mixing water in with the fuel. I have never had any trouble myself.
- The law stipulates that you always have to carry a spare tyre, a jack, an extra headlight bulb, a first-aid kit, a tow rope and a hazard triangle. During a routine police check you may have to show that you do indeed have all that.
- In the winter period, snow chains are vital.

It takes three hours to reach Sarajevo from the border at Metković/Doljani in southern Dalmatia. The route going through Trebinje and Stolac takes one hour more, but nonetheless has my personal preference every time I go to Dubrovnik, as the route is scenic and quiet. From the Split area the best route goes through Kamensko, Livno, Bugojno and Travnik. The route through Tomislav-Grad to Jablanica is stunning, but much of the road is not asphalted, and there are a few forks without signs. There is a road from Sinj via Bili Brig to Livno as well. It may look tempting on the map but is all but inaccessible in reality. From the north, the quickest route to Sarajevo is from Slavonski Brod and Bosanski Brod. However, this route is *not* advisable if this is your first trip to the country. The reason is the war damage you'll see along the road between Brod and Doboj. With every single house completely destroyed for kilometers on stretch, this is perhaps the most depressing road in the country. The routes going through Bihać or Banja Luka are longer but do not look so awful.

Renting a car is easy but costly. Daily rate vary from 75KM to 150KM (with occasional offers at lower prices), with discounts offered if you rent for a longer period. All major cities have car-rental companies. If you arrive at the Sarajevo airport you will find several rental places at the airport. F Rent a Car SA (Kranjčevićeva 39; tel: +387 33 219 177; email: fracsa@team.ba; web: www.frac.co.ba) does airport pick-ups and offers some of the best rates in town, but occasionally fails to give you the car they promised. Avis (tel: +387 33 463 598; fax: +387 33 523 030), Budget (+387 33 234 842 ext. 216), Europcar (tel: +387 33 289 273; fax: +387 33 460 737; email: asa-rent@bih.net.ba) and Hertz (tel: +387 33 668 186) all have desks at the airport. It's usually not a problem to rent a car without reservations when you arrive. Local information on many of the major car-rental companies can be found via links from the international websites and international toll-free phone numbers. Budget offers automatic transmission cars.

Hitchhiking

Unlike hitchhiking in Western Europe, hitchhiking in Bosnia and Herzegovina is not a thing for young people only. On the contrary: many hitchhikers appear to be well over 60.

In the rural areas of Bosnia and Herzegovina, hitchhiking is common practice. In and around the bigger cities it is slightly less common, but there, too, long waits are the exception. Young women rarely hitchhike alone. As in other countries: don't get in if you don't trust the driver.

By bicycle

Roads are often rather narrow and road biking is rare. With the many fast and reckless drivers, biking is not altogether safe on the main routes. But certain parts of the country are just perfect for biking. You can bike for hours on end without experiencing much traffic at all in Popovo polje from Stolac towards Trebinje, or in the large, picturesque valleys of Livanjsko and the Glamočko fields in western Bosnia.

Mountain biking is better still. Hundreds of highland villages are connected by good gravel roads almost everywhere in the country. Igman-Bjelašnica-Visočica in the Sarajevo area offers days of mountain biking trails in breathtaking mountain landscapes.

Bikers should follow the same safety precautions as hikers and stick to the roads and marked paths. Don't wander if you don't know where you are and where you are going. Roads have been cleared of mines, even the isolated gravel ones, but in some places a mine could be just 10m off the side of the road. If you don't know, don't go – or go with a guide.

Hiking

It is already obvious within town: the people from Bosnia and Herzegovina like walking. The habit of taking the car for whatever errand does not exist here, and leisure time with friends or family is often spent on foot, with long strolls through town or in the park. Municipal authorities respect this hobby, and most towns have designated areas for pedestrians only.

And they don't only stroll: all age groups hike, and the hikes they make are often so heavy that the average foreigner will be unable to keep up. These hikes are made for fun – though they can easily take you from town to town and end in family visits - and the routes chosen are beautiful. Deep canyons, raging rivers, high Dinaric peaks, endemic flowers and plants and breathtaking views wherever you turn. For good reasons, big roads are avoided. Pavements do not exist in between towns, road shoulders are rare, and drivers have little respect for pedestrians.

The former Yugoslavia had one of the best-developed systems of mountain trails in Europe. The 'transverzala' connected the Slovenian Alps with the mountains in Macedonia - these trails went through the heart of Bosnia and Herzegovina. Due to the war many trails have disappeared, but mountain associations are in the process of restoring them. The trails' marks are red circles with white dots in the middle. Seeing one is a good sign that you are on a trail that eventually leads to somewhere. You may find the marks on trees or large stones along the trail. The best marked mountain with trail maps is Bjelašnica. The mountain association sells maps and has done an excellent job of keeping the trails clearly marked.

As said repeatedly before, it is not advisable to walk or hike without first checking the mine situation. If you are on a trail that has obviously not been trekked for some time or has faded trail markings you may not want to be there. Fresh trail markings mean that the mountain associations have had the area checked and that they trek it themselves. It is wise to bring a map, compass and GPS if you have one. Check out the sections on safety and what to take for a few additional notes on hiking and hiking requirements.

If you are into hiking, you might want to buy another book of this series. 'Forgotten Beauty' by Matias Gomes describes all hikes over 2,000 meters throughout the country. Without such a book, even the most experienced hiker is recommended to go with a guide. There are literally hundreds of safe trails to trek and hike on. Best not to do it alone.

TOURIST INFORMATION

There are plans to establish a few Bosnia and Herzegovina tourist offices abroad, but at the time of writing none of them had yet opened its doors. The embassies have little or no tourist information available.

Once you are in Sarajevo, the situation is much better. There is a very good tourist information office located close to the cathedral. (tel: 033 220 721/724; fax: 033 532 281; email: tour.off@bih.net.ba; web: www.sarajevo-tourism.com; stand with your back to the cathedral and walk straight down the walkway past Central Café; turn left on Zelene beretke and look for number 22a, 50m down on the right-hand side). Information on hotels, museums, excursions, city tours and other activities is all readily available, and their maps and leaflets are for free. The staff speak English, German,

French and Turkish. They appear to enjoy their work and will go out of their way to help. The very same people give superb guided tours through town.

Alternatively, you could simply check www.city.ba, an up-to-date website on events in the city. The International Women's Club of Sarajevo has produced a well-made practical 'mini' guide to Sarajevo called Opening Doors to Sarajevo, a Selected Guide. The guide is worth the 10KM it costs. Part of the money goes to a good cause.

There is a reasonable tourism information office close to the old bridge in Mostar as well (tel: 036 580 833; email: info@touristinfomostar.co.ba; web: www.touristinfomostar.co.ba).

MAPS

Good road maps of Bosnia and Herzegovina are available in most travel shops, bookshops and airports around Europe. Due to Croatia's odd shape, most maps of Croatia include all of Bosnia and Herzegovina. In-country, maps can be found at a few petrol stations and in some of the bookshops.

All updated European maps include Bosnia and Herzegovina and its main communication arteries. They lack detail and will make you lose your way. The routes suggested by web-based route finders are OK, but the maps are too vague and the estimated travel times do not make any sense at all as the route finders assume unrealistically high average speeds.

The Freytag and Berndt map of Bosnia and Herzegovina and Europe (1:250,000), the Studio FMB map (1:300,000) and the Trasat Polo map of Bosnia and Herzegovina, Croatia and Slovenia (1:500,000) are all good and cost in the range of 12-16 KM. Maps can also be found at www.kakarigi.net/maps (hundreds of maps of cities, towns, mountains and lakes but no map of the country as a whole), www.mapabih.com (for business people) and www.embassyworld.com/maps (lots of links to all sorts of maps). The maps that are available, free of charge, from tourism information centers around the country show the main routes only. If you are really, really into maps, you might want to buy Povijesni Atlas Bosne i Hercegovine, a book with 350 pages of historic maps. At the time of writing, it exists in the local language only, but there are plans to translate it into English.

HEALTH

The chance of getting one of the standard travelers' diseases is very slight, as drinking water throughout the country is excellent and food hygiene is good. Bosnia and Herzegovina has no legal requirements for vaccinations, but visitors are generally advised to be immunized against hepatitis A and B, tetanus, diphtheria, polio, and typhoid. Note that many people ignore this, and that I have never heard of anybody getting sick as a consequence.

To find a pharmacy, ask for 'apoteka'. In major centers, there are many of them, and there is usually at least one that is open 24 hours a day. These pharmacies will generally have all regular prescription drugs readily available. In villages and smaller towns, you may not find a pharmacy at all. If you do find one, it may not stock what you need. The best pharmacy in the country is probably Sarajevo Pharmacy at Saliha Hadžihuseinovića

Muvekita 11 in Sarajevo (tel: 033 722 666; fax: 033 722 667; email: apoteke@bih.net.ba; web: www.apoteke-sarajevo.com).

Public health clinics in Bosnia and Herzegovina are not what they should be, but there are some very good doctors in most towns. It is best to contact your embassy if you need medical attention, as embassies usually have lists of doctors they have good experiences with.

SAFETY

You are going to Bosnia? Are you sure? Why would you do that? Is it safe there? Aren't there mines?

You can't come to Bosnia and Herzegovina without having this conversation. It is an understandable concern: there *are* mines in Bosnia and Herzegovina and, with the clearing process progressing slowly, there will continue to be mines for the decades to come. But that does not mean that visiting Bosnia and Herzegovina is unsafe. So far, no visitor to Bosnia and Herzegovina has ever been involved in a mine incident.

Mine safety is a matter of respecting a few rules:

- Highly populated areas, national parks and conservation areas are all clear of mines and safe to visit.
- Stay away from taped areas. Whether in yellow or red, whether the markings are new or old: just simply never go there.
- If you are in the countryside, stay away from areas that are not obviously frequented by people. Look for cut grass, tire tracks, footprints or rubbish – all indications of safe areas. Obviously, areas in which people are walking, jogging, BBQ-ing et cetera are safe. Conversely, abandoned villages – however much fun it seems to explore them - may pose a threat.
- The most dangerous areas are the former lines of confrontation in the countryside. Many mountain ranges and some rural areas are still contaminated. As tourists and travelers would not normally know much about the location of these former confrontation lines, it is best to take a guide or a local who knows the terrain. Mountain associations and eco-tourism organizations are your best bet for a safe mountain adventure. There is plenty of safe hiking, walking, wandering and exploring to be done in Bosnia and Herzegovina – it is simply not wise to do it alone.

For more information, you could visit the Mine Action Centre (MAC; Zmaja od Bosne 8 in Sarajevo) or visit the center's website (www.bhmac.org).

Apart from the mines, Bosnia and Herzegovina is one of the safest places in Europe. Violent crime is virtually non-existent. For men and women alike, walking the streets of any town or city at any time of day or night is a relatively safe bet.

Traffic may be risky. Most of Bosnia and Herzegovina's roads are narrow and curvy. Road maintenance is getting better but don't let a pot-hole surprise you. The locals tend to drive fast and have little fear of overtaking on a solid line. Other than that, the main concerns for travelers are car thieves and pickpockets. Always lock your car doors, and engage your alarm if you have one. In trams and buses, keep your purse closed and your wallet in your front pocket. Pickpockets are quick and talented, and you will not even know that you have been had until later. They usually work in pairs.

Mountain safety

Bringing a few extras on your hikes adds weight but could save your life in an emergency situation. It is always good to bring high-energy food items. Even outside the summer months a hat and 15+ sunscreen are essential in the mountains. The high mountain sun exposure can be particularly dangerous in summer and a sunstroke is a bad thing to get when you are hours away from help. To prevent sunstroke, also protect your face and back of the neck when the sun is particularly fierce.

Bring water, but also try the sources you'll find on your way. Most water sources are perfectly safe for drinking. Stay away if a source is clogged with moss and algae. Mountain huts on spots without sources closeby generally have water storage reservoirs. If you come across a metal lid near a hut it is probably a rain collection tank. Check it first, but they are usually good for drinking.

Bosnia and Herzegovina is a mountainous land and each valley and range has its own unique system. A rainy day in town could coincide with a sunny afternoon on the mountains around it and freezing winds on their peaks. A consequence is that the weather conditions in town should not affect your packing. The high altitude mountain ranges can experience drastic temperature changes. When a storm or fog rolls in, the temperature can easily drop 10-15° C in a matter of hours. Consequently, even if it is pleasantly warm in town, a warm fleece and an extra shirt and socks could help prevent catching a cold in the mountains.

Many trails are not as well-maintained as they were before the war, so it is best to wear good boots that give you adequate ankle support. Loose rocks, fallen tree limbs or erosion can be enough to twist an ankle and abruptly end your hike.

There are two types of poisonous snakes in Bosnia and Herzegovina. Although their bites are rarely fatal, your first aid box should contain a snake bite kit. These kits can be purchased in most outdoor shops in the West. They are compact, easy to carry, and normally come with very clear instructions. Prevention, of course, is the best protection. Be aware of where you are stepping. In the summer months snakes can be found in clear water rivers and streams. They will also gather on the sunny side of mountains. Be careful around rocky areas with cracks and holes; these are snakes' favorite hiding spots. In the early autumn they tend to linger on tree limbs. The colder air makes them rather lethargic and they are less of a threat than during the hot season. Poisonous snakes only inject venom 25% of the time. If you are bitten it is best to stay calm. The faster your blood circulates the faster the poison travels through your system. Don't let this information scare you. Snakes are more afraid of you than you are of them, and anxious to get out of your way.

Lightning strikes occur frequently on high ridges during a storm, particularly above river canyons. If you see lightning while you are trekking on a ridge get out of there quickly. There are often signs (such as struck-down black pines) that indicate you're in a dangerous area.

It is good practice to let someone know if you plan to hike solo. If you are going with a guide, safety precautions have probably been taken – but it might be wise to check. A mountain rescue service (Gorska služba za spašavanje - GSS) exists but is not present in every region. Rescuers do not always have access to helicopter assistance and it may take some time to reach you in case of an emergency.

WHAT TO TAKE

Almost anything can be bought in Bosnia and Herzegovina, and most items are relatively inexpensive.

In addition to the usual, you might want to take:
- An international driving license if you are not from the surrounding or EU countries.
- Adapters for UK or American plugs. These adapters are not for sale in Bosnia and Herzegovina. The country uses the standard European size and shape (220V and 50Hz) with twin round-pin plugs.
- Sunglasses. Summers are bright, spring and autumn have plenty of bright days, and the reflection of the sun off the snow in winter is blinding.
- A light pair of slippers if you plan on staying with Bosnians or in private accommodation. Most homes have extra slippers, called papuče, but I always find it nice to have my own.
- A jumper. Spring and autumn are similar in that many days are warm and sunny but evenings are chilly. The air is very refreshing but not if you're not dressed adequately. Even on the hottest days in the summer, evenings can be cool.
- The right footwear. The beaches are rocky and full of pebbles, walks require comfortable walking shoes or more, and even in the midst of town many pavements are covered with ice and dirty, cold slush in winter.
- Good winter gear. Thermal underwear, gloves, hat, scarf and rain gear are recommended.

If you intend to hike, you should not forget:
- A water bottle, to be filled at the many springs that you'll pass by on your walks.
- A sunhat, especially if you are planning to do high mountain hikes.
- A snake-bite suction kit, as it's better to be safe than sorry.
- Very sturdy mountain shoes or boots, as many of the trails are not well maintained and loose rocks or roots could cause a serious ankle injury.
- A warm fleece, light rain gear, walking sticks if you use them, and a comfortable rucksack.

- Camping gear, although some of the campsites in Bosnia and Herzegovina provide tents, mats and even sleeping bags.
- Good waterproof gear (gaiters, poncho, waterproof trousers, a protective coat on your shoes) is a good idea if you visit the country in any season other than mid-summer.

Two warnings:
- Winter hiking in this country is an amazing experience, but be prepared for more than 1m of snow above the 1,000m mark during the coldest months. Bring whatever waterproof gear you have. Warm fleeces and thermals are a must. If you plan to hike to over 2,000m, boots that can be worn with crampons are best. If you don't have such gear, you could rent it from a local eco-tourism operator.
- Many travelers find it cool to dress down. Bosnia and Herzegovina is not the country for that. People tend to dress casually, even in fancy places, but their casual clothing matches and is clean and refined. In general, people attach importance to appearance

MEDIA

In the war years, television and radio stations functioned as propaganda machines. There were three main stations, each with limited reach. In addition, there were many dozens of small broadcasters, often focusing on not more than a single municipality. A few years ago, each of these stations was scrutinized and many were closed down. Although many small broadcasters still exist, if only for a few hours per week, most people in Bosnia and Herzegovina have by now moved to one of the larger stations.

There are three main television stations. Luckily for foreign viewers, none of them dubs English language programs. The Federation television station (FTV) and its Republika Srpska counterpart (RTRS) are the two stations envisioned by the Dayton Peace Agreement. They air foreign movies, news, documentaries, music specials and soaps. The best independent station is the Sarajevo-based Hayat. On air 24 hours a day for the people in Bosnia and Herzegovina and for the large diaspora in Europe and North America, Hayat broadcasts local and foreign movies and series, local news, talk shows and documentaries from all over the world. Hayat produces programs as well, for its own use and, on occasion, for CNN. Refreshingly, Hayat does not limit itself to bad news, and managed to give Bosnia and Herzegovina a bit of positive coverage through CNN.

Bosnia Daily is the only English language newspaper in Bosnia and Herzegovina. It is available by electronic subscription only (www.bosniadaily.co.ba; bdaily@megatel.ba). Most subscribers are members of the international community in Bosnia and Herzegovina, and the daily's very strong focus on the role and activities of the international community is therefore logical - but nonetheless somewhat annoying for the outsider. Other than that, this is a relatively good newspaper that carries interesting articles in surprisingly good English.

Apart from Bosnia Daily, all newspapers and magazines are printed in the local language. Perhaps more than anywhere else in the world, the written press feels that bad news sells better than good news, and tends to look very critically at whatever they see around. Endless training from the British and the Americans – through BBC and IREX – have not changed the media's inclination to criticize anything and everything. Going through the local language newspapers, one gets the wrong impression that there is no progress and no hope of progress in this country.

COMMUNICATIONS

Post

Letters to a home address tend to arrive but may take a long time. Packages are a bit riskier and collecting them can be time-consuming. You will receive a yellow slip at the place you are staying, indicating a period within which you should collect your package. With this yellow slip and an ID, you have to come to the post office and go through quite some form-filling and fee-paying. Do not be surprised if your package looks opened and tattered.

There appears to be no service standards and the post office experience depends entirely on the individuals behind the counter. It happened that I walked into a post office, bought stamps and telephone cards, sent a letter by registered mail, and was done within a few minutes. On another occasion, I found the post office staff in the midst of their coffees and cigarettes, seemingly unaware of the people waiting at the counter. Eventually they looked up and started to help people in random order (the discretion line meant nothing to most customers), charging dubious fees in the process.

Telephone

Phoning to Bosnia and Herzegovina: **+387**

Phoning from Bosnia and Herzegovina: **00** – country code – city code without the **0** - number.

Phoning from hotels is often senselessly expensive. Check the prices before you chat away. Phone booths – you will find them at the bus stations and post offices – are a lot cheaper, but still charge more than what you are probably used to. The phones do not accept coins. 10 KM and 20 KM cards can be bought from the post office or at the small newspaper kiosks. Beware: different phone companies provide their services in different parts of the country and your phone cards may not be valid once you leave the town you bought them in.

The companies charge different fees and their nationalist agendas shine through these fees. From Sarajevo, a phone call to Belgrade will cost you quite a bit. Conversely, a call to Belgrade from Banja Luka is considered a local call, and there is no need to even dial the country code. If you intend to make long phone calls, you might even want to cross the entity line if that is only a bus stop away from where you are. In all cases, it is cheaper to phone after 19.00.

Mobile phones have taken Bosnia and Herzegovina by storm. Currently, there are three GSM servers in the country: BiH telecom (061), Eronet (063) and Mobi (065). Unlike the phone card systems, the signals of these servers overlap. This means that, unless you are in the midst of nature or in an isolated village, the signal is generally good.

CENTRAL & NORTH BOSNIA

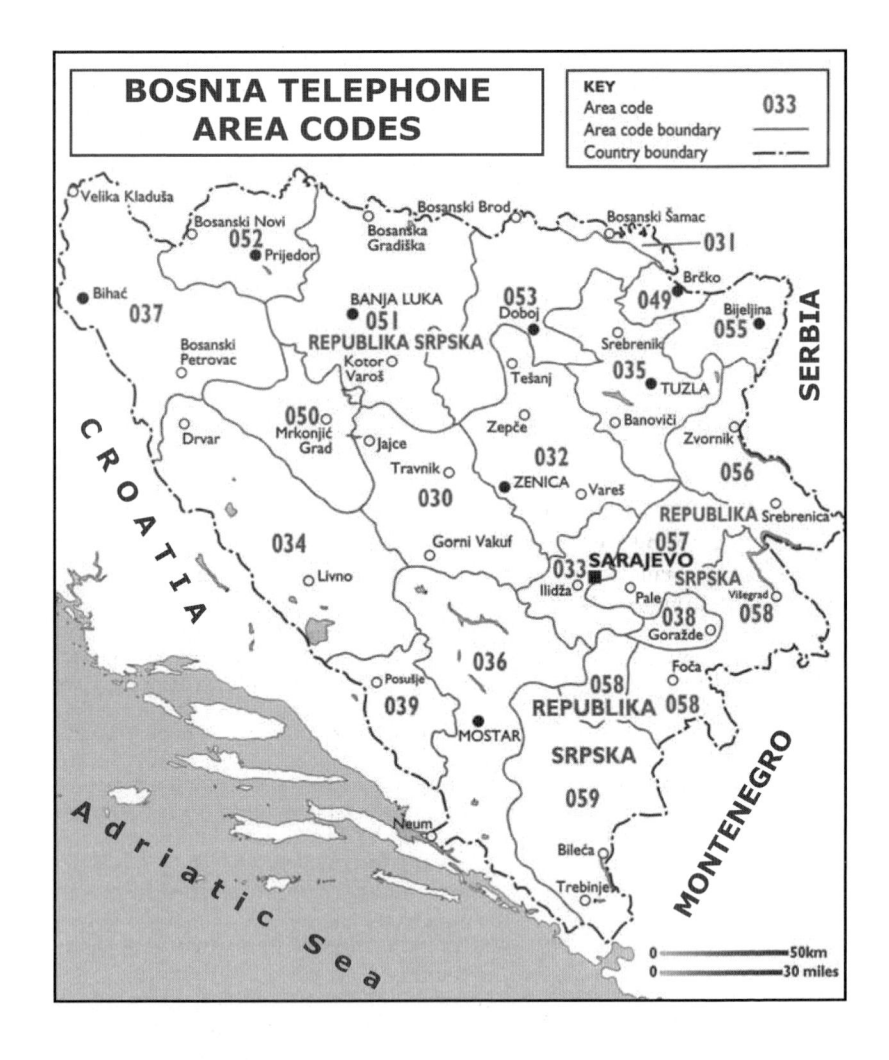

BOSNIA TELEPHONE AREA CODES

KEY
Area code — 033
Area code boundary
Country boundary

THE COUNTRY   63

European GSM mobiles have roaming agreements with Bosnia and Herzegovina, but roaming prices are high. American and Canadian mobile phones do not allow for roaming at all. In either case, you might want to buy a local SIM card. The first purchase of a local SIM ultra card costs 50 KM, including 10 KM call credit. Call credit is available in the form of 20 KM and 50 KM cards, and can be bought from the post office or at the small newspaper kiosks.

Telephone numbers

Emergencies	124
Police	122
Fire	123
Ambulance	124
Emergency roadside service	1282, 1288
Telegram service	1202
Express delivery (EMS)	1417
Operator, local numbers	1182, 1185, 1186, 1188
Operator, international numbers	1201

Internet

Bosnia and Herzegovina does not have the quick, fluid internet communication that is now common in the West, and has just started to scratch the surface of cyber culture. An increasing number of businesses, including hotels and tourist attractions, have websites and email addresses, but the information content is often limited and emails are not always replied to. Since 2001, internet cafes have been popping up. They typically charge 1 KM per hour and the connections are usually slow. In the main towns, many hotels offer internet connections as well, at various fees.

MONEY

Originally, the KM was pegged to the German mark. With the introduction of the Euro, the KM changed its peg without the least bit of trouble (1.95 KM for 1 Euro). Most shops will accept payment in Euro bills, using a 1 to 2 ratio. There are many ATM machines in all major towns and cities.

US dollars, British pounds, Yens and other major currencies can be exchanged at the banks and exchange offices that are present in most major towns. They also swap your leftover KMs back into any of these main currencies. Most banks do not have a fixed fee, but take a percentage of the total amount. As this percentage varies, you should do a bit of research before exchanging large amounts of money. Travelers' cheques are unusual, and appear to be taken by the Central Profit Bank in the old town of Sarajevo only.

Although credit cards are increasingly widely accepted in major towns, you should not rely on them. Even in the bigger towns almost nobody accepts American Express.

Make sure you have all the cash you need before leaving the major towns, as it is next to impossible to find a money machine or anybody who accepts credit card payments in smaller towns and villages.

In case of emergency: Raiffeisen Bank handles Western Union money transfers.

> **Normalizing life in Bosnia and Herzegovina**
>
> People sometimes get frustrated because, almost a decade after the end of the war, the standard of living is still far below what it was in pre-war Yugoslavia. But there *is* obvious progress in many fields. Take money. In the early post-war period, different parts of the country used to have different currencies. Today, the 'Convertible Mark' (KM or BAM) is fully trusted, experiences little or no inflation, and is accepted anywhere in the country.

BUDGETING

This country is not quite as cheap as the 10 dollar-a-day destinations in the developing world, but if you are used to Western Europe and North America, you will find Bosnia and Herzegovina surprisingly inexpensive. Food, going out, transport: it all costs very little and the prices get even lower when you leave the urban centres.

Most food in Bosnia and Herzegovina is of high quality and very affordable. A fine three-course meal in a good restaurant will cost some 20 to 30 KM, excluding modestly priced beverages. If you have much less to spend it is possible to have a 3 KM meal with pies and yoghurt or to get affordable food from any of the many supermarkets.

Going out is possible whatever your budget. If you have little, do as many Bosnians do: stroll, drink espressos for 1 KM and eat ice cream for 0.5 KM. If you have a little more, a world of possibilities opens up. Cinemas cost 5 KM and theatre tickets set you back between 5 and 25 KM. Discotheques ask relatively high prices (3 to 5 KM) for their drinks but do not usually charge an entry fee.

Transport between cities is very reasonably priced. Mostar to Sarajevo will cost you between 10 and 18 KM, for example. Within town, buses are always cheap, but taxi prices depend on the town you're in. The general rule appears to be: the smaller the town and the lower the number of taxis, the more expensive they are.

In comparison, accommodation seems a little overpriced. Most hotels will not accommodate you for less than 60 KM per night in a single, or less than 75 in a double. If you are a budget traveler, you should not stay in such hotels. Instead, you should pay anything between 15 and 25 KM per night for a bed in a private house. That cuts back costs significantly. If you then spend most days enjoying the city's lively streets and parks, not its restaurants and organized tours and trips, Bosnia and Herzegovina should not cost you more than 40 KM (20 euro) per day.

For hikers and adventure-seekers, day trips cost between 20 and 75 KM. A weekend trip with food, guide, transport and accommodation will cost around 150-200 KM. Week-long trips in the mountains are 700-1,200 KM, fully inclusive.

ACCOMMODATION

Hotels

The war destroyed many of the country's hotels, and in the post-war years many of the remaining hotels housed displaced people rather than tourists. But many new hotels have been built recently and many old ones have been reconstructed or renovated.

The number of stars won't tell you much. First, the categories in the Federation and the Republika Srpska are not the same, and two three-star hotels can be worlds apart. Second, the rating does not consider either the cleanliness or the hotel's atmosphere. To avoid ending up in an uncomfortable pre-war state-owned hotel, it is always wise to check out the hotel before booking in.

The main cities generally have one or more nice and fairly large hotels. Elsewhere, hotels and motels are smaller and usually family-owned. They tend to be affordable and well-kept, and you might be able to bargain a little. Most places include breakfast in the price. Breakfast might be continental or even English in the larger hotels but you are more likely to be served a thin omelet and cheese and jams with bread. Hotels usually offer half board (polu - pansion, with breakfast and dinner) or full board (pun pansion, with breakfast, lunch and dinner), but the price on the price list usually includes breakfast only. Dining out in Bosnia and Herzegovina costs so little that it may both be cheaper and more enjoyable to try out some of the restaurants in town.

There is a 2KM accommodation tax that is not usually included in the price.

Private rooms/apartments

Private accommodation is not as well-organized as in neighboring Croatia but many travel agencies in towns throughout the country do offer accommodation in apartments and private homes. Hosts are invariably friendly, but do not always speak English. A few German words are usually helpful.

In the countryside, you are unlikely to find a room sign or anything else offering private accommodation. But the locals are extremely friendly and it is not offensive to ask somebody for the possibilities. They will probably refuse money but leaving 10KM for coffee and cigarettes is a welcome gesture. Solo women travelers planning to stay in private accommodation should make sure there are other women around.

Campsites

There are quite a few campsites in Bosnia and Herzegovina. Some are close to town, but most are hard to get to and from if you don't have your own transport. Quite a few have a snack bar and toilets only, and cater mostly to day trippers. The best camping opportunities are hard to find, but can be booked through the rafting operators on the Tara, Neretva and Una rivers. It is possible to camp even if you didn't bring either a tent or mats, as some campsites pitch and equip a few tents in the summer period.

Pitching a tent on your own is possible but could be risky if you are not fully confident that you are in a mine-free area.

Mountain lodges

Unfortunately, many of the mountain lodges were destroyed during the war. But some have survived and some others have been reconstructed in the past few years. They have dormitories and a great location, and sometimes offer food. They do not normally have any single or double rooms.

EATING

From whatever angle you look at it: the people in Bosnia and Herzegovina take eating and drinking very seriously. Meals for guests are elaborate and everything is made from scratch. The number of coffee shops, bars, terraces, snack bars and restaurants around the country is mind-blowing. Picnicking families roast their lambs in their entirety. Workers generally receive a 7 to 10 KM 'hot meal allowance' per working day, meant to cover lunch but in reality often a quarter or more of their total remuneration.

Bosnia and Herzegovina's culinary traditions are very strong, and people do not like change. If what you are looking for is not within the tradition of the region, you will have difficulty finding it. The only places that might serve a typical English breakfast are the larger hotels. Pizza has been embraced (if occasionally with mayonnaise), but the Chinese, Indian and Mexican restaurants largely depend on foreigners. If you end up cooking for local people – excluding the people working for one of the international organizations – the chances they'll genuinely enjoy your food are slim.

It's best to go local. Bakeries open early and sell hot rolls, croissants, brown bread and apple and cherry strudels. You can take your breakfast to a café and enjoy it with your morning coffee. Most bakeries will make you a sandwich upon request: white bread with thick slices of cheese and bright pink processed meat with a lot of mayonnaise, generally. A little heavy for breakfast but a must-try for lunch are the famous dishes of burek, zeljanica, sirnica and krompiruša. As everything else, these filo-dough wrapped pies are made from scratch and have been a traditional meal since Ottoman times. Burek is a meat pie. Zeljanica is made from spinach and cheese. Sirnica is made from a fresh, home-made cheese and krompiruša is filo-dough with diced potatoes and spices. They may ask if you like pavlaka spread on top. Pavlaka is a fresh cream that tastes wonderful with the pita. Alternatively, try yoghurt alongside your pita. If you are into local cuisine, ask if you can watch them making these pies: it's amazing how they stretch that dough!

Dinner has more options than breakfast or lunch. The following lists include the most common dishes. Be forewarned that most people in Bosnia and Herzegovina smoke and that non-smoking restaurants do not exist.

Meats

People like eating meat

Soon after my first arrival in Bosnia and Herzegovina, I organized a workshop in a large mountain hut near Zenica. The prices were modest, the rooms looked good, and the food, the man assured me, was excellent. I ordered lunch and dinner for 25

> people. At 13.00, we got five types of meat and fries. At 19.00, we got six types of meat, fries and a small salad. When I expressed my surprise, my colleagues all assured me that these meals were exactly as meals should be.

If you like meat, you will like Bosnia and Herzegovina. Meat is a standard for any meal. With the exception of chicken, most meat is fresh from the mountainside. It is common practice here to raise all animals free range, with plenty of space and without any hormones or chemicals. You will taste the difference.

Bamija	- okra with veal.
Begova čorba	- the most popular soup, made of veal and vegetables.
Bosanski lonac	- meat stew cooked over an open fire.
Ćevapi	- small meat sausages of lamb and beef mix. They are usually served with fresh onions and pita bread on the side.
Filovane paprike	- fried peppers stuffed with minced meat and spices.
Ispod saća	- similar to a Dutch oven. A metal dish is placed on hot coals, the food is placed in the dish and covered by a lid which is then completely covered in hot coals and left to bake.
Janjetina	- lamb grilled over an open fire.
Musaka	- a meat pie made of minced beef, very similar to shepherd's pie.
Pršut	- air-dried ham, similar to Italian prosciutto.
Sarme	- meat and rice rolled in cabbage or grape leaves.
Sogandolma	- fried onions stuffed with minced meat.
Sudžuk	- beef sausages similar to pepperoni.
Suho meso	- dried beef.
Slanina	- dried bacon-like pork.
Teletina	- veal, usually served in cutlets. Veal in Bosnia and Herzegovina is not produced by locking calves in a cage to ensure softer meat.

Cheeses

Iz mjeha - sheep's milk poured into a specially sewn sheepskin 'bag.' After a time the dry cheese is taken out of the skin container and the result is a strong, dry cheese that resembles parmesan.

Kajmak - the most difficult of all cheeses to translate. It is the top layer skimmed from milk, creamy and extremely tasty. Kajmak and uštipak (doughnut-type roll) is a wonderful appetiser.

Livanjski - similar to the dry yellow cheeses of Dalmatia. It is very tasty and usually more expensive than other types of cheese. It originates from the west Bosnian town of Livno.

Mladi sir - literally means young cheese. There isn't an equivalent to it in English. It has a soft texture and is unsalted. Often it is served with a cream sauce on top. It is very healthy.

Travnički - a white, feta-like cheese from the Travnik district in central Bosnia. It is a bit salty and very popular with 'meza', which is the tradition of slow drinking and eating throughout the course of a whole day.

Vlašićki - similar to travnički cheese. It is a highland cheese from the mountain villages on Vlašić Mountain in central Bosnia.

Sweets

Baklava	- cake made with pastry sheets, nuts and sugar syrup.
Hurmašica	- date-shaped pastry soaked in a very sweet syrup sauce.
Rahatlokum	- Turkish delight, a jelly-like candy covered in powdered sugar and often served with Turkish coffee.
Ružica	- similar to baklava but baked with raisins in small roll.
Tufahija	- stewed apples stuffed with a walnut filling.

DRINKING

Water

Tourism promotion requires simple images. Bosnia and Herzegovina's first countrywide promotional brochure used the country's ancient tombstones. They are old, unique to the country and quite beautiful. Discussing the importance of national symbols at the Sarajevo University, one of the students said she didn't think the tombstone was a very appealing symbol, as the tombstone is linked with death. She suggested using the opposite - life - for future promotion material. She suggested using the country's abundant natural springs.

The student had a point. Pretty much everywhere around the country, water just comes straight out of the ground or the mountainside. Many local water supply systems are not more than a few pipes connected to one of those springs. Almost every town has one of more public fountains – often to be found in front of the mosque – and the water is invariably excellent. There are roadside fountains as well, built long ago for travelers, and most mountain walks will pass by small springs and streams of sparkling fresh water. In short, you have no worries when drinking the water in Bosnia from the tap or elsewhere. It is probably higher quality water than you have at home!

'Mineralna voda' is bottled throughout the country. Try Ilidžanski dijamant, Sarajevski kiseljak, Tešanjski dijamant or Oaza.

Coffee and tea

When in Rome, do as the Romans do. In Bosnia and Herzegovina, they drink coffee. It is the backbone of social life. During the war, when everything was scarce, coffee was amongst the most sought after commodities.

Immediately after the war ended, coffee was the main symbol of a post-war reconciliation campaign. "Tolerance. Let's have a coffee".

Nowadays, coffee is widely available and affordable. The traditional coffee is *'bosanska kafa'*. It is similar to what the rest of the world calls Turkish coffee, and it is served with oddly-shaped sugar cubes and 'rahatlokum' (Turkish delight). By now, espresso and white coffee are available everywhere in towns and cities. In town, an espresso will cost you 1 KM. The other coffees are more expensive. In villages, you may well get your Bosanska kafa for 0.5 KM.

There is a tea drinking tradition as well. You'll enjoy your tea most if you drink what the locals drink. Don't ask for black tea with milk. People here don't drink it, don't know about it and don't serve it well. Try the herbal teas instead. There are a great many types and they generally have a very nice fragrance. They are often organic and come straight from the forest.

Juices

In most places, lemonade and orange juice are the only fresh squeezed juices available. Bottled juices, however, come in all sorts. The locally produced brands – *Swity* being the largest one - are wonderfully delicious. Historically, Croatia and Slovenia produced and sold the final consumer goods, while Bosnia and Herzegovina had specialized in raw commodities and half fabricates. They didn't sell directly to consumers and, consequently, they don't know *how* to sell. The result in the fruit juice sector is that Slovenian and Croatian brands dominate the market, and that the various local brands are still struggling to get the substantial market shares their products deserve. Enough of the economics though, buy local goods – it's good for the country and it's good for you!

Beer

Local beer is cheap. The first word learned by many foreign visitors is *pivo*. If you like beer, this word is crucial to your trip. A half-liter bottle costs 1 KM in the shop and only 2 or 3 KM in restaurants and bars. Try *Sarajevsko*, *Nektar* and *Preminger*. *Ožujsko* is a good Croatian beer that is also produced locally. In some parts of the Republika Srpska you can find Nikšičko pivo from Montenegro – it's a great beer and according to many locals one of the best in the region. Other imports are available everywhere. They are reasonably priced, but of course more expensive than local beers without really tasting any better.

Wine

The lack of advanced marketing skills shows in the wine sector as it does in the fruit juice sector. The wine-making tradition of Herzegovina dates back to Roman times, and in terms of price and quality the savory reds and dry whites of Herzegovina easily deserve a share in the world wine market. In reality, Herzegovinan wines are rarely seen outside the region. While you're in the country, try them. Stankela, Gangaš žilavka and a range of other sorts will cost you 5 to 20 KM in the shop and 15-35 KM in restaurants.

Spirits

Made from plums, pears, apples or grapes, the local spirits are amazing. They are strong, very strong, with alcohol levels commonly exceeding 40 percent. They are drunk at all times of the day and at all times of the year. Šljivovica (plum) or kruška (pear) are found more in Bosnia. Loza, made of grapes, is the specialty of Herzegovina and Dalmatia (which share the same climate and topsoil and therefore produce very similar grapes). There are a few brand names that you will find everywhere, but the best spirits are home-made. The careful process of making spirits is a male-dominated skill. The Croats in Herzegovina make the best wine and loza, the Serbs make the best šljivovica and kruška. The men who are into producing it will offer a taste of their products as if it were coffee – but with a lot more pride.

PUBLIC HOLIDAYS

Changing every year	Bajrams (Muslim Holy Days)
January 1	New Year
January 7	Orthodox Christmas
January 14	Orthodox New Year
March 1	Independence day
May 1	Labor Day
November 25	Day of the State
December 25	Catholic Christmas

SHOPPING

If you are in any of the main towns, there is a good chance you are close to a 24-hour bakery that took its fresh bread out of the oven just now. The closest grocery shop is probably less than a few minutes away. It is open from the early morning to the late evening, and quite possibly all through the night as well. It sells the exact same products as a thousand other grocery shops around the city. If you need products they do not have, you will succeed in one of the hypermarkets. Snack stands and newspaper kiosks are just around the corner, down town is for fashion and souvenirs, and everything else is spread around the city. There really isn't a thing you can't buy here, and items that are covered separately in guide books to many developing countries (film, sanitary napkins, sun lotion) are all widely available.

Prices in Bosnia and Herzegovina are fixed. While you might successfully try to reduce the price for a room in a family-owned hotel, you would look silly negotiating in Mercator or at the hair dresser. Souvenirs are the exception. When buying souvenirs, you need to bargain a little. Gently though: with rare exceptions, people are not inclined to rip you off at all. Similarly, somebody offering you coffee is not somebody trying to pull off a sales trick: it's what people *do* here.

Certainly unique to the country and the period are the war-related souvenirs. Mortars and bullets are carved and turned into anything from umbrella and candle holders to key chains and pens. Although very contemporary, these war souvenirs are carved in the same Ottoman tradition as the plates and tea and coffee sets. Made of gold, silver, copper, and bronze, all these metal works are good value for money. And they are not merely souvenirs for tourist consumption: unless you buy a plate saying 'best wishes from Bosnia and Herzegovina', you buy something that many Bosnians have at display in their homes. Similarly, the oriental-style rugs and all sorts of woodworks are no pseudo-historical tourist traps, but things that survived the centuries and are still part and parcel of Bosnian life.

INTERACTING WITH LOCAL PEOPLE

Even though there hasn't been a tourist boom since the end of the conflict, the locals are more than familiar with guests from every country in Europe and North America. Ever since the war began in 1992, tens of thousands of people came here as aid workers, soldiers, curious visitors, peace activists, diplomats, businessmen and pilgrims paying homage to the Virgin Mary in Međugorje. Consequently, you will be no surprise to the locals. The locals in the rural areas may stare a bit at first but that seems the thing to do in any small town or village in any other country that I've visited as well. You'll hardly be noticed in places like Sarajevo, Mostar or Banja Luka, where there is a significant international presence.

    Local people will almost always be very friendly. This is common to the region but Bosnian hospitality is something special. Bosnians will go out of their way to assist you in finding something and often invite someone to their home for a coffee. Once you enter someone's home as a guest, expect the red carpet treatment. Rich or poor, your host will most certainly serve you coffee, followed by an offer of cigarettes. The unwritten rule is never to light up without offering the people around you a cigarette as well. More than likely the host will bring out sweets (biscuits or chocolate) and if the energy is right out comes the local spirits and food. Coming from the west, one might see it as going a bit overboard, but the tradition of treating guests like one of their own is taken seriously. My advice is to sit back and enjoy, and if you're in a rush – too bad. The best way to turn down the ninth or tenth coffee, or a chunk of meat for the vegetarian (many villagers don't understand the concept) is to say 'ne mogu', which means 'I can't.' Saying 'no, thank you' simply does not work. If you find yourself shaking from the strong Turkish coffees and just want the host to stop filling your cup then leave a bit of coffee in it. As soon as you finish the host will first give you a refill and then ask if you would like some more.

    Most young people will speak at least a little bit of English, as it is taught in all the schools from an early age. American movies are popular here and many people have learned English from watching films. In western Herzegovina and northern Bosnia many people speak German. Over 300,000 refugees lived in Germany during the war and many more lived and worked in Germany before the conflict began.

    For the most part, young people here don't want to speak about the war or politics. They would rather hear about new music, cool movies, good books or just shoot the breeze with you. The older generation often brings the war and politics into conversation. Many find it therapeutic so lending an ear may be the best service you can offer someone. Comments aren't even necessary. Everyone here bears a burden from the war and oftentimes they cannot handle dealing with someone else's despair. Being a good listener can have a greater effect than one can imagine.

It's nice to exchange addresses, emails, and phone numbers with people. A postcard or phone call when you get home is always much appreciated.

A few rules

People in Bosnia and Herzegovina are very tolerant. It is not easy to offend them, and the warnings that do apply are all in line with common sense.

- People have different ways of dealing with the war. Many prefer not to talk about it. Respect that.
- Begging is one of the very worst forms of child labour. If you give in to it, you encourage it. If you do not give in to it, these poor children may have to continue begging until late at night to ensure a meal or to avoid a beating. It's a dilemma. You might want to consider giving something edible (but no sweets, as these children's nutritional status is generally awful, with a deficit in everything except for sugar).
- In summer especially, the forests get very dry and there are lots of forest fires. Be very cautious.
- Dress whichever way you like, but make sure you are covered when entering a place of worship. Mosques generally have headscarves available at the entrance.
- Ask before you take photographs – refusals are rare. If you promise to send somebody a copy, send that person that copy.
- People are likely to treat you as a guest. Consequently, they would be inclined to pay for you. Remember that most people you will meet have less money than you have. If you want to pay, act quickly and be persistent, or you will fail.
- Tips are optional. Remember that people in the catering business do not normally earn a lot. On the other hand, tips are not really all that common.

Superstitions

Some Bosnians might tell you that they're not superstitious. Well, don't believe them. What some may call superstition many Bosnians take as a natural fact. Where these beliefs have come from nobody knows in full, but rest assured the pagan Illyrians, heretic Bosnian Church, mystic rituals of eastern orthodoxy and Islam have all contributed to them. Here are just a few of the long list of superstitions....

- This one can be refuted (at least by the Bosnians) as a medical fact instead of a superstition. Drafts. Yes, drafts. All diseases are carried in drafts so if its 40 degrees outside and you see all the windows rolled up it's not because everyone has AC. Any earaches, colds, sties, headaches – well, just about any ailment is blamed on that little nip of wind from open windows. Don't be surprised to see people dashing to close the window if there is another one open in the building

THE COUNTRY

or car that you're in.
- Drinking anything cold is another great excuse, even in the middle of summer, for why someone is sick. Don't be disappointed, especially American travelers, to find no ice in most places. You'll get sick for heavens sake!
- Wet hair. On more than one occasion during the war one could find Sarajevans taking a brisk walk through sniper fire and shelling – that was normal. God forbid, though, if you stepped outside with wet hair. That is a big no-no. Wet hair, with the combination of wind (yes, even in the summer) will give you pneumonia, guaranteed. If the receptionist looks at you as if you've just been released from a 'home' she or he is simply worried about you. The general rule is you must first dry your hair with a hairdryer, wait at least an hour and then its safe to walk the streets. And you think I'm kidding.
- If you knock a glass over or spill something while speaking – that, of course, means its true.
- When describing an injury or sickness never ever show or explain it on your own body. Never.
- If you spill your coffee, don't fret it, it simply means you are about to be rewarded some material gain.
- An itchy left palm means you are about to get something (positive).
- An itchy right palm, naturally, means you are about to give something.
- An itchy nose means you are about to get angry.
- If you say something you would like to come true be sure to knock on wood three times, but from underneath – the underneath thing is key.
- Whenever entering a building always enter with right foot first.
- Whatever you do don't whistle in the house. It is a sure bet that you have summoned demons and when you leave there is no guarantee that they haven't.
- Bread is heaven's gift. Never throw it away. This rule gained strength in the war due to the extreme lack of food, every crumble was held in high regard.
- Always stir clockwise, it's the natural flow of things.
- It's bad luck to cut your nails after dark. Only daylight cutting please, you don't want to jinx yourself.
- Never stand in the middle of a doorframe...nobody knows why, it's just 'bad.'
- People talking about you makes you hick-up.

That's what we think you need to know to start your journey. Enjoy your trip through the next section!

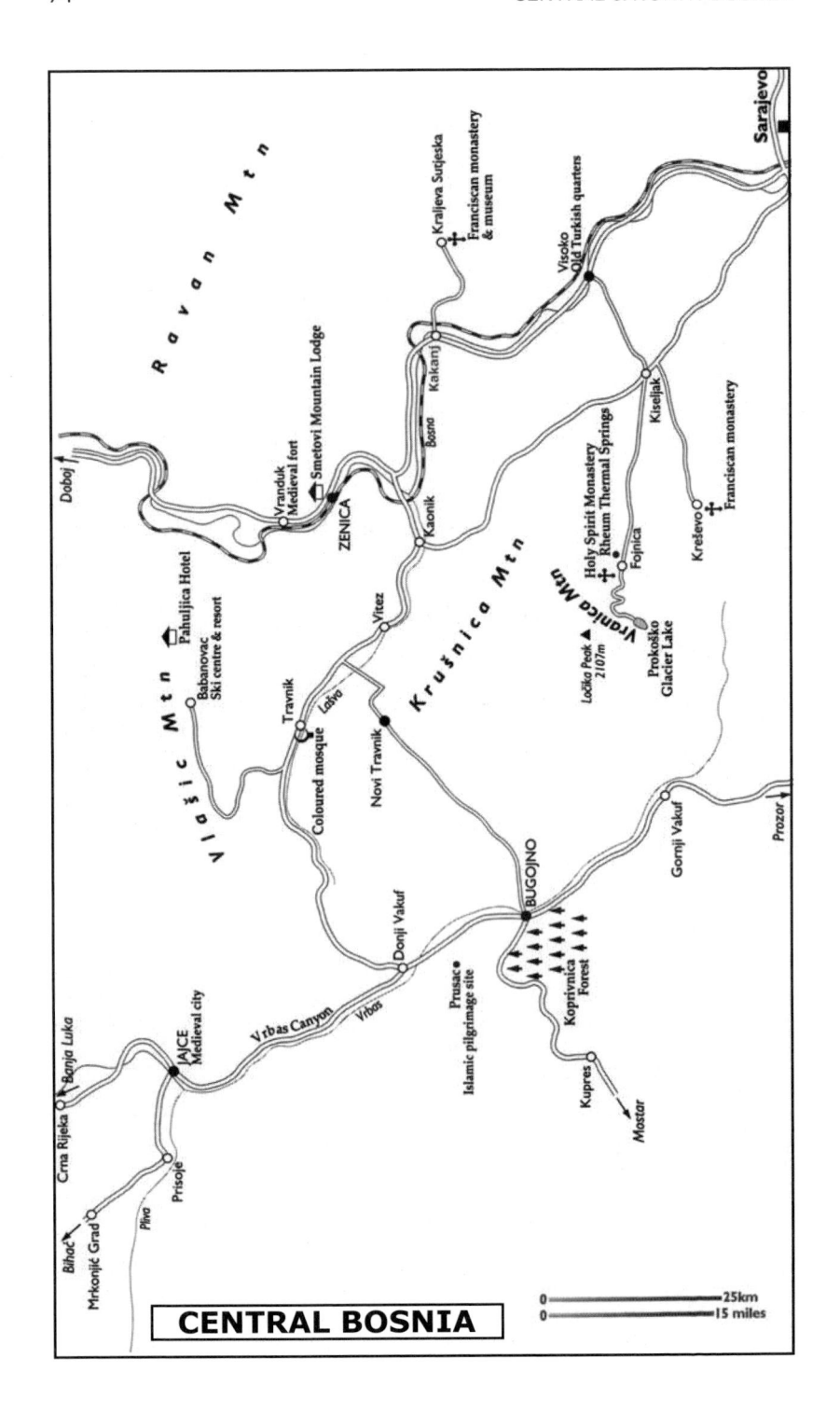

CENTRAL BOSNIA

CENTRAL BOSNIA

As the birthplace of the Bosnian state, this region has shaped much of the cultural and historical heritage of Bosnia and Herzegovina. Today, monuments around the region and, more strikingly, the region's everyday culture bear witness to Central Bosnia's rich and diverse history.

The Croat-Muslim war of the early 1990s shook Central Bosnia's multiculturalism to its very foundation and split the traditional alliance of the Bosnian Croats and Bosniacs. Recent times, however, have seen significant strides in both communities reconciling with the dark days of their past. Although the political and economic situation has greatly improved in the course of the past decade, life in this region is still immensely challenging and, as elsewhere in the country, the healing process will take decades. Meanwhile, both communities remain mutually dependent and there is little doubt that the similarities in language, culture, traditions and ways of life will overcome the few differences there are. Even today, an outsider will find it difficult to see the divides in some communities and even more difficult to understand why they exist.

A short history

The central part of Bosnia and Herzegovina was the seat of the Bosnian state in medieval times. Known as the **Srebrena Bosna** (Silver Bosna) region, it was the political, cultural and religious heart of Bosnia. All the Bosnian kings resided here. The unique 'heretic' Bosnian Church was the spiritual backbone of the small Slav communities that dotted the lush, green countryside until the 14th century. By 1340 the Franciscans had established their first order in Bosnia and in a short space of time Catholicism spread and monasteries were built in Kraljeva Sutjeska, Visoko, Kreševo and Fojnica.

With the arrival of the Ottomans in the mid 15th century, Ottoman culture asserted its influence in places like Travnik, Visoko, Donji Vakuf and Jajce. Travnik became not only the main city in central Bosnia, but also the centre of the Ottoman Empire's establishment in Bosnia and Herzegovina. Mahalas sprang up in many towns and the spread of Islam had a major impact on life in the region. Small settlements developed into towns and cities, and the once isolated mountain communities became more interconnected. The Lašva Valley was a main trading route from Dalmatia, Serbia and beyond. Travnik, heralded as the European Istanbul, soon became known for its magnificent oriental architecture and bustling trade centers.

Of all the ethnically mixed communities in Bosnia, this region in particular enjoyed a harmonious balance of Catholic and Muslim inhabitants (with a much smaller Orthodox community). The Catholics feel strongly rooted and view themselves as the only continual line of defenders of the ancient Christian Bosnian state. The Central Bosnian Franciscans are the heart and soul of this sentiment and, unlike many of their Franciscan counterparts in western Herzegovina, remain loyal to the preservation of Bosnia and Herzegovina's sovereignty.

It is impossible to find a central Bosnian town or community that hasn't intimately meshed with the other. Exploring central Bosnia's ancient fortresses, monasteries, mosques and highland villages is a journey into the very heart of the original Bosnian state and its long line of Slavic ancestors who have inhabited these lands since the 7th century.

Getting there and away

With a highly efficient bus system, both public and private, every destination in central Bosnia has daily buses from any of the main centers: Zenica, Travnik, Kiseljak, Vitez and Bugojno. The only city in central Bosnia on the train route is Zenica. Daily buses from Zagreb and Bihać travel via Jajce, Donji Vakuf, Travnik and Vitez to Sarajevo. With the exceptions of Kreševo, Kraljeva Sutjeska, Fojnica and Vranica Mountain, all towns listed in the guide are located on main roads and are clearly marked on any map of Bosnia and Herzegovina.

ZENICA

Zenica is the largest, most industrial town in central Bosnia and is the political, administrative and cultural centre of the **Zenica-Doboj Canton**. There is more to Zenica than the rather intrusive industrial zone that dominates the city's image.

Prior to the Bosnian war, Zenica was mostly known for its massive steel industry and the city grew significantly during Tito's Yugoslavia as many apartment blocks were erected to house growing mining communities. The city's population has slightly diminished since the war but at the last count there were approximately 120,000 people in Zenica, making it the fourth-largest city in the country. Peeling back the socialist layer of crude architecture and bulky industry reveals the old Zenica and the true heart of the city - a quaint downtown district with mosques, Catholic and Orthodox churches, and a Jewish synagogue.

Zenica is far from a must see destination and its industrial image does tend to deter foreign tourism. Those who do opt to take a closer look will find there is much to see and enjoy.

Getting there

Zenica is a main transit town for both trains and buses. The bus and railway stations are at the same location. All of central Bosnia and the northeast are covered by a very efficient public and private bus system. The railway

Challenging rafting: the Štrbački Buk, close to Bihać

Una River

Downtown Bihać

Rafting on the Una

An Orthodox church in the Pliva region

A chapel in Šipovo

The widespread Balkan Green Lizard (Lacerta trilineata)

station is along the main Sarajevo-Zagreb route. There is one train daily to Zenica from Sarajevo and one from Zagreb.

Tourist information

The **Tourism Board of the Zenica-Doboj Canton** (Maršala Tita 73; tel/fax: 032 441 050; email: turzedok@bih.net.ba) is located in the centre of Zenica. Although it is not an information centre they do offer some general advice in English, particularly about accommodation. Much of the information is somewhat vague and poetic and doesn't necessarily give you the detail you might need but it is certainly better than in many other areas of the country where literally nothing exists in terms of proper information. The Tourist Guide Book to Zenica, created by the now defunct Municipal Tourism Association, is helpful. 'Tourism in Zenica/Doboj Canton' is also in English but does not offer much concrete information.

Where to stay

Dom Penzionera (1 Zeničke brigade 1d; tel: 032 419 424; fax: 032 414 488; single 75KM; double 104KM) – the initial plan was that this building be used as a retiree home. Plans changed and it became one of the nicest hotels in Zenica. The rooms are spacious and have modern fittings.

Hotel Internacional (Bulevar Kulina Bana 28; tel: 032 401 888; fax: 032 416 944). The Internacional is the best of three socialist era hotels on Bulevar Kulina Bana. Singles and doubles cost 60 and 100KM.

Apartmani Fontana (Zacarina 17; tel: 032 403 309; email: restoran_fontana@yahoo.com) offers bed and breakfast accommodation. Singles and doubles cost 72 and 100KM.

Where to eat and drink

Eating out in Zenica means eating either traditional dishes or pizza.

Restaurant Fontana (Zacarina 17; tel: 032 403 309; email: restoran_fontana@yahoo.com) is on Krivače Street. It has an attractive mahala ambience. The food is fantastic and the terrace along the stream is on the sunny south side. They also have a few good and modern rooms.

The Gatto-Club is a microbrewery that has live local rock music every weekend. The beer and music are great. Like most good bars in Bosnia, it gets very smoky in here.

Restaurant Kod Kasima, next to Gatto, serves traditional Bosnian meat dishes, mainly lamb and beef, in many tasty forms. Both places are on Dr. Abdulaha Aska Borića Street running parallel to Bulevar Kulina Bana.

What to see

The most attractive part of town is known as **stara čaršija**, meaning old quarters. This has been the main gathering place since Ottoman times. In the square between Serdarevića and Maršala Tita streets, you will find the **Čaršijska Džamija, Medresa, Hadžimazića House** and the **Austrian fountain**. The Hadžimazića House is similar to the Svrzina House in Sarajevo: it is an old beg family house that has been preserved in its original form.

The house is open to visitors from Monday to Saturday. The entire square is lined with café's and competes with the **Kamberovića Polje** walkway across the Bosna River as the most popular pedestrian area in town. The **synagogue** on Jevrejska Street has been converted into the **City Museum** and **Art Gallery** (032 402 020). It is a very basic 'museum' of the old synagogue with a hall for local art exhibitions. It is open from 08.00 to 20.00 from Monday to Saturday and admission is free.

On the side of town where Branilaca Bosne and Dr. Abdulaha Aska Borića streets meet are the **Svetog Ilije Catholic Church** and school. Behind Branilaca Bosne on Travnička cesta is the **Old Orthodox Church**. I've never found it open but the architecture is admirable even from only the outside. Along the **Kočeva Stream**, not far from the church is the **Sučića Mlin**, an old family mill that is still functional.

Perhaps the most significant relic of Zenica's historical heritage is the **Vranduk Fort** on the River Bosna, 14km north of town. Vranduk is where the Baton uprising during Illyrian times ended. After the Roman army had finally been victorious, the women and children preferred to leap into a fire over becoming slaves to the Romans. During medieval times the fort had great military significance for the defense of Srebrena Bosna. To this day this walled medieval village is still inhabited. However, little has been done to preserve it and nothing has been done to make it the tourist attraction it deserves to be. At best you'll find a small sign on the side of the road pointing to Vranduk. Once you get there (a mere few hundred meters off the road) there isn't a sign in sight, or even a restaurant or café. It's safe and open to explore, but all you'll find on the historical events that occurred here is what your imagination provides you with.

Mountains

As with all Bosnian towns there are several 'izletište', recreational areas, in the proximity of Zenica. The most popular picnic area is at **Bistričak**, about 26km north of Zenica (turn at Nemila). You'll find Zeničani, people from Zenica, along the clear Ograjina River preparing a BBQ, playing volleyball and football and enjoying the sunny fields. There is a small but very popular bed and breakfast named after the recreation area with a massive terrace that seats 100 people (30KM per night per person; tel: 032 678 154).

The surrounding mountains of **Lisac, Pepelari, Vepar, Zmajevac and Smetovi** have nice hiking areas. The **Smetovi Mountaineering Hostel** is generally known as the lungs of Zenica. During the heyday of the steel industry, Smetovi was a welcome escape from the air pollution. With the town's industrial collapse the air pollution in Zenica has been reduced a lot, but people still come here in large numbers. There are well-marked trails, a restaurant, great walking paths and even a mini ski lift for beginners. **Scorpio Extreme Sports Club** organises hiking, biking, alpine climbing and paragliding on and around Smetovi (tel/fax: 032 289 770; email: clubscorpio2004@yahoo.com; the club's organizer, Edin Durmo, also organises high Alpine climbs in Herzegovina, tour skiing on Vlašić Mountain, and a varied range of extreme sport experiences around the country).

Lisac Mountain Hostel (tel: 032 281 250) is my personal favorite. It is run by the Tajan Mountain Association and is the only lodge that is not accessible by vehicle. There are big open fields surrounded by large beech trees and the two-part lodge is perched 1,000m above sea level on a ridge that overlooks the surrounding mountains. It's a great getaway and is only

12km from Zenica. If the phone is not answered by an English-speaking person, you could contact Scorpio instead (tel/fax: 032 289 770). At the time of editing this guide book the Lisac Mountain lodge was struck by lightning and burned to the ground. There is an action to raise money to rebuild this lodge and we hope that by the time the readers have this guide in hand the mountain lodge will be rebuilt and open for business again.

VAREŠ

This tiny mining town is situated in the centre of the middle Bosnian mountain massif of **Kapija, Stijene, Zvijezda** and **Perun** mountains. The newer part of town is centered on the mining industry, whereas the old town is the site of the ancient **Oglavić Church**, the early **Christian Basilica in Dabravine** and the **old Illyrian city** on Zvijezda Mountain to the east. The Catholic church was built here after the first Franciscan order was established in the area in 1340. Artifacts from Vareš can be viewed at the Kraljeva Sutjeska Monastery Museum. **Šarići Mosque** is a fine example of Ottoman architecture and design.

Those of you unable to resist the tempting pine-covered mountains surrounding Vareš should try the excellent hiking and walking areas on Perun Mountain. The mountain lodge **Javorje** is situated at 1,427m and there is perfect terrain for easy hiking. The lodge has a restaurant that serves traditional highland food and some national dishes, and a dormitory that sleeps up to 30. It has no direct phone line but you could contact Damir Grabovac, the president of the Mountaineer Association, at 061 877 496. The fishing society has a mountain hut and hatchery **Bukovica** to the northeast. Try the same Damir Grabovac if you want to get information before going there. Both places are accessible by car on gravel roads.

OLOVO

Olovo means 'lead' in the local language. This ore-rich area has been mined for centuries. Its most valued natural resources, however, are the thermal wells with temperatures of 36°C. The spa **Aquaterm** (032 825 008) is well known for healing joint and muscle problems, nervous and cardiovascular system diseases or just a tired body.

The Bosnian Church obviously left its mark in this mountain town. The holy site of **Gospa Olovska** from the 14th century has been visited by people of all religions - but mostly by Catholics - since the early Ottoman days. The belief that miracles have occurred in this church still draws people who seek help or peace of mind.

Olovo sits in a bowl completely surrounded by a lush green forest of mainly pine trees. Three rivers cross in Olovo, the largest being the **Krivaja River** that flows to Zavidovići and has several spots for some great kayaking. By the Krivaja River it is perfectly safe for a walk, kayaking trip, fishing or picnic, but Olovo to the east and southeast was a front line town. Be careful not to wander into the forest on that side.

On the main road coming from Sarajevo is the **Restoran Panorama**, obviously named for its great view. The food is just as good and they have a small bed and breakfast with ten beds (tel: 032 826 866; email: panorama@bih.net.ba; web: www.panorama.olovo.net). If you plan to stay the night after a long day of kayaking or waiting for a miracle from the

Mother of God Church, you could also choose to stay at **Motel Onix** (Tuzlanska-Olovska Luka bb; tel: 032 826 252). It offers simple, clean and inexpensive accommodation.

Not far from Olovo are the **Bijambara Caves**, located only 30 minutes from Sarajevo on the main road to Tuzla via Olovo in the municipality of Ilijaš. These caves were first recorded during the Austro-Hungarian period in the early 1900s, but it is assumed that they have been used for centuries. There are guided tours into the five-cave complex that goes over 300m into the belly of the mountain. The trails are lit all the way to the fifth dome, which has been named the 'music hall' due to its acoustic quality. Large stalagmites and stalactites can be seen in the caves. It is thought the cave system as it is known now is only a fraction of what remains to be discovered.

In the area around the caves there is a mountain lodge that sleeps 50 and serves homemade meals of varying quality throughout the year. There are marked walking and hiking trails in this area. The walking trail is about 3km of flat walking through open meadows and thick pine forests. The hiking trail of over 3km is a bit more challenging. It travels uphill and finishes at the mountain lodge. There is a picnic area at the lodge and a smaller area on the ledge of the upper cave with a magnificent view of the surrounding area, just above the tree line. Trips can be organized through the Tourist Information Centre in Sarajevo, Green Visions, the Bijambara Mountaineers Club (tel: 033 401 017) or by contacting the lodge directly on 033 401 017 (more than likely you will not reach an English speaker at the lodge).

Further down on that main road towards Sarajevo, you will find a small but popular open air swimming pool and, 20 minutes further down that same road, **Imidž**, an exceptionally nice and child-friendly restaurant (033 436 437).

KRALJEVA SUTJESKA

Arriving in Kraljeva Sutjeska feels like stepping through a time warp. The filthy streams and dust-covered roofs of Kakanj disappear as you near this tiny, ancient village with its large Franciscan church and monastery. The houses are well-kept, the gardens are in perfect shape and the reflection of the sun off the water is caused by the white stones and not the usual discarded tin can. You'll find that many of the women, particularly the older ones, still dress in traditional attire. Most are farmers but you'll find the odd carpenter or shop owner hammering away or selling his wares as well. The **Dusper House** in the village is the oldest house in central Bosnia, dating back to the early 18th century. The house has been designated a protected national monument. Restoration has not yet begun but the house can still be visited and is an impressive example of authentic Bosnian architecture. One of the oldest **mosques** in Bosnia and Herzegovina is situated at the entrance of this village. It was built in a few days only, and has never required any maintenance since - or so the story goes. The mosque and its wooden minaret are open to visitors. You'll enjoy the (local language) accounts of its past, told proudly and with a twinkle in the eyes by the lady who maintains this beautiful little place of worship.

Kraljeva Sutjeska and the citadel at Bobovac were once the seat of two Bosnian kings, Tomač and Tvrtko, of the Kotromanić Dynasty. The last

Bosnian queen, Saint Katarina, is mourned today by the local townswomen who still wear black scarves as part of the traditional dress. When the Ottomans conquered the fortress at **Bobovac**, Queen Katarina either fled or was exiled to Rome, never to return to Bosnia. It was reported that her children were taken to Istanbul, where her son converted to Islam and became a major figure in the Ottoman administration.

To see it all in a one-day trip, contact Josip Brđanović (tel: 061 433 470; 30 KM per person, with a minimum group size of three). Josip doesn't speak English but shows up with an interpreter (Darko or Saša) and is a truly excellent guide. The day includes a forest walk to Bobovac and a traditional lunch prepared by Katarina, Josip's wife.

Getting there

There is a bus line from Kakanj to Kraljeva Sutjeska. If you have your own vehicle, turn off into Kakanj before the fly-over when coming from the M17 from Sarajevo. Follow the road and turn right under the railway bridge. Continue without turning for another 15 minutes, then pass again under a railway bridge and turn immediately right. Stay on this road until you see the sign for Kraljeva Sutjeska

BOBOVAC

The fortress of Bobovac was built because the ancient town of Kraljeva Sutjeska was vulnerably located in the valley. The fortress is strategically situated on a high ridge above the Bukovica Stream, some 5km from Kraljeva Sutjeska. It is in the middle of nowhere. Initially, the inhabitants of Kraljeva Sutjeska sought shelter here when they were under attack. In the dangerous years before the final invasion by the Ottomans, they moved here permanently. The fortified town had quarters for the noble family on the western end, while the central and lowest part of the ridge housed the townspeople. The church, horse stables and military barracks were situated on the upper eastern hill overlooking the entire fortress and the surrounding mountains.

Bobovac is not accessible by car. Getting there is a pleasant and well-marked one-hour walk from Kraljeva Sutjeska, along the **Bukovica Stream** through thick beech tree forests. In the summer months the trail is lined with blackberries and fresh mint growing near the water. The only fully intact structure remaining at Bobovac is the mausoleum that Queen Katarina had built following the death of Tvrtko. His remains were removed during the last conflict and moved to an undisclosed location. Some of the outer walls and part of the horse stables can be seen on the high ridge behind the mausoleum and the king's quarters are slowly crumbling away. The view from this little nest in the valley is extraordinary. If possible, go to the monastery first and take a tour around with one of the Franciscans. The monastery's old drawings of Bobovac will help create a much clearer picture of how things looked in 13th and 14th century Bosnia.

Monastery, museum and library

Today's church is much more recent than the rest of the monastery. It was built just before the turn of the 20th century when the Austro-Hungarians lent considerable support to building and/or reconstruction of sacred Christian objects in Bosnia and Herzegovina. Designed in Venetian style, the high vaulted ceilings are now cracking in places as a result of earthquake damage and, as was recently discovered, because of some flaws in the original design. What is assumed to be the oldest organ in the country was previously hidden in the monastery and is now displayed in the church. A massive statue paying tribute to Queen Katarina (she was deemed a saint by the local church but has not yet been officially acknowledged as such by the Pope) dominates the east side of the church. Even on the hottest summer days the church is chilly. The energy inside is quite humbling, as is listening to the monks tell tales of the trials and tribulations of the Catholics during Ottoman times. I found that most monks at Kraljeva Sutjeska are rather objective in their depiction of history and do a fair job of separating historical facts from folklore. Some speak English.

The monastery is a complex so large that it infinitely exceeds the requirements of the six monks now residing in Kraljeva Sutjeska. It burned down several times during the Ottoman period. The last reconstruction was completed in 1891, with some additions and renovations made since then.

The museum houses a limited collection of art, documents and artifacts gathered or discovered at Bobovac or brought back from monks traveling the Christian world. The paintings are mostly from local artists, dating as far back as the 17th century and are more a source of local pride than of any great artistic significance. The collection of crosses, robes and artifacts is quite impressive for a small three-room museum somewhere in the hills of central Bosnia. A cross from 7th-century Syria is displayed amongst the elaborate crosses collected in Germany, Venice and Rome. Miniature models of the village's old architecture and a rich collection of traditional dresses illustrate the traditional ways of life. Lastly, the original permits issued by both the sultan and the local vizier from **Visoko** are displayed. At the time, these two documents cost more than the construction of the monastery itself.

The old chapel bell was recovered when Bosnia was annexed by Austria. Church bells were illegal during Turkish times and were hidden by the monks. When the bishop was ordered out of Bosnia, only the Franciscan monks were permitted to stay. They went to great lengths to hide and protect the sacred objects that the priests left behind.

The role of the ujak (uncles), as these monks were called, was key to the spiritual survival of the villagers. They were called 'uncle' so as not to attract the attention of the Turkish officials. The Franciscans documented births, deaths, marriages and migrations from the area in a time and place in which there was little or no public record-keeping. These records show the increase or decrease of the Catholic population, and describe the plagues that hit many Croatian areas. They are a rare treasure for historians.

The library, for me, is perhaps the most interesting visit, its books and documents illustrating a colorful past. The largest collection of incunabulas is housed here. Volumes and volumes of philosophy, theology, chemistry and history written in Italian, Latin, German, French and the local language line the shelves. The books were all collected from local boys who went to the West to be educated and brought back literacy and Catholic teachings. The first Bible to be translated into the local bosančica language also has an introduction to the local alphabet so the illiterate villagers could learn to read and write.

Towards the end of the library are the diverse collections of all the monks who ever passed through here. An enormous Bible was printed in order for several monks to read at the same time over each other's shoulders. Printed material for Catholics was often difficult to come by. The monastery was also the final resting place for the monks who served the Srebrena Bosna parish. They would come here to die and all their belongings became the property of the monastery. Their legacy is a fascinating collection of books.

The monastery is open to visitors upon request and on Wednesdays, Fridays and Saturdays. Admission is free of charge but it is always a kind gesture to leave money in the donation box of the museum (tel: 032 779 015/779 291).

VISOKO

Despite only being a 20-minute drive from Sarajevo, Visoko falls politically under the Zenica-Doboj Canton in central Bosnia. The town is best known for its leather smiths, whose craft has been practiced for over 500 years. High-quality, reasonably priced leather goods can be purchased in the old čaršija. **KTK Leather Company** is the largest factory of its kind in the country. Their products can also be found in Sarajevo's čaršija but you're likely to pay more than if you bought them here. The old part of Visoko is a mini version of Sarajevo's Baščaršija.

Visoko reached the peak of its development during the late Middle Ages. It became a strong social, political and economic centre and had the status of a royal town. Its name was recorded for the first time in 1355, in a chart issued to the merchants of Dubrovnik by ban Tvrtko I. On the vast plain near the town were the residences of the bans and the kings. Foreign envoys were received and state assemblies of all Bosnian territories were held in Visoko.

Visoko was also an important trading centre and, like many central Bosnian towns, had a considerable colony of merchants from Dubrovnik. The numerous charts and letters issued and registered in Visoko or its surroundings show the significant role of the town at that time. Today its main role is that of a small industrial and trading town.

KREŠEVO

Famed for his Christian writings and as a master of the Slavic language, Father Grga Matić was recorded in history, particularly Franciscan history, as one of Bosnia's greatest writers. He taught and wrote in a remote valley tucked below the **Bitovnja** and **Lopata mountains** in the tiny town of Kreševo. The Franciscan monastery there has been serving its community for centuries and the Catholic traditions here are very strong. The monastery has a rustic **museum, library** and **gallery**, and, as in most Franciscan monasteries in Bosnia and Herzegovina, the monks are very welcoming to visitors.

With no more than a few thousand inhabitants, medieval Kreševo expanded with the arrival of German blacksmiths. In several areas of Bosnia, small German and Ragusan (present day Dubrovnik) mining communities were established. The noble families of the Bosnian state were keen to exploit the plentiful resources of gold and silver but they didn't have the skills to do so. The craft was passed on from these migrant miners and can be found today in the old town.

Kreševo is known for its old Bosnian architecture. The walls are made of clay and straw plaster and the roof tiles are specially treated cherry-tree shingles. The village of **Vranići**, just a few kilometers from Kreševo, is home to the finest examples of this old type of building. It's a great place to visit and one of a handful of places that didn't suffer the destruction of war. There is also an interesting 'holy spot' at a medicinal water spring at **Dezevice** called **St. Jakov Water**, named after a 15th century Bosnian vicar.

If you pay Kreševo a visit, there is an unwritten rule that every traveler must stop at **Restaurant Banja** (Banjska 13; tel: 030 806 820). The food and service are great but the real attraction is the mysterious spring that flows from a hidden cave next to the restaurant. It creates a natural swimming pool of mineral water in which you are free to take a dip. Some swear it has healing powers. I found it, at the very least, wonderfully refreshing. **Restaurant Ribnjak** (Vrela bb; tel: 030 806 670) grills fresh trout plucked from its own fishpond. If you like trout, you'll love this place.

FOJNICA

It is thought the Illyrians had major settlements here and during the Roman conquest the town rapidly gained importance because of its rich gold deposits.

Handicrafts and trade were well established even before the arrival of the Ottomans in the towns of **Kozograd**, **Zvonigrad** and **Kasteli**, all located in today's Fojnica and surroundings. Kozograd, a fortress located on the slopes of Zec Mountain is presumed to have been in existence since at least the early 15th century, when the Dubrovnik miners would hide here with their treasures from invading forces. It is also believed that this fortification was the last place Queen Katarina stayed at before she fled to Dubrovnik and further on to Rome, never to return to the conquered kingdom she left behind. Zvonigrad is more than likely a prehistoric settlement where ancient miners sought refuge. Kasteli, in the near vicinity of the hunting lodge Zahor, was a temporary shelter for the Franciscan monks from Fojnica during the Ottoman invasion of Bosnia. These three towns are ruins now.

Fojnica as a town was first mentioned in 1365, when miners had come from Germany and Dubrovnik to develop this ore-rich area. In the late 15th century, after the invasion of the Ottomans, Fojnica recorded 329 families. In the same period Mostar, a city now 20 times the size of Fojnica, recorded only 19 dwellings.

The Catholic traditions of Srebrena Bosna are best represented in Fojnica and Kraljeva Sutjeska. The **Holy Spirit Franciscan Museum** (030 832 082), part of a hilltop monastery, holds over 17,000 volumes of books, records and documents, and the second-largest collection of incunabula (books printed before 1500). The museum also exhibits the **Ahdnama**. This document is one of the most important orders issued by *Sultan Mehmed Fatiha* to the Catholic communities of Bosnia and Herzegovina. The 16th-century decree, signed at Milodraz to the northeast of Fojnica, allowed Christians to freely retain their religious life and to propagate their beliefs. Although there were random persecutions at a local level, it was the policy of the empire to grant religious freedom to its Christian citizens.

Ćazim Musa Hadžimeljić in the village of Živčići is an Islamic sacral place where dervishes gather annually. It is also a small family museum, open daily from 8 to 4, that has some fascinating examples of dervish traditional dress from the Ottoman period, and a few paintings and other relics from Ottoman times.

Fojnica is home to one of the 19 spas that operate in Bosnia and Herzegovina. Although the spa is not quite up to western standards there has been significant improvement in service over the past few years. You can get a good massage for 10 KM. The spa, **Reumal Fojnica**, is located in the center of town (Banjska 1; tel: 030 838 804; email: reumal.f@bih.net.ba; web: www.fojnica.com). They have begun to build a new unit exclusively for foreign guests and will offer more modern facilities in the future.

In the vicinity of Fojnica, just off the main road from Kiseljak to Busovača, is the **Naksibendi order tekija** (old dervish house) in **Živčići** village. The area is blessed with the many beautiful waterfalls of **Kozica River**.

VRANICA MOUNTAIN

This is another one of these places in Bosnia and Herzegovina of which visitors wonder why it isn't a national park. **Vranica Mountain** is central Bosnia's highest mountain at 2,112m. Like most of the ranges in the central part of the country, the slopes gently climb to great heights leaving much of the mountain accessible even by car. Vranica is located in between **Gornji Vakuf** and **Fojnica**. The easiest and most common access is from the eastern slopes near Fojnica.

There is an 11km gravel road to the heart of Vranica at **Prokoško Glacier Lake**. Before the lake is the **Jezernica Mountain Lodge**. Set in a pristine forest along the cascading waters of the **Fojnička**, this is one of the best spots on the mountain for a peaceful stay. The lodge sleeps approximately 25 and an overnight stay costs around 10KM. The food is prepared on site, in the traditional way. There is no phone number or address, but it is the only lodge on the only road leading up to Prokoško from Fojnica. Ask any local or contact an eco-tourist group if you don't feel comfortable finding your way.

Prokoško Lake is another half-hour's drive away. Famed for its endemic **triton salamander**, there have been a growing number of local scientists and ecologists calling for its protection. The salamanders are gradually becoming an endangered species as the lake continues to shrink in size. The lake is also home to a large trout population that continues to thrive in these high mountain conditions. The lake formed as a result of melting glaciers from the high peaks of Vranica. As the glaciers continued to melt they carved out the mountain stream of **Borovnica** that flows into Fojnička River in the valley below. The excess water collected in a karst sinkhole. As the glaciers retreated **Borovnica River** was reduced to a stream and the lake took on the form seen today.

For centuries highlanders have used Prokoško Lake as a summer shepherd settlement. The famous katunis (shepherds' huts) dot the countryside around the lake. Katunis are known for their wood shingles and steep roofs designed to prevent snow from accumulating. The interiors are usually rather primitive as these places were used for summer grazing and most of the time was spent outdoors. Town dwellers soon caught on to the wonders of Prokoško Lake and began building weekend huts in the vicinity. Luckily the small valley at 1,635m will not allow for much more development and Prokoško will maintain its traditional look. The highlanders are very friendly and walking up to someone's hut is actually expected. They will, of course, treat you with the great hospitality that most highlanders bestow on foreign guests. While you are guaranteed success if you go fishing in the lake, please remember to limit your catch so as not to adversely effect the trout population.

Vranica is a paradise for hiker and walkers. The landscape above the lake is rather bare, which makes it much easier to keep one's bearings. The hike to **Ločika Peak** (2,108m) is only about an hour's hike from Prokoško. Central Herzegovina opens up from the top and the views of **Čvrsnica**, **Prenj** and **Bjelašnica** are amazing. You'll more than likely come across a herd of sheep, as well as many of the shepherds who gravitate to the sunny slopes of Ločika. Bears, wolves, boars, deer, martens and the occasional chamois inhabit this mountain's pristine landscape. The deep valleys to the northwest are covered in thick forests and much of the wildlife seeks shelter there.

TRAVNIK

Travnik is situated in the valley of the **Lašva River** and bordered by **Vlašić Mountain** to the north and **Mount Vilenica** to the south. The first inhabitants of this narrow valley settled some 5,000 years ago. They lived off the land and the wars they fought were local and tribal. This changed in Roman times, in the early centuries AC. The Romans recognized the valley's strategic importance as the connection between the regions of the river Vrbas in the west and the river Bosna in the east. They conquered the valley and turned it into a regional centre that controlled trade and coordinated the region's defense system. In a matter of years, the valley changed from a series of relatively isolated rural settlements into a hub that linked Salona with Sirmium, two important centers of the large Roman Empire. This, as well as the gold mining that intensified with the arrival of the Romans, brought economic development to the area, and many signs of that new wealth – in the form of coins and inscriptions about prosperity and fame - continue to be found in what is now Travnik and its surroundings. This golden age lasted until the Slavs settled in the region in the 7th century. These Slavs left little evidence of their presence and the valley disappeared from history until 500 years later.

The valley reappeared in 1244, in terms of primary historical records, when the Hungarian King Bela IV gave one of his notables a piece of land in Lašva. By that time, the area was a feudal estate of the Bosnian state. Although remains from these centuries do not show the wealth the valley had known in Roman times, the era did have its share of castles and mansions. The Travnik Fortress was the most impressive fortress at the time, and still stands out as the best preserved of them all. This era gave Travnik its name. At the time, taxes were collected in the form of a grass levy, charged to livestock owners whose livestock grazed in the area. Travnik is named after the official collecting these levies, the 'travarnik'.

The Ottoman era renewed the glory of Travnik. It was the principal city and military centre of the Ottoman Empire. It was from here that the Ottomans orchestrated their invasions further towards the southwest. They brought mosques, religious schools, roads and water systems. They fortified the medieval fortress and built a mini-city within its high stone walls. For over 150 years, the vizier – the Ottoman Sultan's representative in Bosnia - had his headquarters in this town, attracting both consulates and trade. Unlike the Roman period, in which Travnik was important as part of a trade route but was not itself a significant trading partner (other than of gold), the Travnik craftsman benefited from the Ottoman trade links, and the town thrived. Travelers visiting Travnik in this era were impressed by the town and called it the European Istanbul and the most oriental town in Bosnia. Ivo Andrić's brilliant 'Travnik Chornicle' gives you a feel of this period.

It started to go downhill in the mid 19th century. The vizier moved his seat back to Sarajevo, and much of the local talent followed him. The Austro-Hungarian Empire took over Bosnia and Herzegovina in 1878, and the final blow came in 1903, when a fire destroyed most of the town. Very little of the Ottoman heritage survived.

The Austro-Hungarians industrialized Travnik. They built factories (timber, matches, tobacco), a train line, and an electricity network. They also made Travnik a centre once again, this time not of Bosnia but only of its central part.

Passage from Ivo Andrić's *Travnik Chronicle*

...No one in Travnik ever thought it was a town made for a simple life and everyday happenings...

Their town is in fact a tight and deep cleft, built up and cultivated by generations as time passed, a fortified pass in which people remained to live forever, adapting themselves to it through the centuries, and adapting it to themselves. The mountain comes down steeply on both sides and joins in a sharp angle in a forge in which there is hardly room for a thin river and road beside it. It all looks like a half-closed book on whose pages, on one side and the other, like illustrations, are gardens, small streets, houses, fields, graveyards and mosques.

No one ever worked out how many sunny hours nature denied this town, but it is certain that the sun rises later here and sets earlier than in any other of Bosnia's many towns and villages. The inhabitants of Travnik do not deny this, but they also say the sun, while it does shine, shines nowhere as it does above their town.

In that narrow gorge through whose bottom runs the Lašva, and whose sides are criss-crossed by springs, gaps and streams, full of dampness and draft, there is almost no straight path or flat place, where a foot may be placed freely and without thought. Everything is steep and uneven, intersected and intertwined, linked or cut up by private paths, fences, gardens, and garden gates, graveyards or places of worship.

Here, on the water, that secretive, changeable and powerful element, the generations of Travnik are born and die...

Generations replace each other, passing on not only established physical and mental characteristics, but also the land and faith,

> not only an inborn feeling for measure and limits, not only the knowledge and power to differentiate between all the paths, garden gates and passes of their complicated town, but also an inborn capacity for knowing the world and people in general. With all that the children of Travnik are born, above all is pride. Pride is their second nature, the living force that follows them through their lives, moving them and giving them a visible mark that makes them different from the rest of the world.

Tourist Information

Very recently, information posters appeared next to the town's tourist attractions. The poster quality is rather poor, and after a few months the texts were getting a little vague, but the information these posters provide is interesting. In addition, there is the **Tourism Association of Central Bosnia**, located on Bosanska 75 (tel/fax: 030 511 588; email: tzsbk@bih.net.ba). They have brochures and information about Vlašić Mountain and might be able to point you in the right direction around town, with due emphasis here on the word 'might'. **San Tours** on Bosanska 135 (tel: 030 511 910) offers general information on hotels, restaurants and Vlašić Mountain.

Where to stay

Bajra Dolac na Lašvi bb; tel: 030 516 110. This is an excellent new motel just a few kilometers from the center of town. The rooms are modern and quite nice. The restaurant is excellent as is the service. Single rooms are available for around 40 KM.

Aba Šumeće 166a; tel: 030 511 462. This is a small pension near Plava Voda. They have very nice apartments for 75 KM that are equipped with a new Jacuzzi and modern furniture. Do check it out!

Hotel Lipa Bosanska bb; tel: 030 511 604. This is the only hotel from the pre-war period still operating in Travnik. It most certainly is a socialist relic, a bit run down and bit too old. Singles go for 52 KM and a double room is 84 KM.

Motel Consul Pirota bb; tel: 030 514 295 is near the stadium. It is a new motel with modern facilities and a restaurant. A single with breakfast costs 52 KM.

Pansion-restoran Oniks Donja čaršija-Žitarnica bb: tel: 030 512 182. This B&B is located in the old quarters of Travnik, not far from the colored mosque. The rooms are small but nice and the restaurant serves traditional food. Singles and doubles cost 35 and 60 KM.

Motel Bosna (Donje Putićevo bb; tel: 030 707 666) is just a bit outside of Travnik towards Vitez, along the E761. It is an excellent hotel with a great restaurant and attentive service. The rooms are very nice and they have meeting room facilities in the hotel. During the conflict this was the only place Croat and Bosniac officials could meet safely. With the war days gone it is now probably the nicest hotel in the Travnik area. Singles and doubles cost 48 and 86 KM.

CENTRAL BOSNIA

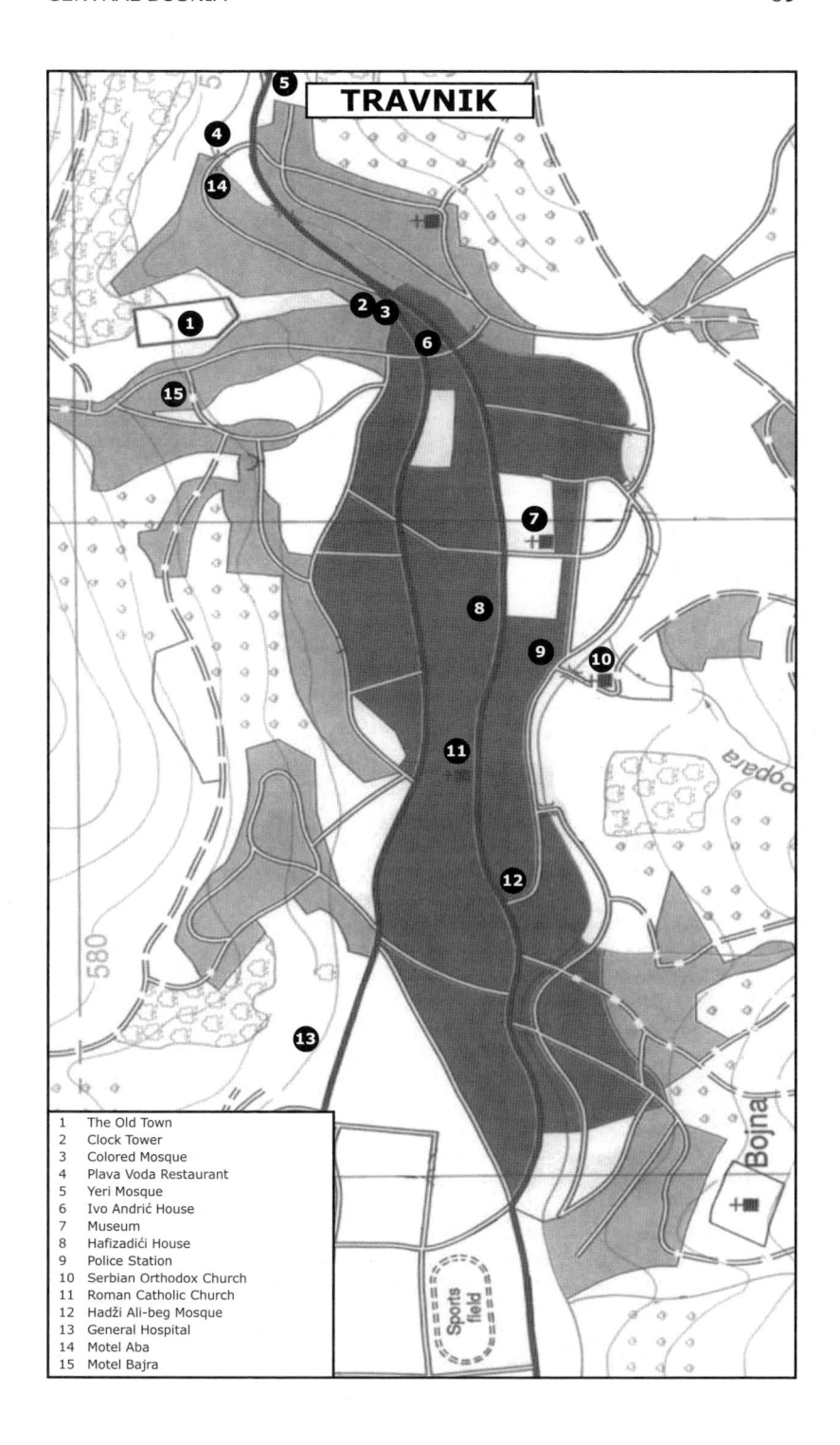

TRAVNIK

1. The Old Town
2. Clock Tower
3. Colored Mosque
4. Plava Voda Restaurant
5. Yeri Mosque
6. Ivo Andrić House
7. Museum
8. Hafizadići House
9. Police Station
10. Serbian Orthodox Church
11. Roman Catholic Church
12. Hadži Ali-beg Mosque
13. General Hospital
14. Motel Aba
15. Motel Bajra

Where to eat

Plava Voda Šumeće 14; tel: 030 618 222. This restaurant is somewhat of a historical monument and the rule is that anybody visiting Travnik should visit Plava Voda, both for the lovely water and for the food. Don't miss this one.

Ivo Andrić House (Zenjak bb; no phone) is a relaxed, but somewhat classy place with a great summer garden. They serve traditional meals, many of which are made in the *ispod saca* (Dutch oven). It is very reasonably priced and a great place to have a meal after visiting the museum upstairs.

Restoran Lutvina Kahva Sumece-Plava Voda bb; tel: 061 154 520. This cozy place is also on the crystal clear waters of Plava Voda. They serve traditional meals on the summer terrace that are delicious. The service is good and the food is very reasonably priced.

Ćevabdžinica Hari Žitarnica bb; tel: 030 511 727. Hari's a perfect place for backpackers looking for a cheap but high quality meal. Ćevapi is grilled sausages served with pita bread and for meat lovers is a great and inexpensive way to eat. They have fresh salads too.

Things to see

The Travnik **Medieval Fort** was one of the survivors of the 1903 fire, and the imposing structure, which for centuries defended the city from outside invaders, still dominates the horizon. The fortress is open to guests - the only question being when. Try your luck and climb the stone steps leading to the main entrance. There may be a gatekeeper to let you in and then again, there may not. The walk up is lovely and the old quarter around the fortress has some very impressive traditional homes.

Without any historical or archaeological confirmation, it is believed that King Tvrtko II had built this impressive structure in the early 15th century. Today, this is perhaps the best preserved fort in all of central Bosnia. This type of structure can be found in other areas of Bosnia and Herzegovina as well (in Tešanj, Doboj and Gradačac, for example) but due to its strategic location, Travnik was usually behind the main lines of confrontation and was able to preserve its original medieval character.

Apart from being the administrative headquarters for Ottoman rule in Bosnia, Travnik is best known as an ancient trading place. The markets were always filled with visitors and traders from Dubrovnik, Serbia and other Ottoman territories. Just as Mostar's and Sarajevo's čaršija developed into craftsmen's quarters so too did the **old town** of Travnik.

Travnik is the birthplace of *Ivo Andrić*, winner of the Nobel Laureate for Literature, author of Bridge on the Drina. He also wrote *Travnik Chronicles*, which portrayed his view of life in Travnik during Ottoman rule. The **Ivo Andrić House** is now a museum and a restaurant, although it has been said that the museum is not the actual house in which he was born. The restaurant, built as an old-style Bosnian room with the walls covered in local art, has one of the best atmospheres in town. Enes Škrgo, the museum's custodian, knows everything there is to know about the place, and indeed about Travnik as a whole. He speaks good English and thoroughly enjoys his job.

The **Sahat Kula** is a yet another trademark from Ottoman times. This clock tower was built in the 18th century and towers 20 meters in the town center.

You'd be ill-advised to ignore **Plava Voda** (Blue Waters), a large source that flows out of the base of **Vlašić Mountain**. There is a path all the way to the source. The water is freezing cold and wonderful for a cold drink or a refreshing splash in the summer. Plava Voda restaurant is situated just below the source and prepares ćevapi which is, according to many, as good as Željo's in Sarajevo and would certainly satisfy the appetites of all but vegetarians. There are, of course, other items on the menu and apart from the oily, sometimes lukewarm chips (a curious culinary feature of many Bosnian dining establishments) the food is great. Near Plava Voda is the **Elči-Ibrahim pašina Medresa**, built in a neo-Moorish style. Its construction in 1706 was due to Travnik's growing importance within the Ottoman Empire not only as a major trade town but for Islamic Studies as well.

It's hard to miss the **Šarena Džamija** (Multi-Colored Mosque), built in 1757. With its bright colors, its unique and intricate artistic details on the outside walls and its carved wood, it is said to be among the most beautiful mosques in the Balkans – and the only one in the country that people believe stores hairs of the prophet. It has unusual flower motives painted on the outside, and it is one of only two mosques in Bosnia and Herzegovina in which the prayer room is positioned on the first floor, with the ground floor used to conduct business. If the door is open and it is not prayer time you are welcome to enter. Remember to take your shoes off and if you are a woman to cover your head with a scarf or shawl. Muslims here are very understanding and tolerant of foreigners who may not know all the customs so don't feel bothered if you've wandered in uncovered or in shorts. At the same time of the construction of the mosque a 27 store bezistan (covered market) was built under it. The taxes collected from merchants were intended to pay for the upkeep of the mosque. The mosque burned to the ground in 1815 and was rebuilt by Suleyman-pasha Skopljak. It was Skopljak who had the outer walls colored as they are today.

Jeni mosque is the oldest mosque in Travnik dating back to 1549. It has been reconstructed and renovated several times since its 16th century construction by dervish orders. The **Lončarica and Hadži Ali-begova mosque**s are also worth a peek as great examples of Ottoman architecture. The Hadži Ali-begova mosque is the only one in Bosnia and Herzegovina to have a sun clock-dial. This **'sunčani sat'** was apparently built in 1886 by the Smoljan brothers to assist the winemakers Bašbunar.

Travnik has always boasted of a rather diverse local population. In town, there is the Catholic Church of **St. Ivan Krstitelja**, built in 1887. Just outside of Travnik in the north Lašva Valley region is the **Gospina Kapela**. This kapela was built by a water source thought to have healing powers and has since became a small pilgrimage site for Catholics in the region. The **Church of the Lords Source** has been built on the same premises. The orthodox church of **Znamenitosti** from 1854 is home to many icons from the 17-19th centuries.

Southeast along the Lašva River from the Šarena Džamija is one of the few remaining old-style **Bosnian mahalas**. These old homes, built with steep roofs to counter the effects of heavy snow, are prime examples of traditional Bosnian architecture. The houses are inhabited, giving them all the characteristics of living museums.

In the middle of town is the **Zavičajni Museum** on Mehmedpaše

Kukavice 1 (tel: 030 518 140; email: zmt99@bih.net.ba). There are interesting artifacts documenting Travnik's long history but guides in English are not available and opening hours are irregular. At **Galerija Terra** on Bosanska Street 161 (tel: 030 511 428; 061 983 003) one can find a rich collection of local paintings, many of them depicting life in Travnik.

Eight kilometers from Travnik towards the town of Vitez is the famous **Franciscan Monastery of Guča Gora**. Although the Franciscan church had significant difficulties during the Ottoman times many of the monasteries continued to function. The small village of Guča Gora is situated on a hilltop overlooking the Lašva Valley. The monastery, as most Franciscan monasteries in Bosnia are, is open to the public and has an interesting library collection.

VLAŠIĆ MOUNTAIN

Inhabiting high, isolated areas was the tradition of the first settlers in Bosnia and Herzegovina. Vlašić was not only home to old Illyrian highlanders and followers of the medieval Bosnian Church but also to a large shepherd community that continues to live off the fertile lands across the vast plateau of Vlašić Mountain. The lives of the highlanders were dramatically affected by the recent conflict and many of them were forced to abandon the lifestyles that they and their ancestors had enjoyed for centuries. However, much of that life has now returned to Vlašić and the highlanders have resumed their age-old customs of sheep-raising and cheese production.

Getting there

The revitalization of many of the villages has also brought back many domestic tourists to the ski resort and mountain lodges that were popular holiday spots before the war. **Babanovac** ski area is only 28km from Travnik and a good road keeps it accessible all year round. Only 2km west of Travnik, before the town of Turbe, is the turn-off for Vlašić. The climb will take 15-20 minutes before you reach the first plateau. After driving another 4-5km the only turn-off to the right (which is well marked) leads to Babanovac. There aren't many roads on Vlašić so it's pretty hard to make a wrong turn.

Where to stay and eat

Around the ski lifts there are several new hotels and pensions:

Pahuljica Hotel (tel: 030 540 022; fax: 030 540 021; email: info@pahuljica.com; web: www.pahuljica.com; 75 KM per person) is the newest and best hotel that has recently expanded to a capacity of 80. All rooms have a minibar, satellite TV and phone. During the winter the large fireplace room often has live traditional music and the restaurant is rumored to be the best on the mountain.

Villa Ugar (tel: 030 540 140; fax: 030 540 141; email: dho2342@yahoo.com) in the centre of Babanovac offers hostel-type accommodation and has a good pizzeria. They are also one of few places in the country to rent out snow scooters. Singles and doubles are 55 and 83 KM.

Vila Sax (tel: 030 537 012; sax@bih.net.ba; www.sax.ba; 55 KM per person) is a new place with nice rooms, good food and friendly service. It is one of the largest new places to open and is close to the ski slopes. Open all year round.

Vila Stella (tel: 061 140 840; vilastella@hotmail.com; www.villastella.com, if you read Italian) is also a new motel with nice, modern rooms for 25 KM per person per night, and a good restaurant.

Dom Karaula (tel: 061 790 582; 061 154 543) is owned and run by the ski club. It is geared towards youth and is more like a hostel with nice, clean and warm accommodation. They have a capacity of 60 with restaurant and café facilities within the hostel itself. 35 KM for adults, 30 KM for children.

Motel Kelly (tel: 061 140 781) is a fairly new wooden structure motel. It is a simple motel but clean and warm with a lovely terrace and placed in a forest of beautiful pines. If it's available: take the apartment downstairs. 40 KM per person per night.

Hotel Babanovac (tel: 030 537 009) is the oldest hotel and dates back from the socialist period. It's conveniently located in the heart of the ski area but cannot really compare to the comfort and service of the other places. 42 KM per person per night.

There is also a large number of weekend homes that are available for rent in both the summer and winter months.

What to see and do

Vlašić Mountain is the second-highest mountain in central Bosnia. Its highest peak, **Paljenik** (1,943m), is not like the steep and sometimes treacherous peaks of the Dinaric chain in Herzegovina. Vlašić is known for its mild and easily accessible highlands. The road infrastructure is excellent and most places can be reached by jeep. The mountain is often used as a shortcut from Travnik to Banja Luka.

During pre-war times Vlašić Mountain was the pride and joy of Travnik. However, during the war it placed Travnik directly in the artillery gunners' sights. In a massive offensive in the winter of 1995, the Bosnian army climbed and conquered the frozen and snow-covered peaks in one of the most dramatic victories of the war.

Skiing on Vlašić is much more child-friendly and family-oriented than skiing on Jahorina or Bjelašnica. There is one central spot only and it is impossible to get lost. The skiing experience itself doesn't compare to the Olympic-quality skiing available on Jahorina or Bjelašnica, but it certainly provides an attractive alternative and the capacity of the ski area of **Babanovac** is, in fact, larger than on Bjelašnica Mountain. Snowboarders too have found a new playground and many clubs set up camp all winter to board. The snowboarding club is located at Babanovac (tel: 030 511 696; email: boardout@hotmail.com; http://www.boardout.org/Info_eng.htm). Ski and board rental is possible at the Babanovac Ski Centre. The 15km of cross-country ski trails and the ski jumps (the biggest being 90m) are not currently in use.

Hiking on Vlašić is a different story. The curse of the beautiful mountain regions of Bosnia and Herzegovina is that they are of the utmost strategic importance during wars and, in the last war, the sides that held high ground were wont to do all they could to hold it. This resulted in post-war minefields of which Vlašić has no shortage. The trails to **Devečani Mountain Lodge** at 1,760m are safe to walk and completely free of mines. The ski area at Babanovac is also mine-free. Other areas are questionable and best trekked only with a guide. The dense pine forests and soft, rolling hills on the high plateau are perfect walking, biking and hiking terrain. For free spirits who love to wander through the mountains, I share in your frustration but it's best to call an eco-tourism group. Green Visions based in Sarajevo and Scorpio Extreme Sports Club in Zenica organise hiking and biking trips.

Don't leave Vlašić without buying some **Vlašićki sir** (cheese). Foreign markets have just got wind of this heavenly, white, salty cheese and the organic and traditional way of preparing it only adds to your appreciation of this local delicacy. The road that passes by Vlašić, from Donji Vakuf to Travnik, is lined with dozens of shops selling it.

BUGOJNO

Located in the upper valley of the **Vrbas River**, this town was a typical example of a multi-ethnic community and is now recovering from the recent conflict which tore that community apart. In the past few years, significant numbers of refugees have returned and Bugojno has started to put on its old face of a Bosniac, Croat and Serb town. The town itself doesn't have much to offer the tourist. As it is a bit off the beaten track, the economy is sluggish and unemployment is high.

To the west towards Kupres is a region called **Koprivica**. This enormous forest was once one of Tito's favorite hunting spots. The dense forest and lack of any human settlements have created a sanctuary for bears, wolves, deer, boar and a plethora of other wild animals. Hunting associations are very active in this region and there are many mountain and hunting lodges dotting the forest. **Duboka Valley** (deep valley) is a designated hunting area covered by thick spruce. **Kalin Mountain** is a popular weekend area for hikers and nature lovers.

To the north of Bugojno near the village of **Prusac** is the largest Muslim pilgrimage site in Europe. Every June thousands of Muslims gather at the holy site at **Ajvatovica**. Prusac, like most places in central Bosnia was badly damaged during the war. The traditional architecture is almost as beautiful as the green hills that roll on as far as the eye can see. Holy spots always seem to have a special energy and, unlike many other sacred places, Prusac has yet to be commercialized. It's a tiny place where people live the way they always have and in June they wait for the thousands of visitors with open arms. There are daily buses from Bugojno and Donji Vakuf to Prusac. There won't be signs in English or even many trail markers but you'll love just wandering around and sipping coffee with the locals.

Legend of Dedo Ajvaz

The legend of Dedo Ajvaz tells of a great drought that threatened the existence of the small mountain community of Prusac. There was barely enough water for the villagers, let alone for the livestock they depended on for their survival. An old grandfather, Dedo Ajvaz, decided to pray for water. It is said that the very fact that he prayed for water and not rain is proof of the power of

> *prayer. Dedo Ajvaz prayed for 40 days and on the 40th day a large rock face near the village began to tremble. The powerful trembling continued and soon the massive rock split in half. From the gap created by the split, water began to flow. News of the miracle spread fast and Muslims and Christians alike came to see for themselves the new spring and the large gorge created by the quake. From that spot water continues to flow from beneath the earth and Muslims come here to give thanks.*

JAJCE

Still blighted by poor economic conditions, Jajce's only success story is an aluminium-tyre-rim factory. The rest of the town is slowly recovering from the effects of the war.

Jajce has had more than its fair share of battles. The town changed hands several times before the independent Bosnian state was finally conquered when the Jajce fortress was the last one to fall to the Ottoman invaders in 1528. It changed hands several times during the recent war as well. In the final offensive by the Bosnian Croat and Muslim armies the Serbs lost the city and retreated to Banja Luka before all three sides were called to the Dayton Peace Talks. Since that joint offensive, Jajce has remained a largely Catholic enclave. Bosniacs and Serbs have returned in small numbers only.

The brighter side of Jajce is the spectacular medieval citadel set on top of the hill in the middle of town. Hugging the old fortress are beautiful old Ottoman-style homes and rushing below them are the two beautiful 27m waterfalls of the Pliva River. No other town in Bosnia and Herzegovina possesses so many cultural layers and architectural styles in a place so small.

The town may seem a bit dead at first but after a good wander around the citadel and through the old quarter things just seem to come to life. The 3rd-century sacred temple dedicated to the god **Mitras** from Roman times sits side by side with a valued example of medieval architecture - the old steeple of **St Luke's Church**. Beneath the church are the **catacombs** where high priests and the nobility were buried. These sites are open to the public. Once again, the only problem is that there is no information office or website, and there are very few signs around town to point you in the right direction. The **Esma Sultan Mosque**, the most prestigious in the region, was destroyed during the last war.

It seemed fitting after so many civilizations had settled and fought over this place that in 1943 the ANVOJ was signed and sealed here in one of the most historical moments of Bosnia's and Yugoslavia's history. The second session of the Anti-Fascist Council of the National Liberation of Yugoslavia on November 29 ratified that Bosnia and Herzegovina, as an equal federal unit, would enter the Democratic Federal Yugoslavia. These resolutions outlined the future democratic and federal organization of the region. The words of the Resolution and Proclamation to the Peoples of Bosnia and Herzegovina read:

> "Today the peoples of Bosnia and Herzegovina, through their single political representative body, the Regional Anti-Fascist Council of

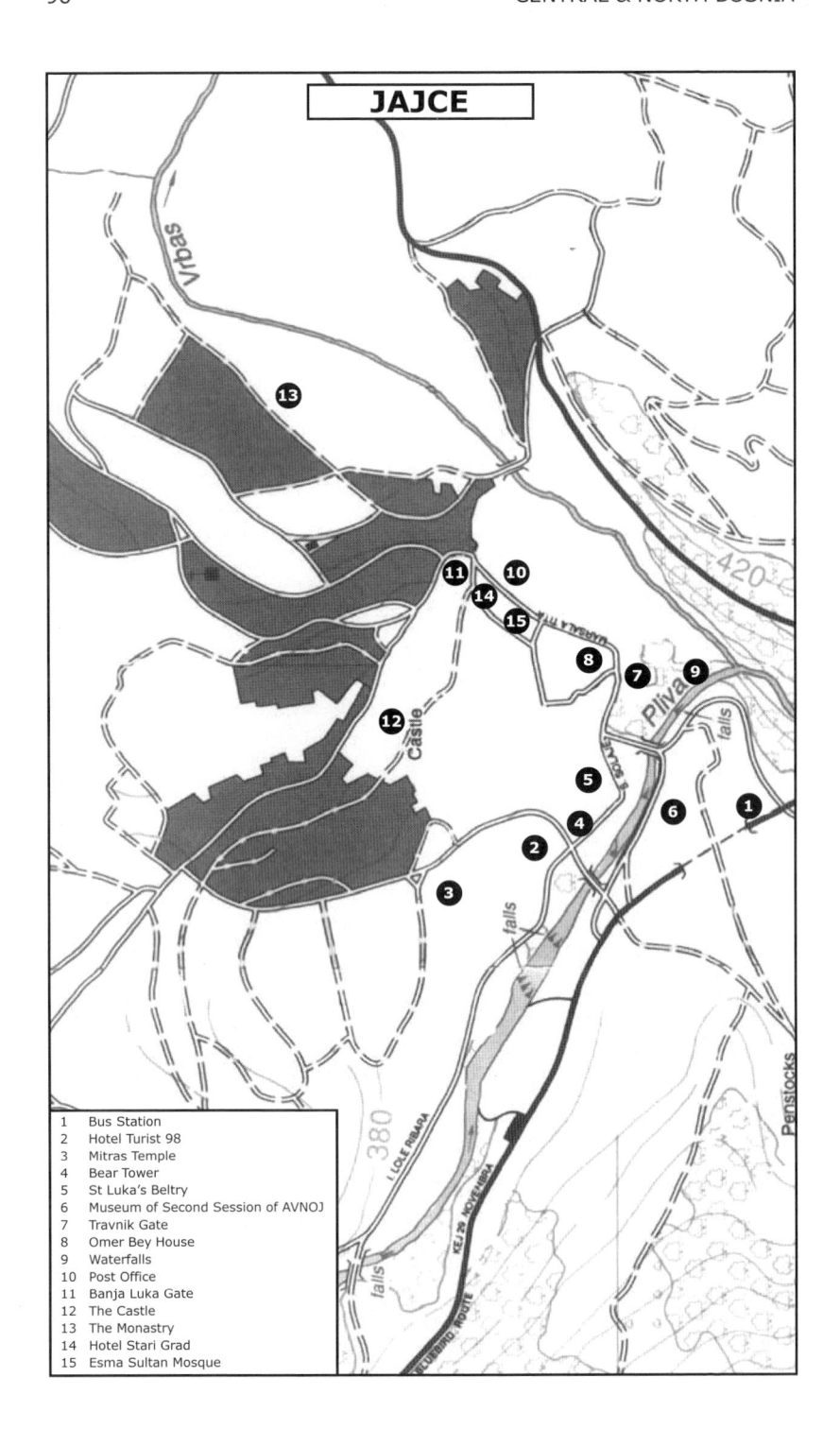

JAJCE

1. Bus Station
2. Hotel Turist 98
3. Mitras Temple
4. Bear Tower
5. St Luka's Beltry
6. Museum of Second Session of AVNOJ
7. Travnik Gate
8. Omer Bey House
9. Waterfalls
10. Post Office
11. Banja Luka Gate
12. The Castle
13. The Monastry
14. Hotel Stari Grad
15. Esma Sultan Mosque

> the Liberation of Bosnia and Herzegovina, express their will that their country, which is neither Serbian nor Croatian nor Muslim, but rather Serbian and Croatian and Muslim, be a Bosnia and Herzegovina characterized by freedom and brotherhood, in which the complete equality of all Serbs, Croats and Muslims will be guaranteed. The peoples of Bosnia and Herzegovina will participate on a basis of equality with the other nations of this country in the building of a national, democratic and federal Yugoslavia".

The outskirts of town are blessed with an abundance of water, which is probably what made it so attractive and practical as a settlement in earlier times. The **Vrbas and Pliva rivers** have been favorite fishing and swimming sites since the hydro-electric dam was built in the 1970s to create the lake. The **Vrbas Canyon** is an amazing drive if you're heading to **Banja Luka**. In the other direction up the Pliva River is the greatest collection of **old mills** in the country. In the wide areas of the Pliva you can find many mills that were built during Ottoman times. Families in the past would gather here to work, grind wheat, wash clothes and gather water. Most of the mills are still in decent shape, some even functional, and they seem a very natural part of the landscape in this area.

Where to stay

Hotel Stari Grad, Svetog Luka 3; tel: 030 654 006; arnoro.jajce@tel.net.ba, is one of the nicest hotels I've seen in the entire country. A Bosnian businessman who lives in Sweden returned to his home town to open this quite elegant place. When construction began they found Roman ruins. Instead of bulldozing them, they preserved these ancient walls and kept them visible by making part of the restaurant's floor out of glass. The rooms, service, food and free-of-charge sauna are all top notch. Single rooms are 80KM and double rooms go for 120KM. All rooms have internet access.

Hotel Turist 98, Kraljice Katarine 1; tel: 030 659 666, is situated at the main entrance to the city of Jajce. It is a pre-war object but one in fairly good condition. The rooms are decent and clean but the hotel still has an air of socialism around in. It's a cheaper alternative with rooms rates usually around 50-60 KM per night.

Hotel Plivsko Jezero, Plivska Jezera bb; tel: 030 654 090, is a good, new hotel on the lake near Jajce. The rooms have modern facilities and the staff is quite friendly and helpful. Singles and doubles go for 30 and 45 KM per night and the hotel is only a hop, skip and a jump from the lake itself.

ŠIPOVO

There have been several failed attempts to place Šipovo and its rivers under national protection. Šipovo is another tiny Krajina town that is overflowing with pure water sources. At Šipovo alone, four rivers meet and flow as one towards the Vrbas River. The **Pliva, Janj, Skočnica** and **Lubovica** rivers crisscross in an impressive display of hydro-power. The rivers and the soft rolling hills covered with thick old forests make Šipovo a fairytale place. One might expect Robin Hood to trot out of the forest for a drink in the clear springs. It's a really beautiful place. Not far from Šipovo is the source of the River Pliva where, as in Jajce, large watermills were erected to provide the local population with flour and other grains.

The **Tetrijeb Hotel and Restaurant** (Sime Šolaje 48, Šipovo; tel: 050 371 629) is a favorite spot for fishers and hunters. The hotel owner, George, is an avid hunter and knows the forests and hills well. The hotel is situated on the Pliva River, near the town centre; rooms are newly renovated and good for 25KM per night. The alternative, **Motel Janj** (tel: 050 371 119), is currently closed.

Šipovo is located off the main road between Jajce and Mrkonjić Grad to the west. There are daily buses from Banja Luka to this little town.

MRKONJIĆ GRAD

This town has quite a history. It was founded, in the late 16th century, by a Bosnian who was taken to Istanbul as a boy, to be converted and educated in the Ottoman tradition and sent back to the town where the Ottomans had killed his father. The town was named and renamed several times until, in 1925, it was given its current name in honor of the Serb ruler Petar Mrkonjić who revolted against the Ottomans in the years before the Austro-Hungarians took over. Because of its strategic location, the town was 'liberated' a full 39 times in the Second World War. In the recent war, the Croats occupied the town in a very quick offensive in autumn 1995, butchering over a hundred Serb civilians in the non-combat related aftermath.

On the brighter side, this beautiful little town largely consists of lovely-looking hill side houses and is surrounded by breathtaking hill forests. It has one hotel only - **Hotel Krajina,** with 50 KM, 60 KM and 70 KM for singles, doubles and triples (tel: 050 211 338). If you have a car or don't mind the walk, it's nicer to stay in **Balkana** (tel: 050 212 505), some four kilometer from Mrkonjić Grad's centre on the main road to Ključ. This is a nature resort, with a campsite, a ski lift, a paragliding club, a very large swimming pool, and forests to explore. If you don't camp, it's best to make sure that Balkana's only apartment is available. For 100 KM per night including breakfast, this is a superbly furnished place, with kitchen and fire place, that sleeps up to four. Otherwise, you'll end up in its very simple and unattractive hotel, for 16 KM per bed.

Zelenkovac is also worth a visit (050 278 617; e-mail: boro@inecco.net; web: http://www.mrkonjic-grad.com/zelenkovac/e_index.html). This is an ecological organization that built a gallery, a few small wooden houses, mills, hanging bridges, observation points and fire places, all in the midst of nature and just a few kilometers from Mrkonjic Grad (first street to the left on the main road to Ključ). Zelenkovac organises eco-volunteer camps and jazz festivals, and hosts artist colonies.

> ### PLIVA RIVER REGION, by John Snyder
>
> This section of the guide book was prepared by the Japan International Cooperation Agency (JICA) for an eco-tourism development project in this region. JICA is working in this area to help small communities create more sustainable economies. The author, John, is the author of many guide books and is an environmental specialist, professional fly fisherman, and has worked

around the world in developing environmentally sound eco-tourism programs. This is the result of his research...enjoy! An all-inclusive website of the region's eco-tourism offers can be found at www.plivatourism.ba .

INTRODUCTION TO THE PLIVA RIVER REGION

Location

The Pliva River Region is located in the north-central part of the Bosnia region of Bosnia and Herzegovina. The region is dominated by major rivers such as the Pliva, Vrbas, and Janje. For many hundreds of years this region was the ultimate stronghold of the Bosnian Kingdom. The castle in Jajce was the fortress of the last Bosnian King. The three largest communities in the Pliva River Region are Šipovo, Jezero, and Jajce. Šipovo is located near the source of the Pliva River, Jezero is located near the Pliva Lakes, and Jajce is located where the Pliva River flows into the Vrbas River. This intersection is the site of a spectacular waterfall that is 15 meters in height.

The Pliva River plays vital environmental and economic development roles in this region of Bosnia. It is the single most important environmental feature of this region because it provides water to sustain human and wildlife populations; it forms a natural transport corridor through the mountains; it offers the best available sites for human settlement; it supports agricultural production; it has hydro-energy resources; and it offers a range of outdoor recreation resources. The Pliva River provides the natural connection between the three towns of Jajce, Jezero, and Šipovo.

Access

The Pliva River Region has an extensive paved road system. Bosnia and Herzegovina route numbers M-5 and M-16 connect the Pliva River Region with the rest of the country. The Pliva River Region is approximately three hours driving from Sarajevo in the south and some four hours driving from Zagreb in the north. Cars may be rented in these cities as well as in Jajce. Bus transport is provided throughout the entire region. All of the towns and rural areas have daily, regular bus service. The buses are very affordable.

Climate and weather conditions

The narrow river valleys of the Pliva and Vrbas Rivers are surrounded by several high mountains. The climate of the Pliva River is governed by these high mountain valleys as well as the region's distance from the Adriatic Sea. The highest mountains in the Pliva Region are Dimitor (1473 m), Vitorog (1907m), Raduša (1956m), Vlašić (1740m) and Ranca Mountain (1473m), Lisina (1337m),

Manjača (1236m) and Čemernica (1388m). The result of the mountainous conditions is a climate that is moderate in the summer months and cold in the other seasons of the year.

Temperature

Temperatures in this region depend on elevation. Summer temperatures average 19 °C.

The region frequently experiences temperature inversions. This is a condition in which cold air is trapped in the bottom of the valleys. Because of these inversions (increase of temperature with height), large areas of fog and frost can occur. This is a typical climatical feature of the Pliva and Vrbas River Valleys. In these valleys, there are over 90 days annually with frost that occurs when the minimum air temperature is under 0 °C.

Winters are often severe in the Pliva River Region. The average temperature in January goes from –0.7 °C in Jajce to –1.1 °C in Šipovo.

FISHING

The pure, spring-fed waters in the rivers and lakes of the Pliva River Region have provided superb fishing opportunities for decades. The Pliva River has a well-deserved reputation as one of Europe's best fly fishing rivers. The middle and lower segments of the Pliva and the other four large rivers in the region provide excellent fishing opportunities for all types of anglers. Enormous fish have been caught in the Pliva Lakes both from the shore and from boats. All of these quality waters are easily accessible from a paved road system that parallels the rivers and lakes.

The rivers and lakes in the Pliva River Region have a diversity of large and healthy fish species that may be caught by the sports angler. Passive to very active fishing techniques may be employed in this region. The sports angler may pursue streamside fishing by either spin casting or fly fishing or considerably more leisurely boat fishing in the lakes.

Fishing areas

The Pliva River

The River Pliva is a mountainous river that extends for 29.5 km from its source at the foot of the Jastrebnjak Mountain, west of the municipality of Šipovo, until it joins the Vrbas River at the Pliva Falls in Jajce. The Pliva Falls are approximately 15 meters tall and provide an extremely picturesque setting. Although the Pliva River is slightly less than 30 km long, it possesses an unusual variety of unique features. The upper reaches of the river zigzags through mountain valleys where it has an extremely fast rate of flow. Across the flat lands the river meanders and its rate of flow reduces considerably. Upon arrival at Jezero, the Pliva is transformed into a series of lakes that are renowned for their calm waters. Beyond Jezero, a short series of waterfalls provide both ancient and modern hydro power. The historic water mills are located near the modern hydro-electric generating facilities. From this location the river proceeds a short distance through the Municipality of Jajce and then it plunges into the Vrbas at Pliva Falls. This incredible variety provides the setting for an equally diverse collection of recreation activities.

The sources of the Pliva River are three enormous underground springs that arise from karst limestone geologic features in the Jastrebnjak Mountain. These springs, located at approximately 489 m above sea level, produce water at an incredible rate that varies from 4 to 15 m^3/s. Pliva River's water temperature at its source is between 7 and 8 °C and this makes the water a perfect, highest quality fishery habitat. Fishing near the source of the Pliva River, especially fly fishing, is amazing.

The Pliva River has distinct seasonal characteristics. During the spring or during long term rainfalls, the Pliva floods the area from Šipovo to Jezero, as well as the part from Draganica to the bridge for Brdjane. The upper reaches will remain clear throughout most of the year, but the lower reaches can be influenced by runoff from snow melt, rainfall, and tributary rivers.

The prize fish species near the source of the Pliva River is the Grayling. The Brown Trout is also native to the Pliva River and this wary fish provides the angler with both challenges and action. The mid-section of the river has California and brook trout, as well as Browns.

There are several streams that enter the Pliva River. The Janj is by far the largest, but the water volume of the Pliva is also increased by flows from the smaller streams that include the Peručica, Sokočnica, and Libovica.

The Janj River

The Janj River is a large, spring-fed river in the Pliva Region. It flows for a distance of 14.5 km through extremely beautiful canyons with sheer rock walls. The source of the Janj River emerges in the River Vaganac canyon. The spring of Janj lies in a deep, dark canyon.

The Lubovica River

The Lubovica is a tributary river of the Pliva River. The character of this river can be torrential. There are numerous creeks along the Lubovica, of which some of the larger ones are Potočić, Vranovina, Mandića potok, Paklarica, Vučajski potok, Jasika, Radovanovića potok, and Trnovica.

The River Volarica

The Volarica is one of the right streams of the Pliva, joining it at Volari. It is approximately 5 km long and drains a small watershed that is approximately 17 km^2 in size.

The River Jošavka

In the centre of the Jezero settlement, the Jošavka joins the Pliva. During heavy rain it floods the area it runs through.

The Pliva Lakes

In the vicinity of Jezero is a series of lakes. The two most prominent of these are called the Great and Small Pliva Lakes. The lakes were originally part of a natural group of lakes associated with the natural course of the Pliva River. Water impoundment structures near Jajce enlarged the lakes substantially and the entire lake system is now some 6 km long. The lake system is divided by a limestone rock into two parts: Gornje or Veliko Jezero and Donje or Malo Jezero. The lakes are quite cold, the highest water temperature being around 21°C.

Lake Trout, Carp, Catfish and California Trout can be caught in the Pliva Lakes. The largest Lake Trout caught in these waters was 24 kg. Sport fishing from both the shore and from boats is very popular.

Sport fishing

Fish species and size

The Pliva River and lakes systems have a remarkable diversity of trophy sport fish species. The name for each species of fish described below is provided in English, Bosnian, and in the Latin biological name.

- **Grayling – Lipen** (*Thymallus thymalus*)

The Grayling thrives only in rivers that have pure and clear water. The Pliva River provides ideal habitat for the Grayling from its source to the town of Šipovo, a distance of approximately 6 km. The steady flow of water from the springs, the nearly constant temperature of the water, and the slow current of the Pliva provide the conditions that are essential for sustaining a quality Grayling habitat.

Grayling may only be found in cold and oxygen rich rivers, with rocky and sandy river beds. The stream conditions in the upper section of the Pliva River provide deep, slow moving water that covers a river bottom composed of sand and rock. The slow pace of the river allows vegetation to flourish and the insects that live in the vegetation provide abundant food sources for the Grayling. The upper Pliva River crosses a wide, flat valley that has a diversity of lush vegetation along its shoreline. These perfect water conditions are becoming increasingly rare and for that reason the Grayling is considered a very desirable sport fish for anglers.

The Grayling is from 20 to 50 cm long and appears to be egg shaped when viewed in cross section. The most prominent feature of the fish is its large dorsal fin that the fish is able to expand like a large fan. Its head is small and pointed. The back of the fish is a gray-green or blue-gray color and the side and the belly are silver or honey color. On the back it's got unevenly distributed dark spots.

Grayling in the Pliva River spawn from mid-March to mid-May on rocks. After fertilization it covers the eggs with rocks. The female hatches from 3,000 to 6,000 eggs that are from 3 to 3.5 mm large.

Grayling feed very aggressively. They will eat both water and airborne insects, terrestrials such as frogs and grasshoppers, as well as larva, snails and small fish. The size of the Pliva River Grayling range from one to five pounds, with an average weight of three pounds. The largest Grayling caught in the Pliva was 58 cm in length.

Flies for Grayling

- Adams Dry
- Elk Wing Caddis
- Gold Ribbed Hare's Ear
- Humpy
- Mosquito Dry
- Light Cahill
- Polar Shrimp

- Mosquito Larva
- Pheasant Tail Nymph
- Salmon Fry
- Tellico
- Zug Bug
- Black Gnat
- Orange Woolly Bugger

- **Brown Trout – Potočna pastrmka**
  (*Salmo trutta morpha fario*)

The Brown Trout is a native species in the Pliva River. It prefers strong flowing rivers and cold temperatures and the Pliva River provides just that. In areas close to the spring the current is stronger and the temperature is lower and this location is an especially important spawning area. The abundant oxygen content of the Pliva River is essential for sustaining the Brown Trout.

The average size of the Brown Trout is about 25-40 cm long and the body shape is mostly round. The fish is dramatically colored. The body is often a bright gold or orange color and there are red and black spots that add to the colorful appearance. The colorful sides of the fish contrast sharply with the back which is mostly greenish to dark brown. The color changes towards the belly. On the upper and lower jaw there are numerous sharp teeth that extend in angles from the mouth.

The spawning season for Brown Trout in the Pliva River lasts from October to the end of December. Females dig a hole in that time with 20 to 50 cm diameter and spawn about 1,000 eggs per 1 kg of her weight. Eggs are from 4 to 5 mm, yellow-red or orange. When they grow up, the fish travel upstream.

The Brown Trout is one of the most difficult fish to catch. They are selective feeders and can be scared away easily when approached. They feed on water and airborne insects, small crabs, larva, tadpoles, small fish, and even on their own species.

The Pliva River has many large Brown Trout. The upstream region has fish that average between four and six pounds. The downstream region has fish that are seven pounds and larger.

- **California Trout - Kaliforijska pastrmka** (*Salmo iridens*)

There are several attractive trout species that have been introduced to the Pliva River. One of these is the California Trout that was introduced from the United States. This fish was brought to Europe from Californian rivers in 1882, and was introduced to the Bosnia region in 1899.

The California Trout spawn in spring when the flow of water is violent. For this reason their reproduction in the Bosnian rivers, such as the Pliva, was minimal. They do spawn very successfully in a fish hatchery, and the Bosnian people along the Pliva River have actively been producing this fish in streamside hatcheries.

California Trout feed on a wide variety of food sources and are well-known as powerful fighters. Once hooked, it is not unusual for these trout to leap from the water several times during their attempt to break away from the line.

Flies for California Trout

Adams Dry	Iliama Pinkie
Bunny Fly	Mirabou Muddler
Egg Sucking Leech	Pheasant Tail Nymph
Elk Wing Caddis	Polar Shrimp
Gold Ribbed Hare's Ear	Woolly Bugger

- **Brook Trout - Amerikanski somic cvergi** (*Amirus nebulosus*)

The Brook Trout is another famous species of trout that was introduced to the Bosnian river system. This species of fish was first brought from Canada in 1879 for breeding in fish ponds. It is found throughout the Pliva River system and especially in the Pliva Lake near Jajce. Another Brook Trout habitat is at the source of the river Bosna, near the spring.

The pectoral, pelvic and anal fins of the Brook Trout are usually orange and edged with black and white. The body is dark, marked with both white and red spots inside blue circles. These fish spawn in the fall and have produced a large population in the Pliva River.

Flies for Brook Trout

Baby Needlefish
Blue Smolt
Gastineau Smolt
Gold Ribbed Hare's Ear
Humpy

Iliama Pinkie
Muddler Minnow
Pheasant Tail Nymph
Roselyn's Sand Lance
Woolly Bugger

- **Lake Trout - Linjak** (*Tinca tinca*)

Lake Trout can grow to enormous size in the Pliva Lakes. For this reason they are a very desirable sport fish. It is an introduced species of trout that was found in select locations of the Mediterranean region and then brought to Bosnia's river systems. Its natural habitat was the Black Sea and the Vardar Region of the Aegean basin. Lake Trout have a golden brown color on their sides and have a dark brown back. Their dorsal fin is especially prominent. Lake Trout may be fished from either the edge of the Pliva Lake or from a boat. The record weight for a Lake Trout caught in the Pliva Lake was 26 kg.

LICENSES

All persons of all ages must have fishing licenses. In Jezero the costs are 10 KM per day for both residents and non-residents. In Šipovo the costs are 10 KM per day for residents and 20 KM for non-residents. Citizens are eligible for seasonal licenses that cost 60 KM in Jajce and 50 KM in Šipovo.

Fishing equipment

- Fly rods of 4, 5, and 6 weights for streams and rivers.
- Rod weights of 7, 8, and 9 for the lakes. To cope with the wind conditions.
- Spinning rods. Usually a two piece sectional rod at 10 feet of length. 15 to 40 grams of action.
- Both open and closed spinning reels.
- Repallas, spinners, and boilies for attracting carp aroma of sweet corn, flour.

Techniques

Specific sections of the river allow the angler to tie on as many as 5 flies to a single line. Other locations require only one fly per line. Spinners and floating dry flies are located on specific reaches of the river.

Catch and release and allowable catch

The fly fishing practice is catch and release. Current regulations for Grayling Trout: one fish of at least 30 cm in length. New regulations will require the fish to be 40 cm in length. The current regulations for other types of trout: one fish of at least 25 cm in length. New regulations will require the fish to be 30 cm in length.

KAYAKING AND BOATING

The Great Pliva Lake was created by impounding the Pliva River near Jajce in order to generate hydro-electrical power. The lake is 3,800 meters long and extends from Jajce to the town of Jezero. The lake is 500 meters wide and has an average depth of 33 meters. The deepest location in the lake is 100 meters. The waters of the lake are generally calm, but high winds occasionally do occur. The Great Pliva Lake never freezes and kayaking and boating take place all year round. The Pliva Lakes' attraction for kayaking and canoeing is that the water is "Heavy". This means that there is a naturally occurring additional atom of hydrogen that provides extra stability to the water. This unique condition results in the water being very flat and stable and this provides the perfect venue for kayak and canoe competitions.

At the Jajce end of the lake, a park with historic and picturesque water mills provides picnic tables and grilles. Other than that park and a few attractive cabins along the edge of the lake, little has been developed here. Unsurprisingly, wildlife such as bear and deer feel at ease and frequently visit the lake's shores.

Since the creation of the Pliva Lake reservoir, a number of islands have been created by sediments continuously being deposited from the flow of the Pliva River. These large islands are densely vegetated, providing migrating and resident birds with both cover and insects to feed upon. Kayakers and boaters go through the attractive channels that split these islands in half, and rest and have picnics on their shores.

People kayak and canoe along the entire 29.5 km length of the Pliva River. Those who like roughing it will enjoy the whitewater runs on the upper reaches of the river, from its source to the Pliva Lakes. For competition-minded people, the real highlight is the Great Pliva Lake. This lake is the site of all sorts of competitions, from local schools competitions to the World Kayak Competition, and 200, 500 and 1,000 meter tracks are permanently marked with buoys. Each year, state and international kayak competitions are held in July and August. On these competition days, the peace and quietness are briefly replaced by large and lively crowds.

Kayaking starts at the Kayak Club, where professional trainers (there are 30 of them!) will determine your skill and experience level, equipment needs, and familiarity with local conditions. Subsequently, you will get some instructions, equipment, and possibly a guide. You can rent two and four seat kayaks. Both come with personal flotation devices, addles, spray skirts, drip rings, float bags, and helmets.

Alternatively, you can rent canoes or peddle boats. They, too, come with safety equipment and instructions. Small sailing boats are allowed to sail on the lake as well. Only motor boats are forbidden, in order to avoid water pollution.

You can rent your equipment for a day or a half day. Once you're done, you might be lucky enough to enjoy a concert on the beach of the small Pliva Lake. A concert schedule is available at the Kayak Club.

Preparations and precautions

Knowledge of kayak and boat safety rules is crucial. Listen carefully to instructors and the licensed guides.

- Whatever you do and wherever you do it – on the lake or in the sometimes heavy-duty whitewater river that leads to it – you should be aware of the water temperature. It rarely exceeds 21 °C, and can be as low as 7 °C close to the source. Appropriate clothing and Personal Flotation Devices are essential.

- Unlike canoes, it is best to get in and out of kayaks while they're in the water.

- Bring waterproof bags (flotation bags of garbage bags) and heavy duty rain gear.

- Accept that, ultimately, the weather conditions will dictate the route you will follow, your speed, and even your destination and choice of landing sites.

- Do not panic if you encounter foul weather and big waves. The boat will not sink. Before you leave shore, make sure your spray skirt is on properly, your life vest is on, and the flotation bags are inflated. Go to shore in a protected area where waves are not breaking. Paddle either into the waves (best) or directly downwind. Do not paddle in the trough, parallel to the waves.

- Never abandon your boat. It can handle more than you can. Never attempt to swim to shore.

- Above all: take no chances with the weather to begin with. Stay on shore and wait if you do not trust the weather.

If you rent your kayak, the rental form will record your time due and destination. If weather or other circumstances prevent your scheduled return, the Kayak Club will be aware of it. In case of an emergency, rental personnel will not fail to notify well-qualified search and rescue groups.

HERB AND MUSHROOM COLLECTION

The forests and river valleys of the Pliva River Region are home to a wide range of herbs (see the table) and mushrooms such as the edible bolete (Boletus sp), morel (Morshella sp), and chanterelle (Cantharellus cibarius). The people of this region use these herbs and mushrooms for food, medicines, and fragrances – and occasionally earn a bit by selling them.

If you are interested in a collection/nature experience, you should ask around: there are plans to turn forest collection into a tourist experience, and guides will be trained to guide you around.

Significant medcinal herbs

Milfoil	*Achillea millefolium*
Monks-hood	*Aconitum variegatum*
Agrimony	*Agrimonia eupatoria*
Onion	*Allium ursinum*
Bear clover	*Anthyllis vulneraria*
Burdock	*Arctium lappa*
Bear ears	*Arctostaphylos uva-ursi*
Wormwood	*Artemisia absinthium*
Asarabacca	*Asarum europaeum*
Woodruff	*Asperula odorata*
Shield-fern	*Aspidium filix-mas*
Belladona	*Atropa belladonna*
Daisy	*Bellis perenis*
Caraway	*Carum carvi*
Forest strawberry	*Fragaria vesca*
Gentian	*Gentiana lutea ssp. Symphyandra*
Common John's Wort	*Hypericum perforatum*
Marjoram	*Origanum vulgare*
Plantain	*Plantago sp.*
Primrose	*Primula sp.*
Lung-wort	*Pulmonaria officinalis*
(Žestika)	*Rhamnus fallax*
Alder buckthorn	*Rhamnus frangula*
Wild rose	*Rosa canina*
Raspberry	*Rubus idaeus*
Blackberry	*Rubus fruticosa*
Dwarf-elder	*Sambucus ebulus*
Elder	*Sambucus nigra*
Dandelion	*Taraxacum officinale*
Thyme	*Thymus serpyllum*
Colt's-foot	*Tussilago farfara*
Grat nettle	*Urtica dioica*
Bilberry, Blue-berry	*Vaccinium myrtilus*

Valeriana	*Valeriana officinalis*
Wood-violet	*Viola sylvestris*

Source: Institute for Urbanism, Banja Luka (corrected by National Museum, Sarajevo)

WILDLIFE VIEWING, BIRDING AND PHOTO SAFARIS

Habitats

Almost half the area of the municipality of Šipovo is covered with forests. This makes Šipovo one of the ecologically richest municipalities in Bosnia and Herzegovina. Mezofilnost and thermopile forests cover the steep hillsides and surrounding mountains (Jastrebnik, Lisina, Vitorog, Stolovaš). There are black and grey alder forests in swampy land areas, and poplar-tree and willow forests dominate the low areas next to the rivers Pliva, Janj, and Sokočnica.

Oak trees (rambling crown) and hornbeam-trees cover the lower layer of the hilly areas, and beech covers the higher parts. In some areas in the north and in exposed valleys, one forest extends into the other - beech-trees are found on the hillsides next to the oak- and hornbeam-trees, and vice versa. The areas covered by these forests suit human requirements and over the centuries, these forests grew smaller and more interspersed with settlements and roads.

In the higher mountains, above the pine-trees on the hillsides, there are beech-, fir- and spruce-trees. The most beautiful areas have been turned into the "Janj" nature reserve just below Stolovaš.

Animals

The remoteness of the region, its enormous size, its rugged terrain, and the few human settlements allowed a variety of rare wildlife species to thrive here for centuries. The European brown bear, wolves, lynx, and wild boar still roam the forests. Small populations of the rare otter (Lutra lutra) and the recently reappearing ream (Lynx lynx) live in the areas around Šipovo and Jajce. The Pliva is a source of life as well. Bear, wolves and deer frequent its shores, and its surroundings provide the peace and food required by a wide range of recuperating migratory birds.

The eco-tourism experience

Wildlife viewing in the midst of the forest is the single greatest attraction to ecotourists. This is the place to do it. This region's diversity and abundance of wildlife species, and the opportunities it offers to see rare and endangered mammals and birds, make a visit to this area an eco-tourism experience that is unique in the world.

Photo safari guide services are provided by the hunting clubs in the communities of Šipovo and Jajce. The members of these organizations have many years of experience and profound knowledge of the forests and wildlife in the entire Pliva River region. They don't just speak about the wildlife you come across, but also explain the environmental conditions that enable the animals to survive.

In line with the eco-philosophy of maximizing enjoyment and minimizing disruption, guides limit the size of their groups. Depending on where you're going you may hike all the way from town, travel a bit by car, or move into the forests with off-road vehicles. Either way, you are likely to be provided with an introduction to the wildlife prior to your departure.

The Pliva Info Centar can provide details and contact numbers (tel: 030 654 100; tel/fax: 030 654 099; email: info@plivatourism.ba or ecohour@plivatourism.ba; web: www.plivatourism.ba).

Guidelines for Photo Safaris

The elimination of human profiles and smells is very important. Don't stand against a skyline. Wear clothing that blends with your environment. Do not act like a predator. Crawl, don't walk when approaching wildlife from short distances. Move in oblique or zig-zag patterns and exercise extreme patience. Adapt yourself to circumstances and be aware of how the animals respect your presences. If you respect their needs and desires, they will often accept you.

Stalking (tracking) is the most commonly used method for approaching wild animals to get a good photograph. Binoculars and spotting scopes are helpful in locating animals at a distance. Be sure to scan the entire area to determine if there is more than one animal in the vicinity. For example, the safe way to photograph a bear is to be certain that there are no cubs in the area. Before stringing off for your animal, have your camera ready to go and mounted on the tripod. Anticipate where the animal will be when you get close enough to get a good picture. Plan your approach to the animal so that lighting and background will produce the best possible picture.

When you get close to an animal and it is aware of you, be patient. Allow the animal to adjust to your presence. Move only when it is busy feeding or otherwise occupied in an activity that will make it less likely to notice your movement. Once you are in its view, it is best to remain in the open where your subject can keep track of you. Never block an animal's escape path.

Take your pictures as discreetly as possible in order to get more natural poses and cause the animal the least distress. Ideally, you should stalk, photograph, and leave without unreasonably disturbing the animal. When you achieve this, you are an excellent stalker and ethical photographer.

A good understanding of the animal's behavior is helpful when stalking. Some species that live in open habitats, such as bear and wolves, may approach rather than flee from you once they spotted you. They come closer to catch your scent before deciding to escape. This behavior often provides an ideal opportunity for photographs.

Special care should be taken around nests and dens where disturbance can lead to abandonment and death of eggs and young. Extreme caution should be used when photographing young animals – the mother is around somewhere and will be very protective. Always consider the consequence of your photographic activities on both the animal's and your well-being.

Safety

Check the safety section in the general part of this booklet before venturing into the forests. If something goes wrong nonetheless, you will probably be brought to the clinic in Šipovo. It has X-ray and diagnostic equipment. For serious injuries, you may have to be transported to the hospital in Banja Luka. The region is covered by a network of field ambulances, each of which is staffed with a trained nurse.

Snakes: There are two species of poisonous snakes in the Pliva River Region. One of them is a viper and the other one is an adder. Both are hemeotoxic (blood poisoning) and bites require immediate medical attention. A bite wound will display swelling and skin discoloration.

Bears: Confrontations with the European brown bear (*Ursus arctos*) are rare. If you do encounter this type of bear: do not run as this will trigger the bear's predator instincts and it will quickly pursue and overtake you. Instead, back away slowly. If an attack is imminent lay on the ground and curl into a ball covering your head and neck with your arms. Never approach bear cubs as the mother will be nearby and is likely to attack you.

Wolves: Wolves (*Cannis lupus*) roam freely throughout this region. They will avoid humans. If you see wolves then attempt to stay upwind of their position. Allow them to migrate through your area.

Wild Boar: These animals also roam freely through the region. Because these animals are hunted they fear man. However, wild boar are belligerent by nature and are especially dangerous when protecting their young.

CENTRAL WEST BOSNIA

Many areas of the western part of central Bosnia have strong political and cultural ties with western Herzegovina. Although this area is not a geographical part of Herzegovina, many of its residents consider themselves part of the its community. This feeling is particularly strong in the towns of Livno, Tomislavgrad and Kupres.

Livno is the cultural and political centre of this vast area. West Bosnia has a very low population density; long open valleys and unpopulated mountains and hills cover most of the region. For nature lovers this region's vast wilderness is an amazingly peaceful getaway. West Central Bosnia is ideal for long bike rides, paragliding, caving, walking and hiking as well as for the many water sports available on the Bušk and Blidinje lakes.

The musical traditions of this region are unique. It is here that the Ganga and Bećarac styles, coupled with the hand-carved gusle, cry out and tell of the hardships and resistance of the hajduks who opposed Ottoman rule. This spirit of resistance never died. Even today, there is a village that declared itself independent from Bosnia and Herzegovina and called itself the Hajdučka Republika or Republic of the Rebels. They created their own seal, don't pay taxes and have their own passports.

LIVNO

Prince Mutimir's **Povelja Charter** from September 28 892 is celebrated as the birthday of the town of Livno. However, as in many other areas in Bosnia and Herzegovina, archaeological research in and around Livno has uncovered human settlements from over 4,000 years ago. Many of these finds are located at **Duman**, a large karst cave that is the source of the **River Bistrica**. This source greatly resembles the one found in Blagaj where the Buna River originates. On the high, steep cliffs of **Teber** there are also the same type of caves as seen in Blagaj. It is most likely that the indigenous Illyrian tribes built the first fortifications atop these cliffs, and the Romans, Slavs and Ottomans later reinforced them. The great rush of water from the caves made it an ideal location for powering mills. The Ottomans built a lovely stone arched bridge over the Duma.

There are daily buses from Mostar and Split to Livno. Livno is also a transit stop for some traffic from Sarajevo and central Bosnia.

The town itself is an interesting blend of Dalmatian, Ottoman and socialist structures. Apart from some good restaurants and café's, the only thing worth seeing inside the town is the **Franciscan Museum and Gorička Gallery** (Gorička bb; tel: 034 200 922; fax: 034 200 923; email: framuzej@hotmail.com). Gorička certainly ranks among the country's best Franciscan galleries and has a permanent exhibition of the works of Gabriel Jurkić. Jurkić was one of the most famous painters in the history of Bosnia and Herzegovina; his work can also be seen at the National Gallery in Sarajevo. The museum traces the history of the church and its followers in fine Franciscan fashion. The **Franciscan Monastery** is in the same compound but separated from the museum and gallery. It is a beautiful and interesting place to check out (Gorička cesta bb; tel/fax: 034 200 311; email: fra.barun@tel.net.ba).

Livno has a longstanding custom of producing a fabulous hard yellow cheese called Livanjski Sir. You don't have to go to Livno to get it, but if you do at least you'll know you're getting the real McCoy. It goes marvelously well with a fine bottle of Herzegovinian red wine and some local pršut (dried ham).

There are quite a few restaurants in town serving the local cuisine. **Restoran Ideal** (Suhača bb; tel: 034 200 428; email: vcolak@acmt.hr) is ideal for a good meal. The name **Restoran MB** may be uninspiring but the food and service are good (Zagrebačka 22; tel: 034 202 280). Prices are about average for Bosnia and Herzegovina and range from 8 to 12KM for a main course. With wine you can expect to spend 50KM for two people. Just a bit out of town there is the brand new **Restaurant Petričević** that also offers bed and breakfast. If you're visiting during the winter months you can hop on the nearby ski lift and hit the slopes for a while. The food is great and they often have live folk music (Zagoričani, Borova Glava bb; tel/fax: 034 201 937).

There are only two hotels in Livno. **Hotel Park** is by far the best choice (Kneza Mutimira 56; tel: 034 202 149; fax: 034 201 009; email: hotel.park.livno@tel.net.ba; web: www.hotel-park-livno.com; singles and doubles are 45 and 80 KM). The entire hotel is renovated and now has very modern facilities. Each room has satellite TV. The suites have a minibar and a mini-kitchen. There are a few suites with small jacuzzis in the bathrooms. For your entertainment there is an excellent pool hall (billiards hall) and within the hotel complex you'll find the Night Flight Disco. The restaurant serves international and traditional dishes. For the budget traveler the **Pansion San** is a simpler and cheaper alternative. The rooms are nice and clean with TV and plenty of hot water (Domobranska 3; tel: 034 202 018; singles and doubles cost 30 and 35 KM). **The Canton Tourism Association** is located in Livno at Stjepana II Kotromanića bb (tel: 034 200 901; email: hbzup@hbzup.com; web: www.hbzup.com). They speak English and have a few vague brochures. If you are looking for directions or accommodation it is better to ask than to rely on the printed material.

TOMISLAVGRAD

There is not much to attract tourists to Tomislavgrad. The most attractive aspect of this sleepy town is its natural surroundings. The largest storage lake in Europe, **Lake Buško**, the surface of which covers 57km2, borders the town. For anglers there are more fish than one can handle. Carp catches of 10kg are not uncommon! The wind from the long valleys **Livanjsko** and **Duvanjsko Fields** provides optimum conditions for parasailing. Water skiing, rowing and canoeing are among the water sports that the tourism association here is developing. There is an annual canoeing and kayaking competition held in August for middle-European countries. You can camp along the banks of the lake, and the entire area is completely clear of mines. Tomislavgrad is also the gateway to **Blidinje Nature Park**. The entrance to the park is marked from the outskirts of town towards **Lipa**. Don't let the dirt track confuse you; good gravel roads connect a large portion of the park. Regular buses to Tomislavgrad travel from Livno and Mostar. There are no buses that travel through Blidinje.

BLIDINJE NATURE PARK

There are many access roads to the park, but it's best to stick to the three main ones: via **Rakitno** northeast from **Posušje**, **Lipa** from **Tomislavgrad**, and west from **Jablanica** via **Doljani**.

The open and barren valley leading into the park is a result of the two past ice ages. The melting glaciers from Čvrsnica created this massive valley between **Čvrsnica** and **Vran** mountains. **Blidinje Lake** is the direct result of a glacial retreat located at 1,184m in the valley below. This runway for ice, water and debris did not, however, manage to stop a wide range of life forms from prospering here. Accompanying some of the rocky and seemingly lifeless slopes are thick forests of pine, including the endemic white-bark pine at **Masna Luka** called Pinus leuco dermis. Three types of wild thyme and dozens of wild flowers cover the valley and mountainsides in the spring and summer. The 3-5km valley, situated at an elevation of 1,150-1,300m, is dotted with the trademark stećci from medieval ages. It is not clear how long human settlements have existed here but research began when Blidinje recently received Nature Park status. Traces of Illyrian graves and Roman roads indicate that Blidinje has been settled for at least 2,500 years. The large necropolis at **Dugo Polje** indicates that the waves of Slavs that came in the 7th century also made this area their home.

The park is set in long sweeping valleys. To the north and southeast are the peaks of Vran and Čvrsnica. Ploča on Čvrsnica is the highest peak in Herzegovina at 2,226m. The peak is unfortunately a military installation and it is forbidden for hikers to summit. The park itself is free of mines with well-marked trails. It's best to visit the hotel by the ski lifts at Risovac for information. They will also have information about the park, its history and the Franciscan monastery that is located within the park and open to visitors.

Croatian people believe that Blidinje is a gift from God. The park's ever-so-tiny population is Croatian. Houses here are traditional shepherd homes with straw roofs that are mainly used during the spring and summer seasons. Winter is harsh and cold in these parts. The ski centre at **Ristovac** opens in winter and has a small hotel that sleeps 42 (Hotel Park Prirode Blidinje; tel: 039 718 515; fax: 039 718 514; 20 KM per bed per night). It is a popular ski destination for folks from Mostar and Split, as well as for the local population from Livno and Tomislavgrad. The park does not, as of yet, have an email address or website. The hotel address is PP 29, 88446, Ristovac, Doljani. **Restoran Žičara**, by the slopes, belongs to the hotel and is open all year round (tel: 039 718 515).

KUPRES

The highest settlement in central-west Bosnia is home to the country's most rugged inhabitants. By rugged I mean that the people of Kupres live a challenging lifestyle closely tied to nature and the elements. At 1,200m above sea level, Kupres is covered in snow for at least five months of the year. The long and bare valley of **Kupreško Polje** creates harsh winter conditions. It also makes Kupres a main winter recreation destination in western Bosnia. **Hotel Adria Ski** (Čajuša bb; tel/fax: 034 275 100; email: hotel@adriaski.com) is the main centre for skiing in the area, along with **Risovac** in Blidinje Park. The hotel has been renovated to attract guests from the Dalmatian coast looking for a nearby ski vacation. They charge 86 and 130 KM for singles and doubles. The ski lift runs right out of the back of the hotel. The slopes aren't steep or super-fast, but the opportunity to ski in the middle of nowhere is, for some, very appealing. **Pansion Kraljica** is a new bed and breakfast that receives most of its guests during the ski season (Splitska 1; tel: 034 274 568; 25 KM per night per bed).

A very rich aspect of Bosnian Croat culture has emerged in this tiny town between Bugojno and Livno. Many of the traditions that are only performed for folk shows in other places are regularly practiced here. The old methods of farming are celebrated on the first Sunday of each May with the Strljanica competition. Expansive fields of long grass are hacked down with traditional sickles to see who is the most skilled in quick cutting. It may seem funny but try it out and you will see not only the skill needed but also the tremendous back and forearm strength that the 'sport' requires. Kupres is known throughout the country for this annual event. Horse races, an almost forgotten rural event, happen each year in the fields of Kupres as well. The traditional Ganga and Bećarac song of the hajduks can often be heard echoing through the valley.

Due to the high altitude, many of the local residents cannot rely on farming for a living and often partake in sheep-raising. Most folks from in and around Kupres will attest to the great grilled lamb and sheep's cheese prepared in the traditional Kupres way. If you have the opportunity to eat with a local family, don't pass it up. Kupres is a transit town from central Bosnia to Livno and the Adriatic coast. Daily buses to and from Vitez and Travnik stop in Kupres if requested.

WESTERN & NORTHWESTERN BOSNIA

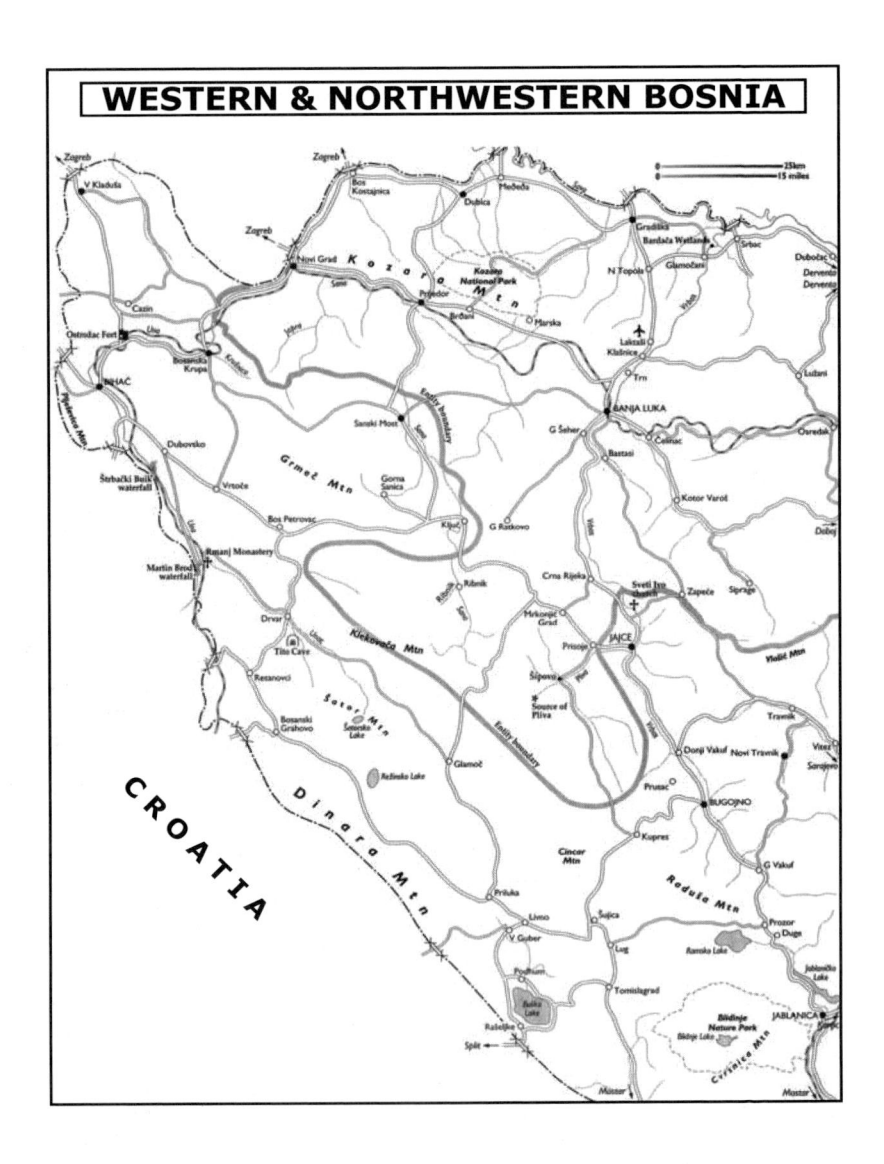

NORTH BOSNIA

For practical purposes this guide to North Bosnia is divided into two sub-sections. The first covers the northwest of the country, which is known as the Krajina. This area is geographically and culturally tied with Banja Luka and Bihać. Similarly the northeast of country shares common ties and also has two main centers in Tuzla and Bjeljina. Brčko, a non-entity district to the far north on the River Sava, is also a large port center where much of the region gravitates to. Travel between the northwest and the northeast is easy and there are no 'borders' to speak of. The northwest is characterized by green rolling hills and an amazing abundance of fresh, crystal clear waters. The northeast is more known for its industrial and agricultural wealth. Both possess an interesting charm, with different traditions and mentalities – but with the common thread of being warm and hospital.

The northern region of Bosnia and Herzegovina, more than any other region in the country, experienced the weight of massive empires vying for its vast natural wealth. Most of the northern region at one time or another was the battleground of the Austro-Hungarian and Ottoman Empires. It was this region that remained under the control of the Hungarian king many years after the fort in Jajce fell in 1528. Much of this land was not fully conquered by the Ottomans until the late 16th century. It has taken on a unique blend of all that have come through here – without ever losing the taste of what is truly Bosnian.

The north does not have a well-developed tourism industry and traveling in this region is considered more 'off the beaten path' than other areas of the country. You won't find information booths or even an adequate tourism office, and you may have to dig a bit deeper to find this region's treasures, but the treasures are there and you'll be glad you came to this part of the country.

The watermills of Jajce

An Ottoman tombstone, Livanjsko Polje

Glamočko Polje

The deserted highlands of Kupres, with Cincar Mountain in the background

Sulejmanija
(the Multi-Colored Mosque) of Travnik

The Franciscan monastery and church of Kraljeva Sutjeska

NORTHWEST BOSNIA: BOSANSKA KRAJINA

The translation of Krajina is frontier. Kraj literally means end. It was this 'end' of the Ottoman front that was for centuries the frontier land against the Austro-Hungarian Empire. The Croatian Krajina, just over the border to the west, was at one time crucial to the Ottoman conquest and was used by the Ottomans as a defence line. As the empire began to decline the frontier slipped back into Bosnia and the entire northwest part of the country became known as the Bosanska Krajina, the Bosnian Frontier. It was the policy of the Ottoman administration to settle this land with janissaries, soldiers and their families. As administrators in the empire, Muslims were given incentives, such as large tracts of land, to settle in the Krajina. Serbs and Vlachs were also given land in order to defend these areas. The Vlachs in particular were sought after by the Ottoman army for their fierce fighting skills. Many Catholics fled or converted during Ottoman times but a significant minority of Croats still inhabit present-day Krajina.

The war carved up the Krajina. In the Republika Srpska section of the Krajina, many non-Serb residents fled or were expelled or killed. The horrific concentration camps you read about in the newspaper or saw on television were all in the Prijedor area. The haunting pictures of skeletal men behind barbed wire are all from the Krajina. In 1995 the large offensives launched by the Bosnian Muslim and Croat armies recaptured almost the entire Krajina region. This sent scores of Serbs fleeing back into Serbian held territory - again displacing a large community. At this time all parties were called to Dayton and the peace accords were signed a month later. Returns to both sides are slow but steady. The towns of Drvar and Bosansko Grahovo, for example, always had a majority Serb population and they have returned in significant numbers. The mainly Muslim areas of Kozarac and Hambarina have also seen part of their pre-war population return, as have many other areas around Prijedor and Sanski Most.

What do all these borders, imaginary or real, mean to the visitor? In practical terms, not much. It is still Bosnia and Herzegovina and there is free and safe passage between the entities. There are no checkpoints or passports needed. It's like driving from England to Wales, where the only noticeable difference may be in the accent or a few road signs in a foreign language. The boundaries between the Federation and Republika Srpska are political, and for all practical purposes should not affect your travels.

However, I would veer away from political or historical conversations in the Republika Srpska; interpretations tend to differ markedly from the Western version.

What is most striking about the Krajina is not its political divide, but rather the beautiful interconnected rivers and the lush, green countryside. The sheer quantity of crystal-clear rivers in this region is phenomenal. The Vrbas, Una, Sana, Sanica and Unac rivers are only a few of the pure water sources that flow into the Sava River. The Bosnian Krajina's greatest tourist attractions all revolve around its natural resources. Just about anywhere in the Krajina one can find beautiful places to hike, walk, bike, fish, hunt or just enjoy a lazy day in the great outdoors. Although there are no tourist cities like Mostar or Sarajevo to visit, Banja Luka and Bihać are regional centres with things to see or do. But chances are you will spend no more than a day there before you find yourself rafting on the Una, or relaxing in the thermal spas at Slatina.

BANJA LUKA

This beautiful town is surrounded by rolling green hills. It is split in two by the Vrbas, a very rough river that, just a short distance from Banja Luka, suddenly loses its waterfalls and cascades, and flows gently into town. Banja Luka is the administrative capital of the Republika Srpska, the second largest city in Bosnia and Herzegovina and by far the largest city in the north.

The town got connected to the world when the Roman trade route from Salona to Servitium got to pass through it. To protect this route (and to enjoy the healing water springs they had discovered in the area) the Romans built a fortress here, the walls of which encompassed an entire miniature town. When the Roman Empire collapsed, the Slavs took over. They defended Banja Luka vigorously when the Ottomans arrived in Bosnia and Herzegovina, and managed to hold on to the town until years after the rest of the region had been conquered.

Once the Ottomans finally controlled the town, they gave it a distinct oriental flavor. The Ottoman governor for Bosnia had his headquarters here for a while, building bridges and mills, and in its Ottoman glory days the town had some 40 mosques. Probably, Banja Luka's name comes from this period: 'banova luka', the governor's meadow. In these times, Christian orthodoxy faired relatively well too, and a number of monasteries were built in the region. Over 400 years later, some of them are still in use.

In the course of the Ottoman centuries, Banja Luka was destroyed repeatedly by Ottoman-Austrian warfare (as well as earthquakes and plagues) until eventually the Austrian-Hungarian Empire absorbed Banja Luka peacefully in the 19th century. They rapidly modernized the town, building factories and connecting it to Vienna and other capital cities.

Although life in Banja Luka was no picnic in the 20th century (there was an awful earthquake in 1969, and the Second World War saw massacres and air raids from both the Germans and the allied forces), the town expanded tremendously. When the Austro-Hungarians did the first-ever Banja Luka census in 1895, Banja Luka had less than 15,000 inhabitants. Less than a century later, more than ten times as many people were counted.

The 1991 census showed Banja Luka to be an ethnically diverse Bosnian city. That is no longer the case. In the recent war, the Bosniacs and Croats

NORTHWEST BOSNIA: BOSANSKA KRAJINA

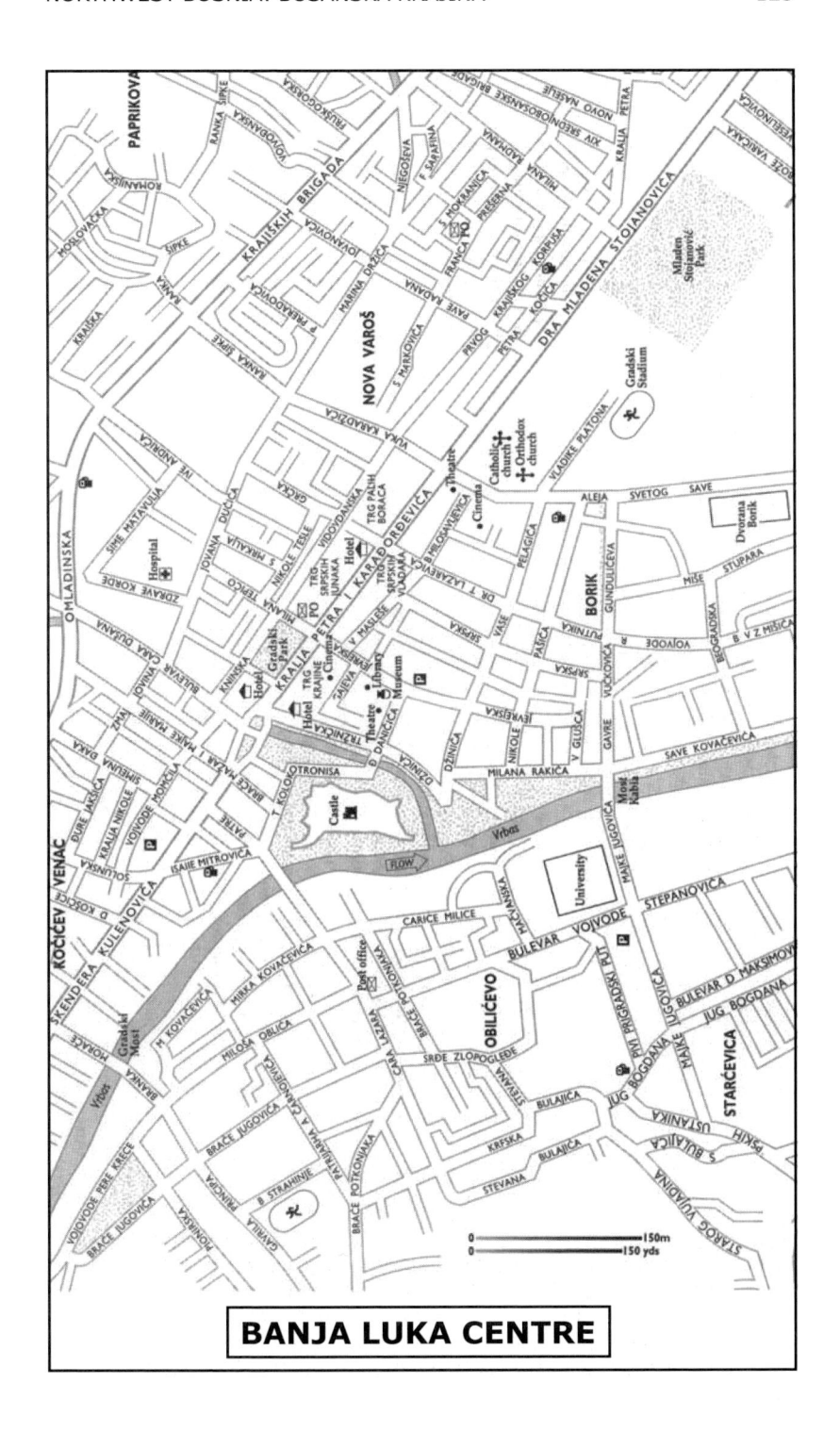

BANJA LUKA CENTRE

were forcefully expelled, and the physical structures they left behind were systematically destroyed to eradicate any signs of their previous presence. As many Serb refugees sought refuge in Banja Luka, and very few Bosniacs and Croats returned to it in the post-war years, Banja Luka today is an overwhelmingly Serb town. You can find out more about Banja Luka at www.banjaluka.rs.ba.

Getting there and away

Getting to Banja Luka is easy. It is the main bus hub of western Republika Srpska, and dozens of buses leave Banja Luka daily to most destinations in the Republika and to the main destinations in the Federation. There are daily trains to and from Zagreb, Sarajevo and Belgrade. The airport in Banja Luka is very small and is experiencing financial difficulties. The only daily flights are to and from Belgrade. Weekly flights go to Vienna. It is more expensive to fly into Banja Luka than into Zagreb or Sarajevo. Air Srpska is the main airline flying out of Banja Luka airport but they too are experiencing financial difficulties and may not always fly when scheduled.

International and domestic bus lines

Banja Luka - Zürich	11:00 every Sunday and 12:00 every Wednesday
Banja Luka - Innsbruck	11:00 every Sunday and 13:30 every Wednesday
Banja Luka - Vienna	11:00 every Sunday and 13:30 every Wednesday and Thursday
Banja Luka - Linz	10:30 every Sunday
Banja Luka - München	10:00; 11:00 every Sunday and 11:00 every Wednesday
Banja Luka - Belgrade	6:30; 9:30; 12:00; 15:00; 17:00; 23:30 every day
Banja Luka - Novi Sad	13:00 every day
Banja Luka - Kragujevac	5:00; 6:00 every day
Banja Luka - Belgrade - Niš	00:45 every day
Banja Luka - Loznica - Niš	18:00 every day
Banja Luka - Zrenjanin	22:00 every day
Banja Luka - Subotica	7:30; 19:00 every day
Banja Luka - Zvornik - Herceg Novi	12:30 every day
Banja Luka - Crvenka	11:00 every Friday and Sunday
Banja Luka - Mostar - Herceg Novi	12:30 every Sunday
Banja Luka - Zagreb	9:45 every day
Banja Luka - Rijeka	22:00 every Monday, Friday, Saturday and Sunday
Banja Luka - B. Manastir	14:15 every day
Banja Luka - Vukovar	7:00 every Monday, Tuesday, Friday and Saturday

Banja Luka - Bihać	7:30; 13:00 every day
Banja Luka - Sarajevo	7:45; 16:00 every day
Banja Luka - Livno	5:30 every day
Banja Luka - Gradiška	8:15; 10:45; 13:05; 18:30 every day
Banja Luka - Kneževo	10:30; 17:30 every day except Sunday
Banja Luka - Novi Grad	8:00 every day
Banja Luka - Kostajnica	11:00; 13:00 every day
Banja Luka – Šipovo	7:00; 7:30; 8:45; 14:00; 15:00 on Saturday and 7:30 and 15:00 on Sunday
Banja Luka - Oštra Luka	10:15; 15:45 every day
Banja Luka - Banja Vrućica	14:45 every day

Train schedules

Banja Luka – Novi Grad	13:20; 19:20
Banja Luka – Prijedor	13:20; 19:20
Banja Luka – Doboj	4:19; 7:30; 10:46
Banja Luka – Dobljin	4:08; 7:30; 10:46; 15:41

Tourist information

There aren't any good guides to Banja Luka, and very few travel agencies actually deal with incoming tourism. The Tourist Organisation of Banja Luka (KP I Karađorđević 75; tel: 051-218022; fax: 051-212323; email: tursavbl@teol.net) has recently begun to develop brochures for the region, and they can point you in the right direction for hotels and restaurants.

Local tour operators

Zepter Passport Banja Luka (Jevrejska bb; tel: 051 213 395; fax: 051 241 138; email: z-passbl@inecco.net; web: www.zepterpassport.com) is the only travel agency that organises tours and guides in the Krajina and in other areas of Bosnia and Herzegovina. They also arrange hunting and fishing trips. Zepter can arrange permits, gear/gun rental, and customs papers if hunters would like to take their trophy with them.

Unis Tours on Kralja Alfonsa XIII 7 (tel: 051-212992; fax: 051-217860) can organise trips to Jahorina or one of the many thermal spas in the Republika Srpska.

Where to stay

Banja Luka's role as a regional centre has spurred a rapid growth in good hotels. They are all in the 50-120 KM range, and appear to compete on the basis of style, service and facilities rather than price. There are no hostels to speak of yet but the tourist information office may be able to help you with private accommodation.

Hotel Firenca (Uroša Predića 1; tel: 051 311 290; fax: 051 311 296; email: firenca@blic.net; web: www.hotelfirenca.com) often caters to foreigners and offers very nice rooms and a quiet relaxing garden. You might want to check out the options, as different rooms have different styles (and different prices). The service in this hotel is a real treat. They remember your name after just one visit, make the breakfast the way you would like to have it, and make you a real quick coffee when you're waiting for a taxi, for example.

Hotel Palace is one of the two main hotels in town and located on the main street (Ulica Petra I Karađorđevića; tel/fax: 051 218 723/4; single 100KM; double130 KM). The hotel is very spacious with 77 rooms, all with air conditioning, minibar, phone and satellite TV. It has a gym. The restaurant and café are always filled with locals. They also have an information centre for things to see and do around Banja Luka and the surrounding area. The hotel's only disadvantage is the mediocre breakfast it serves.

Hotel Bosna (K Petra I Karađorđevića 97; tel: 051 215 775; fax: 051 216 942). Built in 1885, this is the oldest and largest hotel in town. The rooms here are also spacious with all the standard extras – but it's all a little older. Compared to the nicer and newer hotels in town, rooms here are overpriced at 100KM for a single and 140KM for a double room. Breakfast comes in the form of a large open buffet.

Garni Hotel Castello (Knjaza Miloša 64; tel: 051 371 286; fax: 051 371 745; web: www.castello-hotel) is at the east end of town. The rooms are small but comfortable, and cost 60 and 80KM for singles and doubles. The hotel has a café, pizzeria and Italian restaurant. They have internet service and professional translators on hand if you've come for business.

The Olimpus is a hotel apartment complex in downtown Banja Luka (Ivana Franje Jukića 7; tel: 051 212 225; email: olimpus@teleklik.net). This is the only place in town that rents apartments to foreign guests. If you plan to be in town for some time and want to cook for yourself: the apartments come with a complete kitchen. Singles and doubles cost 100 and 150KM respectively.

Hotel Vidović (Kozarska 85; tel: 051 217 883) is new, nice, and two km from the city centre. It is relatively small and has no restaurant, but the staff is pleasant and speaks very good English. A night including breakfast costs 66/77 KM for a single/double room.

Motel Nana (I.G.Kovačića bb; tel: 051 370 667) is on the highway to Zagreb, some 3 km out of town. The motel charges 50/62 KM for singles/doubles.

Hotel Bomi (I.G. Kovačića bb; tel: 051 785 336) is nine kilometers out of town on the same road to Zagreb. It is beautifully situated next to the lake, and surprisingly inexpensive at 50/80 KM for a single/double room and 100 KM for an apartment. The hotel has its own fine restaurant. The restaurant next door is equally good and more modestly priced.

Where to eat

There is no shortage of good restaurants in Banja Luka. Most of them serve traditional local and regional dishes. The prices in Banja Luka are relatively low and there is always a fast food or pita shop for those who are on a really tight budget. Bakeries in Banja Luka are also quite good and I've found some of them to carry more French pastries than I have found in the capital Sarajevo. One may easily find ham and other pork dishes here whereas in some parts of the country they are more difficult to come by. Vegetarians have to make due in Banja Luka: restaurants will all serve you vegetables, cheese and bread but don't expect a vegetarian menu anywhere.

Restaurant Kazamat (tel/fax: 051 312 394) is situated in the Tvrđava Castle and by far the most beautiful place for a summer's meal. They serve traditional foods but also have several international dishes. Even if you just go for a coffee you shouldn't miss this restaurant and a walk through the castle and the surrounding green space.

The mill-turned-into-restaurant **Stari Mlin** on the Vrbas is another experience in traditional dining (Bogdana Marića 14; tel/fax: 051 213 401; email: stari.mlin@blic.net; web: www.starimlin.com; close to this place a competitor opened recently). Many of the dishes are prepared ispod sača (in an open fireplace), and they make a point out of presenting their mixed grills in artfully composed little mountains. Its first floor is particularly dark and discrete, and used by young couples that would like some privacy when dining, wining and kissing. A 1km footpath along the river from the centre of town gets you in the mood and takes you directly to Stari Mlin. You might want to combine a meal with a swim in the lagoon closeby.

Ognjišta (Josifa Pančića 2; tel: 051 307 195) looks like a cottage and serves traditional meals, with a bit less emphasis of meat than most other restaurants in town. It has a nice terrace.

Lanako (051 310 678) is a large restaurant right next to the tennis courts in the Mladen Stojanović Park on Karađorđevića Street. The local elite dine here. It is open until late and the food is excellent.

Mexico Restoran Master (Sime Šolaje 7; tel: 051 317 444; web: www.restoran-master.com) Surprisingly in a country that does not like foreign food, this Mexican restaurant is a local hit and booked out every night of the week. It has good food, real Mexican beer and a great atmosphere.

When the town's Chinese restaurant closed down recently, another one opened its doors in Rudarska in Lauš. I have not seen the place and don't have any contact information, but I heard it's good.

What to see and do

Banja Luka is dominated by the **Vrbas River** and **Tvrđava Kastel** that was built on its banks. Tvrđava survived earthquakes and wars and is one of the best-preserved castles in Bosnia and Herzegovina. Parts of it are still intact and in use. It was originally a much smaller Roman fortress, strengthened by the Slavs and expanded by the Ottomans when Banja Luka became a main frontier town from which the Ottomans defended their empire against the Austro-Hungarians. Eventually, the Ottomans lost it and the Austro-Hungarians renovated and used the castle as a defense structure themselves. The last time the castle was of military importance was as recent as the Second World War, when the German intelligence had a base here. In the last few decades, it has been used to host cultural events and as a children's playground. The Tvrđava has a wonderful restaurant with a large terrace overlooking the Vrbas.

At one point in time, Banja Luka was the headquarters of the Ottoman governor, and even when he moved it to Sarajevo, Banja Luka continued to be of importance to the Ottoman Empire as a frontier town against the Austro-Hungarians. Consequently, the town had a very oriental atmosphere. Today, a few Ottoman houses and mahalas, standing along the Vrbas, are the last reminders of Ottoman times. All sixteen mosques that still existed in the early 1990s (down from 40 at the height of the Ottoman power) were destroyed in the recent war. Among them, there was the **Ferhadija Mosque**, one of greatest mosques in the Balkans, and the centre from which the town of Banja Luka had developed. Reconstruction began recently, ten years after its destruction. Once this reconstruction is completed, a shadow of the traditional oriental flavor may return to Banja Luka.

The main park on **Karađorđevića Street**, called **Mladen Stojanović Park**, has a large pedestrian area, several tennis courts, a café and a restaurant. The park is filled with locals, making it a great spot for mingling with the Banja Lukans.

Aside from the parks and Vrbas River, in the old railway station, the **Art Gallery of Republika Srpska** (Trg Srpskih junaka 2; tel: 051 215 364; email: galrs@inecco.net) exhibits famous works of Serbian painters. They often exhibit local modern art as well. An English-language guide can be arranged and admission is free.

The Cultural Centre Banski Dvor (Trg srpskih vladara 2; tel: 051 305 336; email: banskidvor@blic.net) is situated in a beautiful building-with-park that originally served as the governor's residence. It has programmes of performances, concerts, poetry and other events several days a week. You have to check the schedule when you arrive.

The **Museum of Republika Srpska** (Dur Dannicica 1, tel: 051 215 973; long opening hours and a 2 KM entrance fee) shows archeological findings, war-related exhibits, and traditional costumes. It does not seem to get many visitors.

The main traffic-free strolling street is **Gospodska Ulica**, the first and foremost shopping street in town. The bakery in the middle of that street makes nice sandwiches. Here, as indeed in most parts of town, there is a striking imbalance between the sexes: men seem to be a small minority.

If you're looking to use the internet then visit the Internet Café Click on Majke Jugovića 26.

Festival calendar	
Name of Manifestation	**Date**
Banja Luka Choir Gathering	April-May
Theater Festival "Teatar Fest"	May
The Month of Rock Music	June
Banja Luka Summer Games	August
Folklore Days Banja Luka	July-August, every Thursday
Summer on the Vrbas	July

The eco-tourism experience

There has been a recent revival of eco-tourism activities in and around Banja Luka. Rafting and kayaking trips on the river Vrbas are now available on some of the most attractive parts of this gorgeous river canyon. The **Eco-center,** located 11 km south of Banja Luka, is the main lauching area for the **Rafting Club Kanjon** (tel: 065 420 000; email: info@kanjonraft.com). They offer four routes ranging from an easy 5 kilometer family excursion to a more serious whitewater adventure of 21 kilometers. The **Kayak-Canoe club Vrbas** is in town on Save Kovačevića 44 (tel: 051 303 368; email: kajakkanu@blic.net). They offer a unique opportunity to kayak right through the heart of town by the ancient Roman castle.

Now to dry land and the fun of climbing and caving. The canyon Vrbas offers quite an array of great climbing routes and caves to explore. The **climbing club X-TREME** (Marije Bursać 18; tel: 065 420 000; email: xtremebl@hotmail.com: web: www.xtremebl.com) offers guides and fairly decent gear. Even if you're just up for some free climbing or bouldering it's always best to have a local guide who knows the best rock. The deep karst zone around the Vrbas is a vast change of dolomite and limestone rock that has formed dozens of caves and pits around Banja Luka. The caving club **Ponir** (Sime Matavulja bb: tel: 051 213 904; email: ponir@care2.com) is also located in the city. They like caves so much that they chose to have their office in an old atomic bomb shelter!

Last but not least we take to the air – the paragliding club **Airdrenaline** rounds off the adrenaline junkies agenda with some great low-mountain flights around Banja Luka. They organize paragliding trips for those with some experience and they have all the necessary gear and safety equipment. Their website is out of function at the time of printing but you can contact them by phone at 065 660 333.

AROUND TOWN

Bočac is a 15th century medieval town situated on the left bank of the Vrbas River, half way between Banja Luka and Jajce. There have been several initiatives to create eco-centers to preserve its natural beauty and clean the river from buildup from the hydro-electric dam. It has been placed on the list of national monuments by the government of Republika Srpska. If you're up for a wander, the road leading south out of Banja Luka through the Vrbas Canyon will take you there. It's in quite a beautiful setting but little is organized for the 'tourist.' There is a zoo and a restaurant but no accommodation.

Gomionica Monastery is one of the finest examples of eastern Orthodox monasteries in northern Bosnia. The monastery also has a church on the grounds dedicated to Vavedenje Bogorodice by Bronzani Mejdan, dated 1536. In similar, but not as striking styles as the orthodox monasteries in the Carpathian Mountains in Romania, there are several fresco paintings preserved and a great number of valuable icons and old manuscripts. One can also find an interesting collection of old printed books (all in Cyrillic), as well as other precious objects of art crafts used for the liturgy.

Krupa na Vrbasu Monastery of St. Ilija. Rested above the grounds of the church is the medieval fortress of Greben town situated in the Vrbas Canyon. It is believed that the original church was built within the ancient town but with most of the fortress in ruins and little archeological work completed it has not been confirmed. In the 15th century, the feudal family Vojsalić, successors of Hrvoje Vukčić Hrvatinić, took care of maintenance of the Monastery below the Greben Grad. The Church of St. Ilija in Krupa on the Vrbas was rebuilt in 1889 shortly after the fall of the Ottoman Empire by Sava Kosanović.

Trapisti Franciscan Monastery of Marija Zvijezda. The colony of Trapista was established in Banja Luka in 1869 and the old church of the Trapisti Monastery was built between 1874 and 1875. Apart from the liturgical objects made of precious metals dated from the 19-20th century, the collection of Trapisti Monastery includes two precious paintings: the Crucifixion and St. Filomena, both Venetian works form the 16th century. Like most monasteries it too has a collection of old printed books, among which is the collection of epistles of St Augustin, printed in Bazel in 1493. The monastery is well-known for the delicious white cheese that the monks have been producing for over a century.

Romanovci is a small wooden church located near the town of Gradiška to the northwest of Banja Luka. It is dedicated to St. Nikola by the villagers of Romanovci on the eastern slopes of Kozara Mountain, 20 km south of Gradiška. It was built in the first half of the 18th century and is one of the few remaining wooden orthodox structures in the country.

Bardača Bird Reserve

The Bardača wetlands are a series of 11 lakes situated between the rivers Vrbas and Sava, northeast of Banja Luka near the town of Srbac. This 670-hectare reserve is home to over 100 types of birds. I find it a fascinating place for bird watching; most find it a fun place for bird-hunting and, unlike Hutovo Blato in Herzegovina where hunting is forbidden, the 11-lake reserve is open for fishing and hunting. It is not an official bird reserve so there are no public authorities to contact for information. Zepter Passport in Banja Luka can give information about the reserve or you can go to the Sports and Recreation Centre Bardača (tel: 078 772 55) on site. They have a mediocre hotel with a decent restaurant and a massive swimming pool. Several buses per day go to Srbac from Banja Luka and Bosanska Gradiška.

Spas

Slatina is a small town 13km northeast of Banja Luka. Not much goes on aside from the 43° water that flows from the earth at Banja Slatina (Slatinska 11; tel: 058 788 054). The **Slateks Hotel** (tel: 058 788 010 and 051 788 172) has tapped into the warm waters of Slatina and built a nice hotel complex with thermal baths. It is worth a night or two if you are in the region for a while. There are several buses a day to Slatina from Banja Luka. A 20-minute taxi ride from Banja Luka will cost around 20KM. Alternatively, **Hotel San** in Laktaši (tel/fax: 051 830 092) is also less than 20km out of town. It is equally easily accessible by bus, and has been a functioning spa ever since Roman times. The third spa in the region, in Srpske Toplice, has a no hotel but a pool that is nicely situated under a hill.

PRIJEDOR

As any local can attest to, this town has seen better days. Prijedor enjoyed a rather multi-ethnic make-up before the war. This drastically changed in 1992 with the construction of concentration camps in the region around Prijedor and the systematic expulsion of non-Serb populations. Prijedor is a bit run down to say the least and its former residents have returned in only small numbers as job opportunities are limited and, as any visitor will realize, something just isn't right there.

Many surrounding villages have seen a significant return of their pre-war residents with places like **Kozara** back in full swing after being totally destroyed in the early 1990s. The surrounding hills and valleys are indeed beautiful and ideal for a hike, walk, bikeride, or simply as a pleasant place to get out in nature.

KOZARA NATIONAL PARK

Kozara was proclaimed a protected national forest in 1967. Situated between the rivers Una, Sava, Sana and Vrbas, these 3,375 hectares of dense forest and hilly meadows have earned the nickname 'Green Beauty of Krajina'. Kozara is a popular hunting ground, with a large 18,000-hectare area of the park open to regulated hunting of deer, pheasants, fox, boars, wild hare, and ducks.

A smaller part of the park is designated for nature lovers. Walking, hiking, biking and herb picking are among the many activities in Kozara. Hiking to Lisina, the highest point of the park at 938m, offers a wide panoramic view of this part of the Krajina. The park is unquestionably a lovely nature reserve but even basic information is hard to come by and there are no bike rentals or walking maps with recorded distances.

There are mini ski lifts and there is a ski rental in the winter months. There is a hotel and restaurant in the national park complex (tel: 052-211169; email: parkkozara@prijedor.com).

ECO-CENTRE LONČARI

This interesting experiment is on the halfway mark between Banja Luka and Prijedor. Armed with only a beautiful piece of property, a few men had a vision of creating an eco-centre in the Omarska area. They built a 30-acre park complete with walking paths, ten ponds/lakes for fishing and swimming, and a health food restaurant. The dense hardwood forests cover a good part of the centre and there are walking trails through them. Hunting is not permitted.

Lončari (tel: 052 333 267; email: j.lekanic@mediaproline.net) has camping facilities, and is perfect for backpackers looking for a safe and inexpensive place to camp while traveling through or towards Bihać or Banja Luka. Many buses travel through the outskirts of Omarska via Prijedor and Banja Luka. There are a few daily buses from both those places that stop in Omarska.

BIHAĆ

The area was settled from at least Illyrian and Roman times, but the town itself was first mentioned in 1260, in a document of King Bela IV. It were these far northwest frontier lands that drew the line between the Ottomans and the Austro-Hungarians.

Before the recent conflict Bihać and the entire region was a fairly wealthy area compared to country standards, but the war (partly Bosniacs against Bosniacs in this part of the country) devastated the economy. The town is recovering and already looks much better than in the first post-war years. But its inhabitants are still highly dependent on the money sent by the many people that left Bihać in the war years and now live in Western Europe.

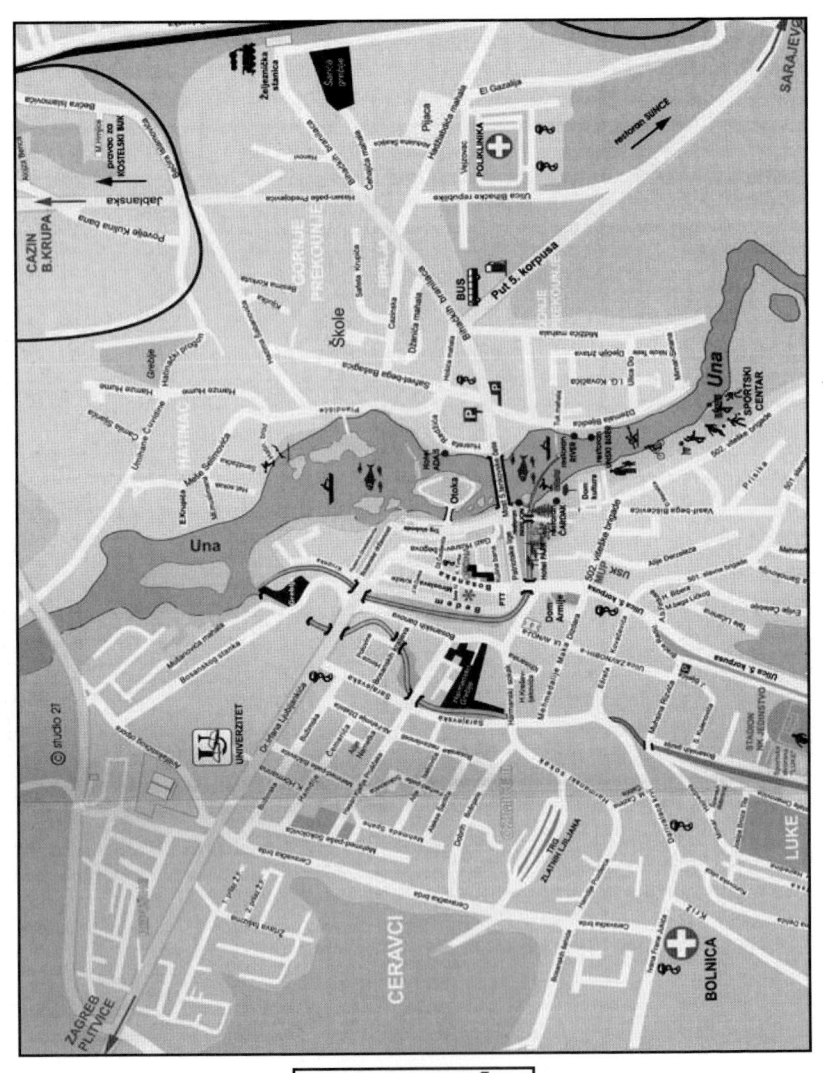

BIHAĆ

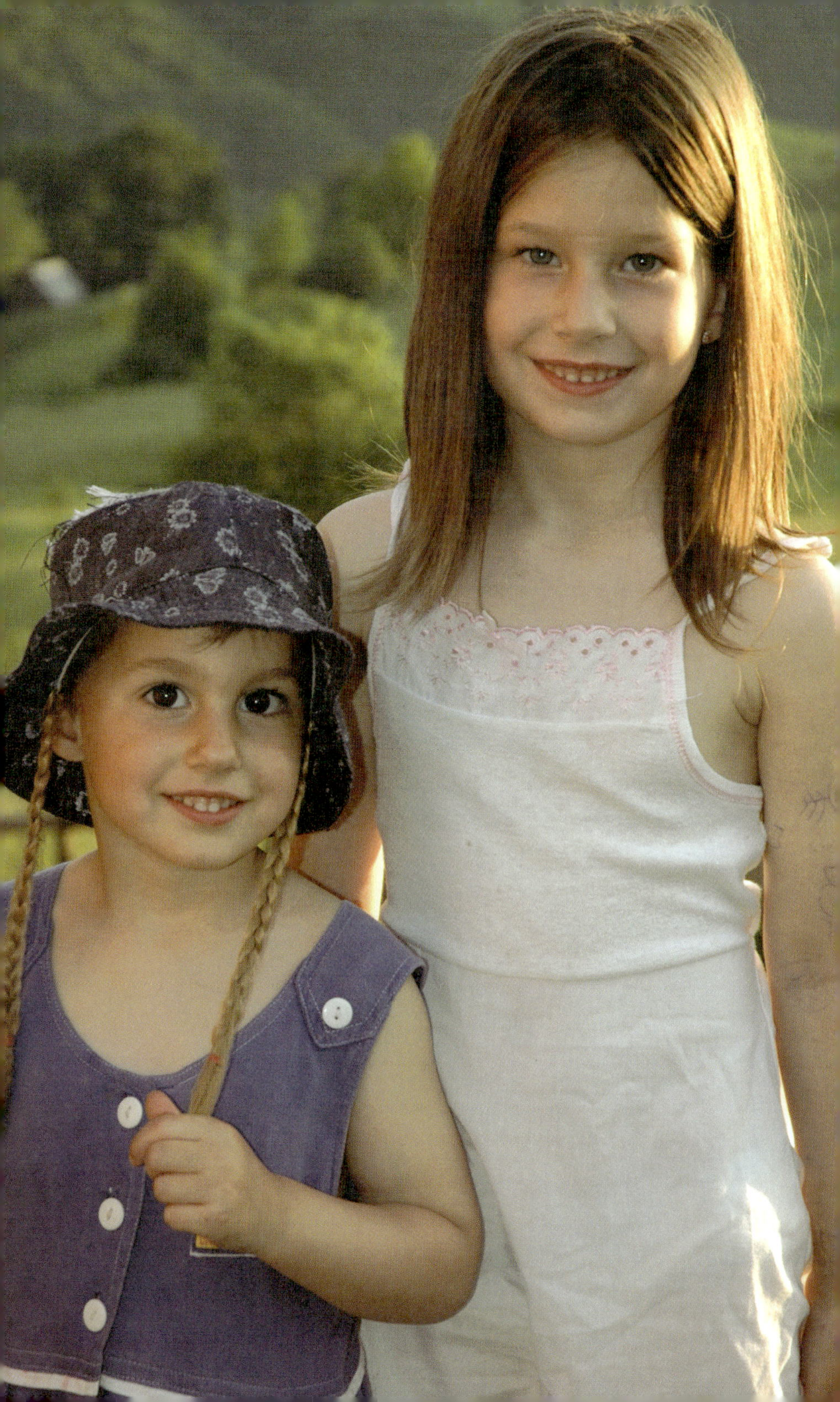

Tranquility

UNA RIVER

The river Una in no way belongs solely to the inhabitants of Bihać. This river, perhaps the most beautiful river in the entire country, is cherished by each community that has formed along her 207 kilometers. The Una is to the Krajina what the Neretva is to Herzegovina – life, and the life-giving forces of the Una have been revered throughout this region's history. I have extracted some interesting points about the Una River from a piece done by Hasan Tijanović from Bihać...

> 'In the underground aquifer systems of Grmeč Mountain the Una River basin is home to the Proteus newt. Over one hundred and seventy types of medicinal herbs grow along her banks. Twenty eight kinds of fish make their home in the Una, the largest being the huchen which grows to over 30 kg. Anglers can vie for the rich supply of trout, grayling, chub and carp found throughout the entire length of the river. Chamois seek refuge in Grmuca Canyon carved by the Una's constant flow and small crayfish can be seen darting along the crystal clear sand basin. The sometimes steep corridors are not always conducive to navigating her beautiful waters yet one of the most frequent motifs of the Una are the small boats with anglers and the ever-increasing number of rafters and kayakers. This river has created a harmony with man, fish, birds, willows, bridges and old mills rarely seen today.'

I, too, doubt that one will find anything like the Una River anywhere else in Europe. It is more than worth a visit to Bihać or any of the towns that live off these emerald waters. It is a great place for a stop over if you're on your way down to the Croatian coast or have visited the Plitvice National Park just across the border. Or better yet, to really experience the magic of this body of water – go stay for a few days, walk along the banks, raft down its amazing falls, or simply sit and listen to the wise tales water always tells.

Getting there and away

The only trains that depart from Bihać's railway station (Bihaćkih Branilaca bb; tel: 037 311 149) are to Bosanska Krupa and Bosanski Novi at 10:07 and 14:20. If you take the morning train, you arrive in Bosanski Novi at 11.50, 15 minutes before the trains to Zagreb and Sarajevo depart from that station at 12:05.

Plitvice National Park is just across the border and many tour buses and tourists come through the Izačić border crossing. By car, this is the best crossing from Croatia. From the southeast there is only one major road leading to Bihać - the Sarajevo-Travnik-Jajce route. You can't miss it on a map.

The Bihać bus station (037 335 590) links all the cities and towns in the upper region of the Krajina. Buses go to Bosanski Petrovac, Bosanska Krupa, Sanski Most, Cazin, Bužim, Velika Kladuša and Ključ several times a day. Bihać is a good five- to six-hour bus ride from Sarajevo and there are daily buses at 07:30, 14:30 and 22:00. Daily buses to Banja Luka depart at 05:30, 07:30, 13:00 and 14:00. There are also daily buses to Zagreb (09.45) and Belgrade (6:30,9:30,12:00,15:00,17:00 and 23:30), and you can travel all the way to Germany and Austria on Wednesdays (13.30) and Sundays (11.00).

Local tour operators

There are two professional rafting operators working out of Bihać.

Sport Bijeli (Pečikovići Klokot; tel: 037 323 502 and 061 138 853; email: raftbeli@bih.net.ba; web: www.raftuna.com.ba) is equipped with modern gear and their skippers are top of the line. What I liked most is that it doesn't just end after rafting. The entire tour with traditional food, camping, fishing, kayaking, playing music or just hanging out is a wonderful experience. Sport Bijeli also provides lessons in kayaking and rents kayaks and canoes without a guide for those who already know their way around the rapids. They can organise fishing trips (licenses in this canton cost 50KM per day) at Klokot River and by the stunning falls at Martin Brod near Kulen Vakuf. Take advantage of their local knowledge.

Una Kiro Rafting is another well-equipped team with a great boarding house for their guests. They focus mainly on rafting and they're quite good at it (M. Ćazima Čatića 1; tel: 037 223 760; email: extreme@una-kiro-rafting.com; web: www.una-kiro-rafting.com).

The mountains of Plješevica and Grmeč are beautiful and rich in wild animals. It is wise to hike with a guide if you are unfamiliar with the area. Bihać was an enclave surrounded by Serbian forces and there are several minefields in the mountains around the city. The terrain around Bihać is ideal for mountain biking and paragliding. The **paragliding club** on V korpusa 5 (tel/fax: 037 229 788; email: paraclub@bihac.org; web: www.paraclub.bihac) offers paragliding adventures and lessons. The **Aero Klub** from Bihać (tel: 037 333 652; email: aeroklub-bihac@hotmail.com) can organise some high flying above the Una with small plane rides from Bihać's mini airport.

For fishing licenses, go to the association of fishermen ('Una', at Krupska bb; tel: 037 311 531).

Tourist information

For general tourist information there is the **Bihać Tourist Information Centre** (tel/fax: 037 322 079; email: turizamb@bih.net.ba; web: www.bihac-turizam.com), which covers Bihać and the immediate area. The **Una-Sana Canton Tourism Association** covers the whole territory of the Federation part of the Krajina (tel/fax: 037 310 043; email: tzusk@tzusk.com).

Where to stay

In Bihać, there are more bed and breakfast places ('Prenoćište') than in most other towns in Bosnia and Herzegovina. If you've come for the rafting adventure of your life, then check with the rafting operators as they often have their own bed and breakfasts or have an arrangement with someone providing inexpensive places to stay.

Hotel Park (V Korpusa bb; tel: 037 331 549) is a pre-war hotel that was privatised in 2003. Renovations have been completed and the hotel is now quite nice, offering singles for 50KM and doubles for 100KM. Although reasonable value for money, a big part of the Bihać experience is the people and nature, and big hotel complexes just don't seem to fit well in the Krajina.

Hotel Ada-s is a new hotel located on H Redžića 1 (tel: 037 311 570) in the town centre near the Una. Singles start from 70KM per night to 200KM for a 60m2 apartment. The rooms have satellite TV and telephone. The gardens have neatly trimmed lawns and nicely landscaped flowerbeds. The receptionist doesn't speak much English.

Prenoćište Pansion Edo on Hanovi 6 (tel: 037 310 537; email: pansione@bih.net.ba) is near the train station. At the entrance to Bihać from Sarajevo there is a fork; the left leads to the centre of town and the right to the train station. About 800m down is Pansion Edo. This place is ideal for backpackers and tourist-class travellers. German and Italian tourists frequently book this place. For the price of 20-30KM per night without breakfast, it's probably the best deal in town. There are three rooms/apartments that have their own bathrooms. The other three rooms share a bathroom. It is in a family home so rest assured it's clean, and hot water is always available.

Hotel MB Lipovača is a decent hotel on Ljubijankića 91 (tel: 037 351 620). The hotel is on the main road heading out of Bihać towards the Izačić border crossing. It's only a five-minute drive to town. The rooms are simple but new and a single costs 45KM. Double rooms go for 80KM and breakfast is included.

Alternatively, you could go to **Hanka** at Čehajić Mahala 1 (037 310 598), **Šaha** at Srbljani bb (037 531 234), or **Una** at I.G. Kovačića 12 (037 312 963).

Where to eat

The plethora of good eateries, most of them along the Una, is the second best way to enjoy the river. The first, of course, is being on the river itself.

Restoran Kostelski Buk (Kostela bb; tel: 037 302 340). A bit out of town on the main road to Cazin. This classic restaurant is a popular meeting place for lunch and dinner. Although it rests right on the main road you'll hardly be able to tell from your table overlooking the Una River that a road is anywhere nearby. They serve mainly traditional meals, which means meat dishes of lamb and beef. If you're a vegetarian you might want to find a pizzeria.

Caffe-bar Picerija Bondeno on Bosanska bb in the centre of town has good pizzas for 6-8KM, as does **Pizzeria Bistro** on the same road.

Gradska Kafana Paviljon is another regularly frequented local spot on Bihaćkih branilaca bb.

Gradska Pivnica Kareka (Bosanske Državnost bb) For a taste of home-brewed beer, a good meal and a great view at a fantastic price this place shouldn't be missed.

Čardak na Uni (502 viteška brigada bb; tel: 037 331 822) Čardak also offers horse and carriage rides along the river and through the park in town.

River (Džemala Bijedića 12; tel: 037 310 014) offers casual dining with excellent food. Dishes are mainly traditional and cost about 8-12KM for a main course. The fresh trout is priced around 10KM.

Unski Biser Restaurant (tel: 037 333 732). Also on Džemala Bijedića road, I wouldn't classify it as fine dining but it is a step up from the other more casual spots.

What to see

Close to town is **Sokolac**, a perfectly preserved fortification built by the Austrians in the 14th century. Christianity and Islam met and often clashed here. The present-day **Fathija Mosque** was once the Church of St Anton. The stećci in the square mark the presence of the heretic Bosnian Church in these parts. The town square is dominated by the **Kapetanova Tower** (used as a lookout tower), the **Zvonik Church** and an Ottoman turbe, proving the multi-ethnic flavour this community has maintained. The **Town Gallery** (Bosanska 15; tel/fax: 037 223 083; email: galbihac@bih.net.ba; local language only web: www.ggbihac.com) has very nice exhibits of local artists. It is open Monday to Friday and sometimes at weekends during the summer. Admission is free. The **Pounje Museum** (037 223 214) on the same street is a tiny museum with many Illyrian, Roman, Austrian and Ottoman artefacts discovered in the area.

If you ask the folk from Bihać what there is to see of their town they may eventually murmur something about their history. But their first answer will be the Una. The **Una River** is treated as a member of the family and the people of Bihać have the strongest collective ecological consciousness in the country. The width of the Una River that runs through the town is about 30m. The full length of the river, beginning in the **Croatian Krajina** and entering the **Sava** at **Jasenovac**, is 207km. It is the fourth-largest river in Bosnia and Herzegovina with a volume of 270m3 per second. But locals won't tell you that. They will tell you about the blue waters that have dug deep limestone canyons, the fertile valleys fed by her water, their favourite swimming hole as a kid and, without exception, the thrill of whitewater rafting on the mighty Una. The legend behind the river's name goes back to Roman times when a legionnaire had his first glance of the sparkling waters and uttered 'Una, solo una' (the only one), suggesting he had never seen anything like it in his life. You might feel the same. Rafting on the Una is becoming a national pastime. The annual international **Una Regatta** has increased so much in popularity that places in the three-day competition are booked months in advance. It's a fabulous experience and more than worth a stop. There are at least four different raft runs on the Una River, from two hours of easy rafting to six hours of up to class VI rapids. The most attractive, interesting and exciting part of the river is the **Strbački Buk**-**Lahovo** run. This 15km route is a class IV-V run that conquers waterfalls you've only seen in films.

KRUPA

Bosanska Krupa, named after a 13th century girl named Krupana, is a small town on the banks of the **Una** and **Krušnica rivers**. The area is well known for its characteristic watermills and the fishing houses built on stilts. The town centre was built around the ruins of a town called **Psata** at the end of the 19th century. Much of the old city is intact and in typical Bosnian fashion a Catholic and Orthodox church stand side by side with a mosque. The most attractive parts of town are the rivers and the source of the Krušnica.

It's a paradise for anglers and walkers. In Krupa, fishing is second only to rafting and canoeing. Large carp and trout can be found in both rivers, but the Krušnica River seems to be the place for bigger catches. Krušnica Spring is home to a diverse world of fish with carp, trout, greyling, pike and chub. The local fishing association can guide visiting anglers to the hot spots and arrange for a license.

There was once an artist colony here and many works are displayed in the **Town Gallery**. Most of the paintings capture the old-style bridges and the unique little islands with natural beaches in the middle of the river. These islands are ideal for camping and bonfires. Even on the hottest days the river makes the evenings cool and sometimes chilly. Of the rafting routes 22km go through Krupa in the **Una Canyon** to **Ostrožac**. Fishing competitions are also held in this part of the canyon. Accommodation in the **Hotel Stari Grad-Ilma** (Trg oslobođenja; tel: 037 471 061; 59 and 80KM for singles and doubles) is not bad but outdated, being yet another large socialist hotel. **Hotel Eki** (tel: 037 473 971) is a brand new and beautiful building right on the riverbank of the Una. They have two rooms and one apartment only, all equipped with modern furniture and facilities. They charge 40 KM per person per night. Their restaurant and bar serve excellent food and drink. **Bistro Una** at Ljušina bb (tel: 037 477 471) is a good spot that serves local specialties. Besides the standard meat dishes, they offer a wide array of fresh grilled fish.

CAZIN

About 26km from Bihać, in a quiet valley surrounded by a picturesque hilly landscape, lies Cazin. Its old town, or čaršija, is its heart and it has a lovely little brook cutting it through the middle. Although small in size, Cazin has played a significant role in the country's history. Since the 14th century it has been a strategic point for the foreign powers that lusted after the land of Bosnia and Herzegovina. The medieval remains of Ostrožac, Pećigrad, Radetina Tower, Stijena and Trzač dominate the town. The most beautiful and impressive is **Ostrožac Castle.** Built in a neo-gothic style, Ostrožac is one of the main attractions in **Una Sana** canton. It was here that the Austro-Hungarian Empire set up camp to defend its frontier (and from time to time launch offensives against the Ottoman foes). Ostrožac was finally captured by the Ottomans but it was one of the last frontier territories to be conquered. Cazin nowadays has an almost 100 percent Bosniac population, and a mayor who boasts that the town is 'ethnically clean'.

Hotel Sedra (Ostrožac na Uni; tel: 037 513 551/331 551) is perhaps the largest hotel complex in the region located directly on the river. The hotel has an interesting touch of oriental and socialist design. Single rooms cost 58 KM with breakfast. The main hotel is a leftover from the socialist era but is probably among the best, if not the best, of the old hotels in the region. The bungalows and apartments on the complex are built in traditional style and are more attractive than the hotel rooms. They go for 40KM for a single and 56KM for a double. The restaurant serves a large menu of traditional foods that are very reasonably priced. A full meal with several courses and wine costs 20-25KM. There are two tennis courts next to the hotel and swimming and fishing areas just metres from the back.

Just across the river is the **Restoran Unski Smaragd** (Srbljani bb; tel: 037 531 190). The food here is said to be the best in town. The service is great and the atmosphere inside and out gets two thumbs-up. Exiting

Cazin towards Krupa you will find the **Restoran Šadrvan** on K. Ljubijankića 1 (tel: 037 514 156).

VELIKA KLADUŠA

The **Velika Kladuša** municipality is the furthest northwest location in Bosnia and Herzegovina and sits right on the border with Croatia. The moderate continental climate and rich unspoiled forests are said to be ideal for hunting and fishing. This was one of the wealthiest towns in Bosnia and Herzegovina during Yugoslavian days, when the large AgroKomerc company, run by Fikret Abdić, was one of the most successful companies in the country. During the war Kladuša was an enclave within an enclave. The townspeople, mainly Bosniac, backed the business and political leader Abdić, who sought to keep hold of his successful enterprise. He formed his own military units and, backed by the Serbs, held a front line against the surrounded Muslim population of the Bihać enclave. Velika Kladuša is now part of the Federation and one of the nine municipalities of the Una Sana canton. The oldest written document about the town dates back to 1280. The remains of the ancient towns of **Podzvizd, Vrnograc, Todorovo** and the old part of Velika Kladuša are remnants of centuries of Western influence in the area. The rivers **Glinica, Kladušnica** and **Grbarska** are well known as quality fishing areas.

An ancient fort in the old town has been converted into **Hotel Stari Grad** (Zagrad bb; tel: 037 770 133 and 061 790 143). It is the only hotel in the region that is a combination of an old castle and authentic Bosnian-style architecture. They have three houses outside the fort walls, and two apartments and a restaurant in the fort itself. Sleeping here is well worth the 80 KM per person per night.

At the entrance to town, from the Bihać direction, you can't miss the large thermal swimming pool in **Mala Kladuša**. This thermal spring is rich in minerals and open to the public.

DRVAR

Drvar is famous for a partisan victory over an elite unit of German paratroopers. Tito and his brave partisans were hiding out in a cave (now called **Tito Cave**). Some say they were waiting to secretly attack the Germans, but I tend to think they were hiding from the relentless air strikes. German surveillance recorded no sign of resistance and when the paratroopers landed they were met by the partisans and wiped out. Drvar had been defended and this battle became the highlight of the partisan recruitment scheme which asserted that the Germans could be defeated by heart and wit. Today, **Tito's Cave** is the only tourist attraction in the sleepy town of Drvar.

The Bosnian Croat army captured the town in 1995, when it still had a 97% Serbian population. The residents fled and have only recently and partially come back.

The area around Drvar is incredibly beautiful, with one of the largest forests in the country. Its isolated geographic position hosts an untouched wildlife population and some of the most stunning water sources in the region. A real highlight is the source and gorge of the **River Unac**, towards **Bosansko Grahovo** to the southwest. The gorge is named **Bastašica** after the village of **Bastihe**. The villagers of Bastihe were the courageous partisan defenders of Drvar. To the northwest by the town of **Martin Brod** are the waterfalls and cascades of the River Unac, which eventually connects with the Una River. The **Rmanj Orthodox Monastery** is in Martin Brod and most likely dates from the 16th century when a large migration of Serbs came to the frontier. The **Lom Klekovačka Forest Reserve** is among the largest forests in the country. It has, unfortunately, fallen victim to uncontrolled clear-cutting in some parts. The rule of law when it comes to the environment in Bosnia and Herzegovina is rarely practised.

Drvar's only hotel, **Bastasi** (tel: 034 820133 and 063 354 634), is situated right next to Tito's Cave. It is large and empty, and singles/doubles cost 63/86KM.

SANSKI MOST

One of the first tourist villages in Bosnia and Herzegovina was built in the upper **Sanica** between Ključ and Sanski Most. Unfortunately it was destroyed during the recent war. Today, Sanski Most, a town on five rivers, only caters for one type of tourism: the Sanski Most Diaspora that easily doubles the town's population in the summer period.

In these months, the area around this 'City of Flowers' springs to life. Hundreds of people sit around in **Banja Ilidža**, famous for its healing waters (061 465 518; not a word of English). It has a large picnic area, an outdoor swimming pool and a mud pool. In the low season that is all closed, but you can still visit the indoor swimming pool, filled with smelly but healthy water, for 2 KM per 30 minutes. Men and women have separate pools.

You reach Banja Ilidža by taking the main road to Ključ (check out that strange-looking mosque on the right hand side!), turning left at the Banja Ilidža sign, and left again when the road forks. If you take the fork's right instead, you drive through a beautiful canyon – admittedly with plenty of destroyed houses on either side of the road. It's good fishing here, and in the summer months many families camp in this area for days on stretch, bringing nothing but bread and beer, fully expecting the river to provide the rest. There has been a lot of destruction in this area, but there are no mines.

A little after the turn left to Banja Ilidža, there is a turn right. Take the bad road to the left after having crossed the orange bridge over the Sanića river and you get into another canyon, also with a river with lots of cascades. This one is very popular with the Sanski Most current and previous population too. The only house you'll see here is Mostiscići Restaurant. Naturally, it serves fresh fish.

The cave closeby (follow the main street after the bridge, follow the 'Merdanovići' road sign and then ask for Pećina) has a gate but no lock. You can get over a mile deep into the mountain. When I went there I felt lucky to spot an entire wild boar family, only to find out minutes later that these poor animals were fenced in. It turned out that the local shepherd bought these boar and allows hunters to train their dogs on them for one KM per minute! In summer, this most entrepreneurial man sells ice cream.

Also close to Sanski Most is the source of the **Dabar River** that swells from an enormous cave, and the **Blihi River** that creates a beautiful waterfall by tumbling 72m. The only thing worth a visit in town itself is the **Hamza-begova Mosque**, dated 1557. It was built on the place where Sultan Mehmed Fatih first prayed after conquering the town in 1463.

There are three hotels in town. **Hotel Sanus** is located in the centre of town (tel: 037 686 138 and 061 144 187; fax: 037 686 204). It has a friendly receptionist who speaks fluent English, and mediocre rooms for 40 KM and 70 KM including breakfast. For the budget traveler there is **Zlatna Dolina,** immediately behind Hotel Sanus: 28 KM per person for a very plain room without bathroom (tel: 037 683 900 and 061 137 414; fax: 037 683 900). By far the best deal in town – and indeed one of the very best deals in the whole of Bosnia and Herzegovina – is **Motel Oaza** (tel: 037 684 530 and 061 105 401; fax: 037 684 530). It is a bit far from the centre of town, but worth the walk. It's brand new and has beautiful and fully equipped rooms for 40 KM (single), 60 KM (double) and 80 KM (apartment), all with an elaborate breakfast. The walls' many large pictures give you an idea of the natural beauty of this area. To get there, pass the 'mašinski most' (the old railroad bridge) and take the second street on the right. It's the big white house.

Buses from Sanski Most travel daily to Ključ and Bihać. Local buses from nearby Prijedor operate several times per day. Banja Luka also has a Sanski Most route via Prijedor. At 05.00 and 07.00, daily buses depart for a 5.5-hour trip to Sarajevo.

The old town and fortress of Tešanj

Typical 'four roof' Ottoman mosque, Tuzla region

The Husein Gradaščević Mosque

The very strong 'Bosanski konj' (Bosnian horses)

One of the many rural Ottoman mosques

The Stari Grad of Srebrenik

Stećak, a tombstone of the Bosnian Church

Ottoman interior

NORTHEAST BOSNIA

The northeast corner of Bosnia and Herzegovina is the industrial backbone of the country. It is also a region with dozens of places to see and visit and, like any other part of Bosnia and Herzegovina, you don't have to go very far to find an isolated mountain, a cool stream or a thick green forest.

The areas along the Sava River to the extreme northeast are the most fertile regions in the country. With over 50% of its territory used for agricultural purposes, agriculture in the entire northeast pocket is the number one industry and employer. Around the central city of Tuzla is the heart of the country's industry. This city, named after its salt mines during Ottoman times, combines enormous coal-fired power plants and the resulting air-pollution with some lovely areas that have existed since far back into the Middle Ages. The mountains and lakes, particularly in the far east, are endless green carpets of magnificent natural terrain. Konjuh, Majevica and Ozren crisscross the middle section of the northeast and create large natural boundaries between the mountain climates and the long flatlands of Semberija in the extreme north of the region. Majevica and Ozren saw quite a lot of fighting during the war so hiking solo is not a good idea. The local mountain associations are very active and have several mountain huts. If you are truly keen on a hike, it will take some perseverance on your behalf to locate an English-speaking member. If your sign language skills are good, local hikers will be glad to take a guest along with them.

During the war the entire eastern border of Bosnia and Herzegovina fell quickly and easily to the Serbian militias. They marched south and west from Bijeljina and Zvornik to secure the border with Serbia and Montenegro to the south, and the northern border of Slavonia with Croatia. This strategy would unite the Serbs in Slavonia with the Croatian Krajina to the west, and those in eastern Bosnia and Herzegovina with Montenegro in the far south. The most challenging part of this was getting past Brčko. Brčko was and is a key city (hence its current 'district' status, not belonging to the Federation or the Republika Srpska). Brčko got pounded by both sides. The Croats fought from the north and the Bosnian-Croat alliance fought from the south to keep the Brčko corridor from being a supply route for the Serb-captured lands to the west. When the Dayton Peace Accords were signed, the future of Brčko was 'to be decided later'. This basically meant that the parties could not agree. As the issue threatened the peace process, all sides agreed to leave the decision to an international arbiter, who gave it the status of 'district'.

The Dayton Peace Accords carved this very multi-ethnic area up into many little pieces. The central region of the northeast falls under Tuzla and Zenica-Doboj cantons in the Federation. West of Tuzla, at Doboj, is the beginning of western Republika Srpska. To the east is also Republika Srpska and to the north is the semi-autonomous district of Brčko. Confused yet? To the west of the small corridor that Brčko creates are the two little Federation 'islands' of the Posavina canton, at Orašje and Odžak, on the Croatian border. The isolated 'finger' of Usora, Tešanj and Maglaj is part of the Zenica-Doboj canton. Gradačac and as far as Čelić near Brčko are part of the Tuzla canton.

TUZLA

Situated on the southeast slopes of the **Majevica Mountain**, the city of Tuzla occupies the central area of northeast Bosnia. The town is 239m above sea level, and it stretches across an area of approximately 15km2. The city's population is approximately 100,000 but the greater municipal area has over 170,000 inhabitants. Tuzla claims to be the economic, scientific, cultural, educational, health and tourist centre of northeast Bosnia, basically taking credit for most things that go on in the northeast. To some extent this is true.

History

The settlement of Tuzla has always been closely tied to its salt resources. The oldest written records, left behind by the Greek, prove that even they were aware of the region's salt.

Tuzla received its name much later. The present-day name is derived from the Turkish word Tuz, meaning salt. The first Ottoman document recording the exploitation of Tuzla's saltwater springs dates from 1548. Salt was produced here all year round and salt wells were located on the present-day Salt Square.

With the arrival of the Ottomans in 1460, production increased fivefold and the settlement greatly gained in importance. Due to vast reforms in the 17th-century Ottoman administration, a freer development of the town economy occurred. With the introduction of modern crafts, Tuzla developed into the administrative centre of the Zvornik sandžak and became an important communications, military, trade and cultural centre in northeast Bosnia. Towards the end of Ottoman rule Tuzla had approximately 5,000 inhabitants, making it one of the largest towns in Bosnia and Herzegovina.

In the early 18th century a rectangular fortification was built in the town centre. Tensions with the Austrians had been significant and raids and battles became commonplace on the northern frontiers. The fortification was built with high walls and one lookout on each wall. The fortification was destroyed in 1870, and the Ottomans left Bosnia and Herzegovina eight years later. Many buildings from Ottoman times remain in Tuzla. **Turalibeg's Mosque**, with a typical stone minaret, was built in the 16th century and still stands today.

The Austro-Hungarians introduced more modern methods for salt and coal exploitation, and Tuzla became an integral part of the empire's economy.

NORTHEAST BOSNIA

The city continued to play an important economic role in Yugoslavia. Today, its factories find it difficult to compete on the world market, and the city's economy is not doing particularly well. In addition, many factories use outdated technology and add to the environmental problems Tuzla faces. The war did not spare Tuzla. Towards its end, when most thought the fighting might finally be over, an artillery round slammed into the old quarters on 'youth day', killing 72 young people sitting in café's. At the **Kapija** (gate) is a monument dedicated to their memory.

Getting there and around

There is a railway connecting Tuzla to Doboj to the east and Vinkovci to the north. The Sarajevo train to Budapest travels via Doboj. From Doboj it is possible to travel at least once daily to Tuzla and vice versa. This route is included in the 2004 InterRail agreement that Bosnia and Herzegovina has just entered.

By car, the easiest access from the west is via Slavonia in eastern Croatia. The major border crossings of Slavonski Brod, Bosanski Šamac, Županija and Zvornik all lead to Tuzla. From central Bosnia the best route by bus is via Zenica-Doboj. The quickest route from Sarajevo travels through Olovo-Kladanj but in the winter this can be slow-moving through the mountains.

Tuzla's bus station is one of the busiest in the country, as illustrated by the schedule below.

Domestic bus lines

Tuzla-Kladanj-Sarajevo	4:00 on working days, 5:30, 6:00, 6:30, 7:00, 7:30, 8:05, 9:00, 10:00, 11:45, 13:00, 14:30, 15:15, 16:00, 16:45, 18:00, 19:13
Tuzla-Sarajevo-Čapljina	5:00
Tuzla-Gračanica-Doboj	5:20, 9:00, 9:50, 12:30, 17:30, 18:40
Tuzla-Gračanica-Zenica-Bihać	5:30
Tuzla-Srebrenik-Brčko	5:30 (not on Sunday), 9:50, 10:10 (not on Sunday), 13:00, 15:10, 17:30, 18:45 (working days)
Tuzla-Srebrenik-Čelić	6:00
Tuzla-Priboj-Bijeljina	6:00, 6:30, 7:45, 8:20, 9:35, 10:20, 11:35, 12:00, 13:00, 15:00, 16:05, 18:30
Tuzla-Kalesija-Zvornik	6:00, 7:30, 9:30, 13:00, 15:10, 17:00
Tuzla-Županja-Đakovo-Osijek	13:00
Tuzla-Kalesija-Sapna	6:00, 13:30, 17:00 (working days)
Tuzla-Doboj-Zenica	6:30, 10:15, 18:30
Tuzla-Srebrenik-Brdsko-Čelić	6:45, 9:45 (not on Sunday), 13:15, 14:10, 16:50

Tuzla-Srebrenik-Gradačac	7:00, 8:10 (not on Sunday), 10:00 (working days), 11:00, 11:30 (working days), 11:40, 12:35 (working days), 13:30 (not on Sunday), 15:40 (not on Sunday), 16:00 (on working days except Thursday), 17:30 (working days), 20:15
Tuzla-Lukavac-Gračanica	7:00 (not on Sunday), 7:30, 8:30, 10:10 (working days), 10:50, 11:40 (working days), 12:55 (working days), 13:20, 14:10, 14:50 (working days), 15:10 (working days), 15:35, 17:25, 19:30
Tuzla-Teočak-Bilalići	7:10 (working days), 10:00 (working days), 11:50 (not on Sunday), 14:00 (not on Saturday), 16:00 (not on Sunday), 19:10 (working days)
Tuzla-G.Tuzla-Čelić-Humci	8:00, 15:10 (working days)
Tuzla-Doboj-Tešanj	8:00, 11:00, 13:50, 15:00 (working days), 16:00
Tuzla-Kamensko/S	8:00
Tuzla-Banovići-Vozuća	8:30 (working days)
Tuzla-Živinice-Kladanj	8:15 (working days), 8:50 (not on Sunday), 10:30 (not on Sunday), 11:00, 11:35 (working days), 12:15, 13:30 (working days), 15:00 (not on Sunday), 15:55, 17:15 (working days)
Tuzla-Doboj-Bugojno	15:45
Tuzla-Srebrenik-Čelić	8:45, 10:25, 11:45
Tuzla-Banovići-Zavidovići	9:25, 18:20
Tuzla-Sarajevo-Mostar	9:30
Tuzla-Kalesija-Vitinica	9:30 (not on Sunday), 14:10 (not on Sunday)
Tuzla-Gračanica-Doboj	9:30, 11:50, 17:05
Tuzla-S.Han-Kalesija	9:55, 10:57, 15:15
Tuzla-Banovići-V.Kladuša	11:15
Tuzla-Gračanica-Tešanj	13:30 (not on Sunday)
Tuzla-Doboj-Zenica-Travnik	16:30

International bus lines

Tuzla-Orašje-Ljubljana	7:10 (Monday, Wednesday, Friday, Saturday), 9:45
Tuzla-Zenica-Split	8:00
Tuzla-Zagreb-Rijeka-Pula	9:15, 18:00

Local tour operators

Receptive tourism for foreign tourists hasn't really taken off here yet. The demand is low and most of the tourism in this region is local/domestic. This undoubtedly adds to its authenticity but doesn't make it easy for the foreign guest. However, the **Tuzla Canton Tourism Association** is helpful for accommodation, what to see around town and regional information. They have decent local maps which are always helpful if you have to get around on your own. They are located at Trg Slobode 2; tel: 035 270 131; email: turisticka.tz@max.ba.

Where to stay

Hotel Tuzla is the daddy of all hotels in the northeast (M Fizovića 22; tel: 035 250 428; fax: 035 250 427; email: hoteltz@inet.ba; web: www.hoteltz.inet.ba; singles and doubles cost 65 and 130KM respectively). Its capacity of 330 makes it one of the largest hotels in the country. It is a relic from the socialist era, as many things are in Tuzla, but the service and feel of the place isn't bad at all. It has a nice indoor swimming pool and sauna, is centrally located and is a good place to get everything you need under one roof. The restaurant has a capacity of 450!

Hotel Bristol (Aleja bosanskih vladara 3; tel: 035 232 845; singles are 50KM and doubles are 80KM) is a notch down in size and sleeps 118 people. The Bristol is a nice hotel with a restaurant, bar and the standard extras in the room.

Big Hilton is a much smaller pension, located on Bosna Srebrena bb (tel: 035 281 588; single 45KM; double 80KM). It has small and simple rooms.

Near Lake Modrac in Lukavac is the **Vila** (Armije BiH 11; tel: 035 553 043; single 40KM; double 80KM) and on the lake itself is the **Senad od Bosne Hotel** (tel: 035 553 222; fax: 035 553 223; single 65KM; double 105KM). They are both very nice places and with regular city buses running between Lukavac and Tuzla you don't need your own transport. The postwar hotels tend to be the nicest and are more in line with what foreign clientele is looking for. These two fit the bill. Expect Senad od Bosne to be quite crowded and a very popular place to eat and drink. The restaurant and terrace seats 220 people.

Where to eat

Caffe bar America (tel: 035 250 058) doesn't serve anything American but the pizza is good. It's downtown on Patriotske Lige 1.

Restoran Sezam (tel: 035 257 123) is a nice traditional restaurant by the old Turalibegova Mosque, on the road of the same name at number 20. On Modrac Lake I've yet to eat at a place that didn't have good food.

The competition for the thousands of hungry holidaymakers here is intense. The strip along the beach is long and there's not a bad restaurant among them.

What to see and do

The mineral-water springs at **Slana Banja** and **Kiseljak** are amongst the greatest natural resources in Tuzla. The underground exploitation of raw materials, however, has created such large sinkholes that a good part of the **old town** has caved in. Due to either poor planning or greed, local officials have had to destroy many of the historical buildings and some Ottoman architecture, including people's homes! Sinkholes as deep as 10m have been a great challenge to fill in an attempt to stop the erosion. Many famous streets, squares and neighbourhoods of old Tuzla have disappeared.

In recent years much effort has been put into a planned revitalisation of the area. What remains of the old town is still charming and while strolling through the centre you forget the obnoxious industry on the far side of the city.

Tuzla is a university and educational centre, so there are always plenty of café's and clubs to visit for younger travellers. Folks from Tuzla have been among the nicest and most genuine people I have met in my extensive travels throughout Bosnia and Herzegovina.

The **National Theatre** (Pozorišna Street 4; tel: 035 251 327) was built in 1898 during Austro-Hungarian rule and is the oldest in the country. Local productions are held regularly and although it's a rarity to have plays or concerts in English, they do have some excellent shows. The **Portrait Gallery** (Ratka Vokića bb; tel: 035 252 002) has continuous exhibitions of work by local and international artists. **Ismet Mujezinović's Gallery** (Klosterska 17; tel: 035 252 350) is mainly dedicated to Mr Mujezinović himself. He was a painter from Tuzla, famous enough to have a gallery established in his name and a monument erected in his honour. The **Eastern Bosnia Museum** (Mije Kereševića Guje bb; tel: 035 280 034) exhibits archaeological, ethnological, historical and artistic pieces and artefacts from the whole region. The content is interesting but the presentation leaves a bit to be desired.

I always find it comforting to see churches and mosques standing side by side. Apart from Tuzla's many beautiful mosques, there is also the **Orthodox church** that went untouched throughout the war. The **Franciscan monastery** in town is still very active and the Catholic community in Tuzla is rather large. Just out of town in the village of Breska is a 200-year-old Catholic church.

Being so far from the sea and not having a Neretva or Una River nearby, the administrations of the northeast have embarked on a mission to create large artificial lakes. **Panonija Lake**, created near the saltwater wells in the centre of town, was visited by 100,000 people in less than two months when it first opened. A fifth of the lake is saltwater which acts as a natural cleanser. The town has several other attractive picnic locations: **Ilinčica** is the closest to town; **Lake Modrac**, a massive lake lined with beaches, restaurants and bed and breakfasts, attracts the biggest crowds; **Konjuh Mountain** is the best area if you're looking to do some hiking; **Majevac Mountain**, as noted earlier, was heavily mined in some areas, and should be avoided if you don't have a guide.

KLADANJ

Kladanj is located on the Tuzla to Sarajevo road along the **River Drinjača**, at the base of Konjuh Mountain. It was first mentioned in documents from the late 1300s. The settlement is a very small mountain community famous for a water source that is said to have special powers. The story goes that **Muška Voda** (man's water) is supposed to increase a man's strength. That's how they sell it in the brochures anyway. The local version is that the water acts as a natural Viagra. That's why they built a mountain lodge, bungalows and walking paths near the source. The 16th-century Turkish travel writer *Evlija Ćelebija* described it as the fountain of youth. Recent scientific research has concluded that this water has a positive effect on blood pressure and sugar concentration, increases water extraction and improves blood circulation.

At 53 different locations in and around Kladanj, over 400 stećci have been discovered. Walking through the mountains you're bound to come across one of the many caves on or near **Konjuh Mountain**. Among the largest caves are the **Djevojačka and Bebrava caves**. The Djevojačka Cave is a pre-Islamic sacred spot where the followers of the heretic Bosnian Church made pilgrimages. There's a good chance that in this area you will run across a black bear or see a grey eagle soaring above the rock faces.

The only reasons to go and stay in Kladanj would be to walk, hike, hunt or drink from the fountain of youth. Although there are no guides per se, you'll find the motel owners more than willing to show you around. **Motel Amerika** (Hamdije Selića 36; tel/fax: 035 621 111; email: jelen@bih.net.ba) and **Motel Mimoza** at Kovačići bb might both be closed: check before you go there.

BIJELJINA

In the vast flat plains that stretch from Hungary deep into Serbia is the far northeast corner of Bosnia and Herzegovina. Bijeljina is the pivotal city in this sub-region, with all roads leading there. Like most places in the Semberija plains along the Sava and Drina rivers, Bijeljina is blessed with rich, fertile soil. Agriculture is the largest industry by far.

The abrupt change in landscape around Bijeljina was created 30 million years ago when the area was part of the Pannonian Sea (Paratetis). The erosion during the following ice ages left the marine-lake sediment that has made Semberija so fertile.

Man has long settled here due to the area's easy access and the steady migration of peoples across the great plains. The **Museum Semberija** (Karađorđeva 1; 055 201 292) in Bijeljina has an interesting collection of archaeological finds from the area, including many ancient farming tools used to till the land from the earliest of times.

Bijeljina has a different feel than other places in Bosnia. The houses and gardens resemble those in Hungary and the areas of Vojvodina in Serbia and Slavonia in Croatia. The parks and walking areas around town are neatly arranged with fences and well-kept lawns. The oriental character has been largely erased from the area. A significant Muslim minority was driven from the town at the onset of the war. **Atik Mosque**, dated well before 1566, was destroyed - as were all other mosques in town.

The swimming and fishing areas in the vicinity of the **Drina River** are nice and the area enjoys a mild climate: Bijeljina has 1,800 hours of sun per year. The **Amajlija** recreation area near the Drina has a good traditional restaurant with a great outdoor terrace. **Restoran Drina** (tel: 055 401 041) is a local favourite. **Tina Restaurant** in Dvorovi, near the thermal springs, is a very popular local spot with live music at weekends. The place is very traditional, or one could say very local. It's an interesting experience seeing the locals live it up!

Bijeljina is on a convenient access route to Novi Sad and Belgrade in Serbia. The border crossing is fairly large by Bosnian standards and the highway across the border makes it a quick jaunt to both places. If you're going to stay the night, **Šico** is the best deal (Jovana Dučića 3; tel: 055 210 952; 80KM and 100KM for singles and doubles). Alternatively, **Motel Despotović** (Cara Uroša 52; tel: 065 662 582; 055 203 192; rooms are 30-50KM) and the **Hotel Drina** (Kneza Miloša 1; tel: 055 204 216; singles and doubles are 48 and 75KM) are OK too. The first is a new motel with modern facilities. The second is an older hotel and has a more traditional style.

If you're in town, you might want to check out the **Tavna Orthodox Monastery** from the 15th century, in the middle of town. It's quite tiny, as most Orthodox monasteries are, but the interior is very detailed and beautiful.

BRČKO

Brčko's significance is its location on the **Sava River** which is a tributary to the **Danube** and belongs to the **Black Sea basin**. For industrial towns like Tuzla and Zenica, Brčko is vital for moving goods in and out of the country via rail and boat. For the Republika Srpska it is the only land link between its eastern and western territories and Serbia. The district has always been the centre of the **Posavina region**. All this makes Brčko of strategic importance.

You can cross into Croatia from this point as well but it is more practical to cross further west if you are heading towards Zagreb, Belgrade or Budapest. If you're in the neighborhood, you could visit the 'Arizona Market'. This used to be Bosnia and Herzegovina's largest and astonishingly chaotic open air market. Then Italian investors turned it into a regular set of shops. It lost its charm, but is still very cheap.

Grand Hotel Posavina (Trg Mladih 4; tel: 049 220 111; email: grand_hotel@elinspanic.net) is the best hotel in town. Singles and doubles cost 60 and 80KM. For the best food in town, go to **Restaurant Lime** at Bulevar Mira 4 (049 215 533).

GRADAČAC

This is certainly one of the places to see when you visit the northeast of Bosnia. On the **River Gradišnica**, between the mountains of **Majevica** and **Trebava**, lies the beautiful town of Gradačac.

This town holds great historical significance for Bosnians. Husein Kapetan Gradaščević was a ruling beg during Ottoman times. He was a warrior and leader, highly respected and feared throughout the region, who posed such a tangible threat to Ottoman authority that he could bargain for more autonomy, self-rule and land rights. There are several versions of history but the common one is that he and his army were able to defend the territories of the northeastern frontier when the Ottomans could not. He was greatly feared by the Ottomans, and when the rebellious Dragon of Bosnia (as he was called) decided to confront the Ottomans, he marched his army all the way to Kosovo in 1831. The Dragon's army defeated the Ottomans and further destabilised the empire's hold on Bosnia. This rebellious spirit proved contagious among the local pashas and ruling families, and sparked many more rebellions. Gradaščević was later betrayed and forced to flee across the Sava to Austria. The numerous buildings bearing his name attest to his role in the history of the town. The **family house Gradaščević** was built in 1786 and today is a private museum.

The town is recognisable by the **tower of Husein-kapetan Gradaščević** that was built in 1821. This large complex was damaged in the last war but has been renovated in its original form. The old part of town has a cultural centre, museum, gallery and library, all named after him. Underneath the city gate there is the **Mosque of Husein** which was built in 1826 and is characterised by its high and narrow minarets. In this same period the **Sahat clock tower** (22m high) was built. The town has in general very much preserved its oriental character.

Believe it or not there is yet another thermal spa in the northeast. **Banja Ilidža** (Hazna bb; tel: 035 817 822; fax: 035 817 039; singles and doubles for 49 and 78KM) is a rehabilitative centre for heart disease and rheumatism. Socialist era, yes, but not bad. The charm of the town and its surroundings adds so much to the total package that the bland rooms and ugly reception area won't make any difference at all.

This region is also characterised by its artificial lakes, **Hazna** and **Vidara**. As in Tuzla, there are beaches and organised water sports and fishing, as well as a recreational field. The **Hunting Centre of Gradačac** organises duck, rabbit, and pheasant hunts on 37,000 hectares of land. Every year in Gradačac there is an international **plum fair** and a **literature fair**, both very small and local, making it that much more enticing. **Aščina Grom** at HK Gradaščević bb serves great traditional foods of all kinds. The location is great and so is the service. **Kapija Bosna** at Hadžiefendijina bb has tasty traditional dishes as well, as does **Bosna Restoran** at Mionica bb.

SREBRENIK

Most famous for its old fort above the endless plains of Posavina, this medieval town is an interesting destination. The villages in the surrounding areas have a storybook appearance with quaint, well-maintained homes and beautiful gardens with orchards of apple, plum and pear trees. The clear streams that run from the hills to the encroaching plains paint the fields bright green in the springtime. The old fort is an interesting but quick visit. In August and September there is an art festival called '**Open Town of Art**', where artists from all over the country set up art colonies around the area to exchange ideas, meet and paint the lovely landscapes around the Tinja. Srebrenik is only 36km from Tuzla in the small river valley of Tinja.

DOBOJ

Doboj is at a pivotal point on the rivers Usora and Bosna. It is one of those Bosnian towns where you can find mosques and Catholic and Orthodox churches close to each other. It is also the town where the Rabbi for Bosnia and Herzegovina lives. Doboj's **Jewish Cultural Centre**, destroyed in the Second World War, was restored only recently.

Although life here has been traced back to the Stone Age, the first recorded settlement was in the 1st century when the Romans conquered these territories and built the Kastrum and the small settlement of Kanube. **Kastrum** is now the main fortress in the centre of the town and was enhanced by the Bosnian aristocracy and the Ottomans when they arrived in Doboj in the 16th century. Much of it is still intact and the view from the fortress's hilltop position is worth the climb.

Mount Ozren, the mountain right next to Doboj, is more attractive than Doboj itself. There are a few 13th century monasteries (**Monastery Ozren** near Petrovo being the most interesting among them). For more leisurely entertainment, there is the small, natural and very clean **Eagle's Lake** ('Orlovo Jezero'). If you want to swim *and* eat, you could go to **Goransko Jezero**, some 5 km from downtown Doboj. It is clean and surrounded by forests – and it has a restaurant. It used to be fairly crowded here but nowadays the lake is quiet, as **D'ungla**, the most sophisticated swimming complex in the entire Balkans, opened up in Doboj recently (Nikola Pašića bb; tel: 053 241 273).

Doboj was one the most important railway knots in pre-war Yugoslavia, and it is still possible to take the train from here to Zagreb, Ljubljana, Belgrade, Budapest and Sarajevo. It is a town you have to go through to get from Sarajevo to most places in the northeast, yet very few people stop here. If you do stop here, you could spend the night in the relatively large **Hotel Bosna** (Kneze Lazara 6; tel: 053 242 012; 55 and 80 KM for singles and doubles). The best food in town is eaten in **Restaurant City** (Cara Dušana 37; tel: 053 241 852). It has a really nice interior and is often crowded. Other restaurants in town are **Dalmacija** (Kralja Dragutina 54; tel: 053 231 753); **Fontana** (Pop Ljubina 2; tel: 053 242 716), and **Princ** (Vojvode Sinđelića 16; tel: 053 222011).

GRAČANICA

Gračanica is located in the lower valley of the River Spreča along the main road from Tuzla to Doboj, about 50km west of Tuzla. It is said that this town was formed in the Middle Ages, in the period when the town Soko above the Sokoluša brook was built. From 1580 Gračanica began to develop into a regional and cultural urban centre for the dozens of rural settlements in the surrounding countryside. Agriculture is the main industry in the region and several factories produce natural juices, jams and preserved vegetables.

If you happen to pass by this place, check out the old town. The attractive homes and craft shops line the old quarter which is highlighted by the Ahmed-pasha or Čaršija Mosque, built in 1595. The massive 27m clock tower was built at the end of the 16th century, renovated after a fire in 1812 and again in 1952. In 1889 the medresa was built even though, by that time, the Austrians had established themselves as the new occupiers and the Muslim Ottomans were long gone.

TESLIĆ

Teslić is a tiny town in the **Usora River Valley** about 20km southwest of Doboj. Since Roman times the thermal springs here have brought settlers and travellers to the area. This is another classic example of high-quality thermal mineral waters in an ex-Yugoslav setting. The area around the **Banja Vrućica** (Hot Spas; tel: 053 421 200; fax: 053 431 391) is full of lovely soft rolling hills which are excellent for walking. The accommodation at **Hotel Kardial** (Banja Vrućica; tel: 053 421 200; depending on the season, singles and doubles cost a little more or less than 40 and 60KM) is mediocre with a largely socialist decor - but nonetheless the best in town. The rooms are clean and simple with little or no extras. The hotel has a great indoor swimming pool. There is also access to the natural springs that are used in the rehabilitation centre for rheumatism, heart disease and circulation problems. The water quality is unquestionable but the accommodation and facilities prevent any major influx of tourists. However, the government in Republika Srpska is pushing hard to find investors, and you can expect to see new and more updated facilities in the next few years.

Through the mountains towards Banja Luka is a stunning Orthodox monastery from the 14th century. In my opinion **Liplje Monastery**'s (Liplje bb; tel: 053 441 022) architecture lends itself to one of the most beautiful sacred places in Bosnia and Herzegovina. It is open to visitors. In Teslić town the local **Orthodox Art Gallery and Museum** exhibitions (Svetog Save 60; tel: 053 736 363) are certainly a worthwhile visit. You may find reasonably priced gifts and handmade souvenirs that are distinctly Byzantine in style.

TEŠANJ

Many Bosnians didn't know much about this town until two rather significant events occurred. The first was that Tešanj's Oaza mineral water won a gold medal at the Berkeley Springs Mineral Water Contest in the United States. Rumour has it that even President Bill Clinton drank Oaza in the White House. This event was a great source of local pride and national envy. More recently, producer Pjer Žalica's 2003 film Gori Vatra (Fuse) was set in Tešanj. The film won the Sarajevo Film Festival Grand Prize in 2003 and was nominated for an Oscar. This finally put Tešanj in the limelight.

The old town is dominated by the well-preserved fortress that overlooks the whole city. The fortress is a result of the many different civilisations that have made Bosnia and Herzegovina their home. The fort is open to visitors but it doesn't have information boards to tell you more about the place.

The uncle of King Stjepan Tomašević, Radoje Krstić, was 'given' the town of Tešanj by his nephew in 1461. Tešanj became the seat of the kingdom where the noble Krstić family lived and reigned until 1476. Then, the Ottomans dethroned everyone, and Tešanj was no exception. The main Ottoman figure in the early days of Tešanj's new rule was Gazi Ferhad bey. His most significant contribution was the building of the **Ferhadija Mosque**, which still stands in the old town and dates back to the 15th century. The old **Eminagić House** is the oldest house in Tešanj, and is said to have been built at the end of the 17th century.

The entire town is walkable and is a really lovely quiet place for a day visit. You don't have to buy a bottle of mineral water in Tešanj, you can go directly to the public source called **Tešanjski Kiseljak** and drink your fill. Around the source is a local picnic area and swimming pool. The **River Usora** is a much better angling spot than the **Bosna River** as the Bosna is rather polluted here and wading in the river or eating fish out of it is probably unwise.

If you want to hang around town for a night or two **Motel RM** (tel: 032 650 513) on Muftije ef Smailbegovića 6 is a nice place with small singles and doubles for 53 and 86 KM. **Hotel A-A** is a bit out of town, between Jelah and Tešanj on Huseina-kapetana Gradaščevića bb (tel/fax: 032 663 609; email: ildao@bih.net.ba; web: www.mapabih.com/tesanj; 48 and 86KM for singles and doubles). The traditional restaurants in Tešanj are very good and rather inexpensive. **Aščinica** is a cafeteria-like eatery with a wide range of local dishes (including some for vegetarians). **Aščinica Boem 2** is not far from Hotel A-A on the same road and **Aščinica Saračević** is on Maršala Tita bb. You'll find grilled mushrooms, mashed potatoes, fried okra and almost every national dish noted in the section on eating and drinking. By the old mosque on Gazi Ferhad bega 1 is **Restoran Kahva** which is run by the Islamic community of Tešanj. It has quite a different atmosphere from a normal Bosnian restaurant and the food is excellent.

MAGLAJ

I have visited the town many times over the years and am always impressed by the **Old Fortress** in the old town. Many towns in this region have hilltop fortresses built by the Romans, Hungarians or Ottomans, but there is something special about the one in Maglaj.

Maglaj means 'fog' and the wide valley along this part of the **Bosna River** has mystic fog frequently rolling in, especially in the early morning hours.

I don't know why I always find pictures of a socialist building or an empty pool in tourist brochures about Maglaj, there really is so much more. **Kuršumlija Mosque** in the old town near the fortress is a beautiful example of Ottoman architecture. It was built in 1560 by Kalavun Jusuf Pasha. The town is rich in apple and pear orchards, particularly along the river. If you get a chance, climb up to the tower - the view of the valley is magnificent. It's an easy-walking town and a nice day trip from Tuzla or Zenica.

HAB Motel Chicago (061 376 924) has rooms for 30 KM per person, and a great traditional restaurant with stews, grilled lamb and baked ispod sača. It's on the M-17 motorway from Zenica to Doboj that runs through Maglaj but, regardless of its imperfect location, the rooms are nice and the service is friendly. **Hotel Galeb** is in town on Sulejman Omerovića bb (tel: 032 603 027) and not as busy as Chicago. Rooms are 42 and 64KM for singles and doubles. On Aleja Ljiljana Street in downtown Maglaj are most of the best café's, restaurants and sweet shops. Check out **Izletište Borik** on that street. Sweet shop **Carigrad** on Aleja Ljiljana 10 has great cakes and **Caffe bar Check Point** is a local favourite.

ZAVIDOVIĆI

Zavidovići is located 15km east of the main road from Zenica to Doboj. The turn-off is through the town of Žepče. The town is home to **Krivaja Wood Industries** which sell a considerable amount of wood and furniture to American and European markets. They take full advantage of the 41,000 hectares of forest that cover the municipality.

The town of Zavidovići doesn't offer much for the visitor, but its surroundings are magnificent. On the outskirts of town to the east is the beautiful valley of **Krivaja River**. The long valley stretches all the way to Olovo. The **Krivaja and Gostović** valleys are wonderful fishing spots and have several long runs of rapids for kayaking. There is a mountain lodge on the highest point in the area, **Tajan**, about 32km from town. Scorpio Extreme Sports Club from Zenica organizes kayaking in this wild region.

NATURE PARK TAJAN

This area has recently been acknowledged as a protected area. There has been a wonderful grassroots movement from environmental groups, mountain associations, caving clubs and nature lovers from the Zavidovići area that have put a tremendous amount of energy making this beautiful little corner of northern Bosnia a protected one. The mountains in this area aren't like the towering peaks of the central Dinaric Alps. Nonetheless, the thick conifer forests and endless tracks of hills provide nature lovers with a wide range of nature activities. They are just getting started so expect a few hinges organizational wise – but the knowledge and passion that has gone into the eco-tourism development of this area should be an example for the rest of the country. Here is a walk through the many canyons and caves this area hosts.

What to see and do

Canyon Mašica is one of the most beautiful canyons in the northern part of Bosnia and Herzegovina. It was shaped by water cutting through Triassic limestone with help of tectonic forces. The water divided the limestone massif into two parts, Masica and Middle Rock Face. The deepest depth is about 350 meters. During big rain falls when the canyon is unable to hold all the water, the beautiful brook of Suvodol is formed.

The floor of the canyon in some parts is only three meters wide. Those parts were once even tighter but were widened for the sake of forest exploitation. The canyon floor is full of caves which are ideal for bear hibernation during the winter months.

Canyon Duboke Tajašnice. This canyon, through which flows a crystal clear brook, has not been explored by many. The brook falls very steep from the peaks of Tajana creating a lot of waterfalls. There are some plans of collecting the water of the brook and adding it to the Suha so that the water reduction during summertime can be prevented.

Canyon Suha serves as a travel communication network between Kamenica and Ponijere. At the end of canyon is the Suha source. Along the entire length of the canyon there are speleontological objects as well as archaeological and paleontological findings. During summertime there is almost no water here because of the underground aquifer systems in the area. Hence the name Suha, meaning dry.

The Rock Face Mašička reaches as high as 250 meters on the right banks of canyon Mašice. It is an ideal place for free climbing and offers some fun and challenging routes for climbers. At the base of the rock faces are many small caves, fun for leisurely exploration – but only in the summer. These caves are often inhabited by bears during the winter.

There are over a hundred **caves** and **pits** in the region beside the peaks of Tajan Mountain. The **Atom Pit** is found on northeastern faces of

Tajan Mountain, between magma and limestone rocks. This pit is actually a sink hole which collects water and feeds the source of Suha River. Full exploration has yet to be completed due to its size and difficult access but the depth was measured to be 170 meters and the length is about 1 km. Further research is being conducted. **Lukina Cave** is located at the base of the vertical rock face at Middle Rock. The entire 200 meter length is lined with deposits of crystalline calcium carbonate of varying colors ranging from white to dark red. Similar to the Orlovacko Caves near Pale around Sarajevo the remains of the extinct cave bear (ursus spelaeus), which are dated over 15,000 years, have been found in Lukina. The cave is accessible for even amateur cavers. The **Youth Pit** entrance is on a plateau of Rapte Mountain. It is 114 meters deep with its lowest room of 70m length and 30 meters high.

The Middle Rock Cave is situated close to Lukina Cave and it was found in May 2004. This is a cave with lot of large caverns and domed rooms with beautiful cave decorations.

Interesting Flora and fauna

The dynamic eco-system of Nature Park 'Tajan' hosts a number of endemic plants. Here, you can find the endemic Bosnian lily (Iilium bosnaiacum), which has for centuries been the symbol of the Bosnian state. At the very entrance of Lukina Cave, there is the 30 cm wide ivy (hedera helix). Some 10 km from 'Tajan' Park grows the *Gregersen mlječika* (Euphorbia gregersenii fam, Euphorbiaceas), another protected plant that is on the international red list of endangered plants. The thick forests that cover the entire park host bears, wolves, foxes, deer, rabbits, wild cats, wild boars, and grouses. There are also many cave species of insects and spiders which live in the underground region of the park. The caves mentioned above all house bats, which are gravely endangered in Europe, as well as black bears. The brooks and streams are rich in fish and shellfish. Research has uncovered paleontological findings dating over fifteen thousand years of the cave bear, cave hyena, and red deer.

Activities

The upper flow of Gostović River has all the conditions for fly-fishing. For caving, the region of Nature Park 'Tajan' has over 100 speleological objects that can be explored. Alpine climbing in the park offers a lot of possibilities for climbing fans. The routes are easy and fun for climbers of all ages. The rock faces of Duboke Tajašnice, Suhe, Rujnice, Ljevičkog stone, Mašice, Middle Rock are all doable but the small climbing community there has only developed two routes: Ljevički stone (45 m) and Rock face in Rujnice (15m). Pioneers can set the stage on the other more difficult routes. Mountain biking in Tajan park is excellent. Due largely to forestry roads a large system of bike trails has been developed. Every year in May the hiking association organizes a mountain biking competition.

For hiking and biking, check with the Youth Center in Zavidovići (tel: 032 873 749; their website - www.cmzav8m.com/english.html - is incomplete). Most people here speak English. For caving and climbing, check with the youth centre's Speleological and Alpinism Club 'ATOM' (tel: 032 873 749 - ask for Almir Bajraktarević Ado; email: shima48@bih.net.ba; local language website: www.atom.8m.net/).

Where to stay

Resort Kamenice, with over 100 weekend-houses is only about 17 km from Zavidovići. It is located on the banks of Gostović River at around 400 meters above sea level. Despite its low elevation a real mountain climate dominates the region. There are three pleasant hunting lodges here: **Trbušnica** (20 KM per person; tel: 032 874 206), **Old Kamenica** (20-25 KM per person) and **Predašnica** (20 KM per person). **Kamenica** (tel: 032 871 863) serves good food in a former mountain hut which is located just above the waterfall on river Gostović.

Just 1 km from Resort Kamenice, also on the banks of the river Gostović, the tourism association of Zavidovići started to build a sport-recreation centre called 'Luke'. This place is ideal for camping and one may pitch a tent here. There are a lot of sport terrains for basketball, beach volleyball and football. Next to those there is a playground for young children. There is also a mountain biking trail which is being used for competition every year in May.

Ponijeri is a weekend-place with a much larger accommodation capacity than Kamenice. At over 1,100 meters above sea level this is an ideal mountain getaway. Accommodation is not luxurious but comfortable and quite cheap. A bed goes for about 20 KM (check with Imamovic Mevludin - 061 102 832 - for the possibilities). A ski lift is being constructed. On Ponijeri there are around 400 weekend-houses (some of which can be rented), one restaurant and two small hotels.

Resort Pepelari - this village resort and weekend spot is located on the west side of Nature Park 'Tajan'. It is about 40 km from city of Zenica. There are around 20 beds in the mountain hut (061 679 065).

ZVORNIK

Zvornik is located on the mighty **Drina River** on the border with Serbia. This town was once a micro-region focal point of industry, economy and culture. Today it is a struggling post-socialist city with many ghosts still remaining in the closet. It was a site of ugly ethnic cleansing during the past war. Many mass graves from the Srebrenica massacre are here.

The municipality of Zvornik covers 387 km2 and ranges from 135-600 meters above sea level. It is very rich in natural resources, primarily limestone, wood, and mineral water springs (notably the seven springs of *Vitinicki Kiseljak* which is one of the many tasty Bosnian mineral waters). The Drina River itself is the greatest attraction in Zvornik. Rafting or canoeing around Zvornik has some really fantastic spots as does fishing in the region south of the high dam. The mild climate and land structure suit the production of berries, plums, cherries, and vegetables.

There is not a whole lot to do in Zvornik, and its residents mostly stroll up and down the promenade along the river Drina and in the area of the court and municipal building, where there are quite a few hip coffee shops (one of them – **Galaxy** - serving good fresh orange juice). Apart from the promenades, the town has many coffee shops, pizzerias and a few restaurants serving the usual menu. **Restaurant Avala** (tel: 056 210 001 or 387 65 905 131; email: avalarestoran@spinter.net), close to the pedestrian bridge, is the best amongst them.

If you have to spend the night in Zvornik, you could stay in either

Hotel Vidikovac or Hotel Drina. Both have seen better days. **Hotel Drina** at Svetog Save bb is an old remnant from the socialist days in rather dire condition in the centre of town. Rooms are 39 and 45KM for singles and doubles. At the time of writing, their phone lines (tel: 056 230 360 ; fax 056 210 412) are cut off and you need to phone the hotel manager on his mobile if you want to make reservations: 065 532 197. **Hotel Vidikovac** (Divic; tel/fax: 056 210 245) is slightly better and charges 40 and 70KM for singles and doubles. It used to attract people that would come to Zvornik for a weekend of beaching. Now, the place is normally empty, and people know this hotel mostly because of the secret meetings that Milošević, Mladić and Karadžić held here, and because of a famous war reporter that was thrown off his room's balcony. The rooms are simple, the breakfast and the service are poor.

This town comes to life only twice per year, during its two annual festivals. In July, there is a week-long cultural festival with folk, jazz and rock bands performing on the river bank. In May or June, there is the annual canoeing competition. **KKK Drina Zvornik**, the canoe club in Divić that organises this competition, also rents canoes and water scooters at reasonable prices. If there is sufficient interest, they will also take you to Srebrenica for a canoe trip from there to Bratunac, or even all the way back to the dam in Zvornik.

Papraća Monastery in Sekovići is located about 20 kilometers southwest from Zvornik. The earliest written mentioning dates back to 1550. **Lovnica** Monastery, with a church devoted to St. George, is located several kilometers north from Sekovici. A lot of documents are preserved in this church, as is some of the work of Longina, one of the most famous Serb painters of the 16th century. The tiny convent is open for visitors, and the nuns will open the old church's wooden door with a huge brass key to show you around. Some of the icons and frescoes date back to the 16th century.

In **Kula Grad**, a village that is part of Zvornik municipality, there is an Ottoman fort from which you have a superb view on the town. This was the last Bosniac stronghold in the area, holding out for months after Zvornik had been taken by the Serbs. The area was never mined, and you can walk to and around it. If you come to this fort, you might also want to take a look at the five-minaret mosque. It was built recently and is the only privately owned mosque in the country.

SREBRENICA

It's hard to talk about this place in a guidebook. It's like writing about Krakow and Auschwitz in the same breath, somehow it just doesn't go.

After repeated waves of attack in the earlier stages of the war, resulting in a humanitarian situation in the town so critical that thousands of people slept outside during a long, cold Bosnian winter with pitiful food supplies dropped from airplanes, Srebrenica was declared a UN safe zone and French General Morillon promised that the United Nations would protect the besieged community from the surrounding Bosnian Serb Army. A humanitarian convoy was supposed to bring food and supplies to the encircled Bosnian Muslims. The Bosnian Serb army would not allow the convoy through but they did allow the general and an envoy of UN aid workers in to assess the situation in Srebrenica. When General Morillon arrived he was greeted by a cheering crowd; when he tried to leave his convoy was stopped by a human blockade. The civilians would not let the UN convoy out, fearing it was only a matter of time before they would die at the hands of the Serbian military.

Srebrenica was already overloaded with Muslim refugees who had fled or been expelled from the surrounding areas of Bratunac and Vlasenica. Most Muslims felt that if the UN did not take immediate action, the fate of the 50,000 refugees would be left in the hands of their enemies. After a long night General Morillon came to the window with a megaphone and announced that Srebrenica was now under the protection of the United Nations. However, subsequent to Morillon leaving the enclave and in advance of the UN Security Council finally declaring Srebrenica a 'safe haven', the Serbs renewed their offensive on the town.

On one occasion, fifty six people were killed as the besiegers rained shells down on the town. This prompted even a truly diplomatic and respected humanitarian, Larry Hollingworth, a UNHCR field officer to famously reply to journalists asking for his reaction to the incident: "My first thought was for the commander who gave the order to attack. I hope he burns in the hottest corner of hell. My second thought was for the soldiers who loaded the breaches and fired the guns. I hope their sleep is forever punctuated by the screams of the children and the cries of their mothers".

The Serbs would abide by the resolution only if Bosnian government forces were disarmed, arguing that if the Bosniacs were under the protection of the United Nations they wouldn't need weapons. The UN agreed and disarmed the Bosnian government forces.

In a later stage of the war, Serbian forces began mounting at the borders of the enclave. It has been said that the Serbs did not fear reprisal from NATO or the UN because indicted war criminal and Bosnian Serb General Ratko Mladić had struck a deal with the new French commander, General Janvier; the Serbs would leave the UN alone if no retaliatory action was taken against the Bosnian Serbs. Bosnian Serb troops rolled into Srebrenica without a fight. The Dutch 'peacekeepers', undermanned and poorly armed, simply watched as boys and men were separated from the women. NATO requested pinpoint air strikes to stop the offensive, but General Janvier and UN Special Envoy to ex-Yugoslavia Akashi denied the request. They have never given an adequate answer as to why.

The women were shipped to Tuzla on buses and the men, numbering at least 7,000, simply disappeared. The people's worst nightmares came true. Some men fled through the mountains and were hunted down by Serbian troops. Many committed suicide as Serb forces closed the loop around them. Most, however, were systematically executed, some on the spot and many more in the town of Zvornik in order to avoid UN peacekeepers or Red Cross workers. Mass graves are still being found today and the painful memory of the Srebrenica massacre is still fresh in the minds of many.

Not long ago the memorial cemetery was opened in Srebrenica. The dead are at least able to be buried in their home town. The memorial centre is a beautiful and touching place. Life may be returning to normal in Srebrenica, but the women and children who survived will continue to live their lives without their brothers, fathers, husbands and friends. Srebrenica is a sad place. I can't tell you of the beautiful dense forests that line the hillside or the plethora of bears and wolves that roam the wilderness to the southeast of town. Go to Srebrenica. The wounds are still gaping wide from the tragedy of 1995 but life, as it does, carries on. There are nice places to see in and around Srebrenica. The natural thermal springs, the stunning pine covered hills, and lovely villages that dot the countryside. A young woman travelled to volunteer in Srebrenica and can offer a bit more insight to this area....

Srebrenica Info, by Babeth Knol

Tourism in Srebrenica is still a bit tricky. I think the sentiments are about 50/50 divided. Some people would love foreigners to visit their town (especially young people who can feel very isolated), and some people will not like it at all. An example is the open air concert 'Silver Town' in the summer of 2003. Some people were very happy with it, sharing the opinion that Srebrenica needs to start living again and allow some happiness in town after what happened a long nine years ago. Others feel Srebrenica needs to stay like it is, as a sort of monument of what happened. People need to be aware of that when they go to Srebrenica to not upset people when they are out in the street. But from my experience, the majority of people are just very curious and will cross exam you in a friendly way.

Housing: The best hotel is S.U.R. "Misirlije". The telephone number is 056 385 726. You can find it in the south of town, almost at the end. The owner is called Abdulah Purković and he speaks German. He is the first Bosniac to return to Srebrenica after the war, and if he is not busy he will probably sit down to tell you all about his life, the war, his fruit garden, recipes etc. He charges 25 KM per person per night.

Where to eat
- Omer (little street behind Dom Kulture, cultural centre on main square) Very good soup and cevapi.
- Arrivanas, on beginning of Crni Guber.
- Abdullah (Misirlije), bit more expensive but very good food, especially fish and pastries.

If you want to eat something special, you may have to tell them the day before or in the morning, because they don't always have everything in stock.

What to do
Veneras is a cool hangout for young people near the central square. This is where all the young people gather - in the day for a cappuccino and in the evening for a beer. There are some other bars, but there are rumours that they are quite nationalist. *Calypso* is a popular spot as well. It is located on the road from the center to the north part of town, 30 meters after the park.

Dom Kulture in the centre of town is worth a visit (opening hours from 8 to 3 on weekdays). Among other things, it has a small museum. In just one room, some of Srebrenica's rich history is depicted in pictures, old maps, costumes, carpets and mining tools.

Discotheque A used to be the only disco in the region and it is very busy every Friday and Saturday. A disco has now opened in the nearby town of Bratunac, but there are still a lot of people who come here to dance to local and international pop hits.

Walking: If you walk up the Crni Guber, you will find the different springs that Srebrenica used to be famous for. You can see the remains of ice cream shops and a restaurant at the side of the road. Nowadays, you can still get water from the different sources (there is one for the eyes, one for the skin, and one for body health in general) and if you walk all the way up the hill (where the restaurant used to be) you can find little paths that will lead you a bit further into the forest. Go back if you think there is no path though, as this area is not landmine safe.

Potočari: If you are in Srebrenica, you have to go see the monument in Potočari. It is very impressive. From Srebrenica, take one of the taxis that are waiting in front of the park. Walking is possible (20-30 minutes) but unpleasant as people tend to drive fast.

APPENDIX: LANGUAGE

Pronunciation

Latin	Cyrillic	
A, a	А, а	as in p<u>a</u>rty
B, b	Б, б	as in <u>b</u>ed
C, c	Ц, ц	as in fa<u>ts</u>, ba<u>ts</u>
Č, č	Ч, ч	as in cul<u>tu</u>re
Ć, ć	Ћ, ћ	as in <u>ch</u>eese
D, d	Д, д	as in <u>d</u>octor
Dž, dž	Џ, џ	as in <u>j</u>am
Đ, đ	Ђ, ђ	as in <u>j</u>azz
E, e	Е, е	as in p<u>e</u>t
F, f	Ф, ф	as in <u>f</u>ree
G, g	Г, г	as in <u>g</u>oat
H, h	Х, х	as in <u>h</u>at
I, i	И, и	as in f<u>ee</u>t
J, j	Ј, ј	as in <u>y</u>et
K, k	К, к	as in <u>k</u>ept
L, l	Л, л	as in <u>l</u>eg
Lj, lj	Љ, љ	
M, m	М, м	as in <u>m</u>other
N, n	Н, н	as in <u>n</u>o
Nj, nj	Њ, њ	as in <u>n</u>ew
O, o	О, о	as in h<u>o</u>t
P, p	П, п	as in <u>p</u>ie
R, r	Р, р	as in <u>a</u>ir
S, s	С, с	as in <u>s</u>and
Š, š	Ш, ш	as in <u>sh</u>ovel
T, t	Т, т	as in <u>t</u>oo
U, u	У, у	as in l<u>oo</u>k
V, v	В, в	as in <u>v</u>ery
Z, z	З, з	as in <u>z</u>oo
Ž, ž	Ж, ж	as in trea<u>s</u>ure

Greetings

Good morning	Dobro jutro	Good afternoon	Dobar dan
Good evening	Dobro veče [dobro veche]		
Good night	Laku noć	Hello/Goodbye	Ćao [chao]
What is your name?	Kako se zoveš?	How are you?	Kako si?
I am well	Dobro sam		

Basic phrases

please	molim Vas	thank you	hvala
you're welcome	nema na čemu (reply to thank you)		
there is no	nema	excuse me	oprostite
give me	dajte mi	I like to	želim
I would like	volio bih	how?	kako?
how much?	koliko?	how much (cost)?	koliko košta?
what?	šta?	what's this ?	šta je ovo?
who?	ko?	when?	kada?
where?	gdje?	from where?	odakle?
where is	gdje je	do you know?	znate li?
I don't know	ne znam	I don't understand	ne razumijem
yes	da	no	ne
perhaps	možda	good	dobro/dobra (m/f)
how do you say?	kako se kaže?		

Numbers

one	jedan	nine	devet
two	dva	ten	deset
three	tri	eleven	jedanaest
four	četiri	sixteen	šesnaest
five	pet	twenty	dvadeset
six	šest	thirty one	trideset i jedan
seven	sedam	one hundred	stotina
eight	osam	one thousand	hiljada/tisuća

Food and drink

baked	pečeno	beef	govedina
beer	pivo	boiled	kuhano
bon appetite	prijatno	brandy	loza
bread	hljeb/kruh	breakfast	doručak [doruchak]
cabbage	kupus	cake	kolač
cheese	sir	coffee	kafa/kava/kahva
cucumber	krastavac	bean	grah
chicken	piletina	chips, french fries	pomfrit
dinner	večera	drink (noun)	piće
drink (verb)	piti	eggs	jaja
fish	riba	fried	prženo
fruit	voće	grilled	sa roštilja
home-made	domaće	juice	đus
lamb	janjetina	lemon	limun

LANGUAGE

lunch	*ručak*	meat	*meso*
milk	*mlijeko*	onion	*luk*
orange	*naranča*	pasta	*makaroni*
pears	*kruške*	peaches	*breskve*
plums	*šljive*	pork	*svinjetina*
potato	*krompir*	restaurant	*restoran*
rice	*riža*	salt	*so*
soup	*supa*	spirit	*rakija*
sugar	*šećer*	tomato	*paradajz*
tea	*čaj*	to eat	*jesti*
veal	*teletina*	vegetables	*povrće*
water	*voda*	wine	*vino*

Shopping

bank	*banka*	money	*novac*
bookshop	*knjižara*	postcard	*razglednica*
chemist	*apoteka*	post office	*pošta*
market	*pijaca*	shop	*prodavnica*

Getting around

bus	*autobus*	left/right	*lijevo/desno*
bus station	*autobusna stanica (autobusni kolodvor)*	straight on	*pravo*
train station	*željeznička stanica (željeznički kolodvor)*	ahead/behind	*naprijed/iza*
plane/airport	*avion/aerodrom (avion/zračna luka)*	up/down	*gore/dolje*
car/taxi	*auto/taxi*	under/over	*ispod/iznad*
petrol	*benzin*	north/south	*sjever/jug*
petrol station	*benzinska pumpa*	east/west	*istok/zapad*
entrance/exit	*ulaz/izlaz*	road/bridge	*put/most*
arrival/departure	*dolazak/polazak*	hill/mountain	*brdo/planina*
open/closed	*otvoreno/zatvoreno*	village/town	*selo/grad*
here/there	*ovdje/tamo*	waterfall	*vodopad*
near/far	*blizu/daleko*		

Time

hour/minute	*sat/minuta*	today/tomorrow	*danas/sutra*
week/day	*sedmica/dan (tjedan/dan)*	yesterday	*jučer*
year/month	*godina/mjesec*	morning	*jutro*
now	*sada*	afternoon	*poslijepodne*
soon	*uskoro*	evening/night	*večer/noć*
Monday	*ponedjeljak*	Friday	*petak*
Tuesday	*utorak*	Saturday	*subota*
Wednesday	*srijeda*	Sunday	*nedjelja*
Thursday	*četvrtak*	spring	*proljeće*
autumn	*jesen*	summer	*ljeto*
winter	*zima*		

Other useful words

a little	*malo*	a lot	*puno*
after	*poslije*	bathroom	*kupatilo*
bed	*krevet*	before	*prije*
block (of buildings)	*zgrade*	book	*knjiga*
car	*auto*	child	*dijete*
church	*crkva*	city	*grad*
cold	*hladno*	currency	*valuta*
dentist	*zubar*	doctor	*doktor*
dry	*suho*	embassy	*ambasada*
enough	*dosta*	fever	*temperatura*
film	*film*	hill	*brdo*
hospital	*bolnica*	hot	*toplo*
hotel	*hotel*	house	*kuća*
hut	*koliba*	ill	*bolestan*
key	*ključ*	lake	*jezero*
large	*veliko*	lorry	*kamion*
mosque	*džamija*	never	*nikad*
night	*noć*	nightclub	*disko*
nothing	*ništa*	police	*policija*
railway	*željeznica*	rain	*kiša*
river	*rijeka*	road	*put*
room	*soba*	sea	*more*
small	*malo*	street	*ulica*
to hurt	*boljeti*	to swim	*plivati*
toilet paper	*toalet papir*	too much	*previše*
tourist office	*turistički ured*	train	*voz/vlak*
village	*selo*	you	*Vi/ ti*

APPENDIX: MORE INFORMATION

BOOKS

History/Politics
Simms, Brendan *Unfinest Hour; How Britain Helped to Destroy Bosnia* Penguin Press 2003
Malcolm, Noel *Bosnia, A short history* London Macmillan1994
Maas, Peter *Love Thy Neighbour* Papermac 1996
Lovrenović, Ivan *Bosnia, A Cultural History* Saqi Books 2001
Glenny, Misha *The Balkans 1804-1999, Nationalism, War and the Great Powers* Granta Books 2000 (second edition)
Holbrooke, Richard *To end a war* Modern Library 1998
Gutman, Roy *Witness to Genocide* Element Books 1993

Literature from Bosnia and Herzegovina (published in English)
Jergović, Miljenko *Sarajevo Marlboro* Consortium Book 2004
Selimović, Meša *Death of the Dervish* Northwestern University Press 1996
Andrić, Ivo *Bridge over the Drina* Harvill Press 1995
Hemon, Aleksandar *Question of Bruno* Picador 2001
Hemon, Aleksandar *Nowhere man* Picador 2003

WEBSITES
The web is being used more and more in Bosnia and Herzegovina these days. It is not, however, used on the scale as in the west. Most sites are, logically, in the local language, but there are quite a few good and helpful websites in English as well. Some of them simply offer a different angle as to what is going on in the country. When checking these sites you'll find some better than others but they all have some value for those looking to get to know Bosnia and Herzegovina a little bit better.

General
www.bosnia.org.uk - is the Bosnian Institute site that is a tremendous source of inside info and links to many local sites.

www.unsa.ba – University of Sarajevo gives a little insight as to what programs are available, what people are learning and what students in this part of the world are all about.

www.sarajevo-airport.ba – Flight schedules and other miscellaneous information about the coming and going to Sarajevo are available on this site.

www.imenik.telecom.ba – Online phone directory

www.rtvbih.ba – This is the official site of the Bosnia and Herzegovina National TV.

www.bhmac.org - is the official site of the Mine Action Center. It's not to scare you, it's meant to inform you.

Government

www.mvp.gov.ba – the Ministry of Foreign Affairs site gives an general overview of visa requirements and embassies here and abroad.

www.komorabih.com – this is the website of the Chambers of Foreign Commerce. The info provided is good and has many links to other informative sites in the country.

www.britishcouncil.ba - the British Council supports many cultural and educational activities. They are very up to date on the culture scene in BiH.

www.usis.com.ba – The American Embassy in BiH is very active. The site will give American citizens all the information they need while traveling as an American here.

www.ohr.int – The Office of the High Representative in BiH is the international governing body in the country. There are many updates on the economy, human rights, reform, and general info about who is who and what's going on in Bosnia and Herzegovina.

Tourism

www.bhtourism.ba – We made this site back in 2002. It's an OK site, but won't provide you with any information that is not already in this guide book series. There are plans to expand this site in the course of 2005.

www.sarajevo-tourism.com – Tourism Association of Sarajevo Canton is good site for general tourist information.

www.touristguide-ba.com – is a yellow pages 'tour guide' for the country. It does list an incredible amount of hotels, banks, restaurants, and even car repair garages. It may be of some help if you're looking for something in particular but the organization of it is not totally coherent.

www.sarajevo.ba - a site on the city of Sarajevo, what there is to see and what's happening in the fastest changing city in Europe.

www.city.ba - current events on cultural events in Sarajevo.

www.hercegovina.ba - a comprehensive web site on tourism in Herzegovina.

www.greenvisions.ba - an informative site on general information, eco-tourism, the environment and community development projects.

www.plivatourism.ba - an excellent site on eco-tourism in the Jajce area of central Bosnia.

www.veleztourism.ba - this site covers the cultural and natural heritage of the Blagaj and Mt. Velež area south of Mostar, including activities and accommodation.

Other interesting websites

Country history	http://vlib.iue.it/history/europe/Bosnia/
Country history	http://en.wikipedia.org/wiki/History of Bosnia and Herzegovina
Country history	http://www.kakarigi.net/manu/briefhis.htm
Historical maps	http://www.nytimes.com/specials/bosnia/context/yugo1815.GIF.html
War history	http://www.friendsofbosnia.org/edu_bos.html
Towns and cities	http://www.fallingrain.com/world/BK/
Sarajevo	http://uvod.sarajevo.ba/
Banja Luka	http://www.banjaluka.rs.ba/_e/default.aspx
Mostar	http://en.wikipedia.org/wiki/Mostar
Tuzla	http://www.hr/tuzla/
Bihać	http://www.bihac.org/fotos/indexeng.html
Tourist guide	http://www.bosnie-herzegovina.net/e frames.html?/e toe.html
General info	http://www.bosnia-herzegowina.starttips.com/
Government	http://www.fbihvlada.gov.ba/#
Federation Gov.	http://www.fbihvlada.gov.ba/engleski/index.html
Rep. Srpska Gov.	http://www.vladars.net/en/
Canton Sarajevo	http://www.ks.gov.ba/eng/index.htm
Politics	http://en.wikipedia.org/wiki/Politics of Bosnia and Herzegovina

INDEX

Accommodation 65-66 (see also under the various towns, cities and nature parks)
    Airports Sarajevo 49-50
    Banja Luka 124
    Bihać 134
Art, artists and art galleries **25-30**, 33, 35, 37, 78, 82, 90, 98, 128, 129, 136, 137, 146, 149, 151 (see also museums)

Banja Luka 122-130
Bardaca Bird Reserve 130
Bihać 131-136
Bijeljina 141, **147-148**
Biking 54, 78, 94, 113, 122, 131, 134, 154, 155
Birding 106, 109, 130
Blidinje Nature Park 113, **115**, 116
Boating 106-107
Bobovac 80, **81**, 82
Books (see literature)
Bosanska Krajina 121 (and the entire chapter on the northwest)
Bosnian Church 24, 26, 34, 75, 79, 92, 136, 147
Brčko 119, 141-142, **148**
Budgeting 64
Bugojno 94-95
Buses 51-52, 76
Bus schedules (in addition to the below, most towns and cities include some information on public transport)
Banja Luka 124-125
Bihać 133
    Tuzla 143-145

Campsites 65, 98, 115, 131, 134, 137, 139, 155
Canyons
    Duboke Tajašnice 153
    Grmuča 133
    Janj 101

Mašica 153
Sanski Most's 139
Suha 153
Tajan Nature Park's 153
Una 136-137
Vaganac 101
Vrbas 97, 128, 129
Caves and pits 14, 25, 31 (paintings)
    Atom Pit 153
    Banja Luka's 129
    Bijambara 80
    Kreševo's 84
    Livno's 113
    Lukina Cave 154
    Middle Rock Cave 154
    Tajan Nature Park's 153-154
    Youth Pit 154
Cazin 137-138
Churches 78, 79, 80, 81-82, 91, 92, 95, 114, 129, 130, 136, 146, 147, 150, 156
Climate 14, **17**, 20, 99-100 (Pliva Region), 138 (Velika Kladuša), 141 (northeast), 148 (Bijeljina), 155 (Tajan Nature Park), 155 (Zvornik)
Communication 61-63
Culture (see history, art and museums)
Cultural expressions 25-30, 116
    Mountain culture 20

Dayton Peace Accords 44, 95, 121, 141-142
Demographics 20
Doboj 142, 143, **149-150**
Drinking 56, 58, **68-70**, 73
    Beer 69
    Coffee and tea 68-69
    Juices and soft drinks 69
    Spirits 70
    Water 56, 58, 68, 91, 97, 147 (the 'fountain of youth'), 151
    Wine 69
Driving 53-54, 57-58
Drvar 121, **138-139**

Eating 56, **66-68**, 73 (restaurants are reviewed throughout the text)
    Cheese 67-68, 92 and 94 (Vlašić), 114 (Livno), 116 (Kupres), 130 (Trapisti monastery)
    Meat 66-67
    Prices 64
    Sweets 68
    Vegetarian 71, 126-127, 152
Economy 22-24
Eco-tourism 57, 60, 94, 98-99, 109-110, 128-129, 153
Embassies 46-49

Fauna **17-18**, 65, 109-111 (Pliva Region), 154 (Tajan)
Film **26**, 151
Fishing 18, 79 (Vareš), 79 (Olovo), 86 (Prokoško Lake), 97 and 100-106

INDEX 171

(Pliva Region), 125 and 134 (arranging trips), 131 (Lončari), 137 (Krupa), 137 (Cazin), 138 (Velika Kladuša), 139 (Sanski Most), 147-148 (Bijeljina), 149 (Gradačac), 153-154 (Tajan), 155 (Zvornik)
Flora **17**, 65
Fojnica 75, 76, **84-85**
Food (see eating)
Fortresses 76, 78, 81, 84, 86-87, 90, 95, 99, 119, 122, 127, 129, 136, 138, 142, 149, 150, 151, 152, 156

Galleries 78, 83, 98, 114, 128, 136, 137, 146, 149, 151
Geography 14-16
Getting there, away and around 49-55 (see the town and city sections for more information)
    Air travel 49-50 (Sarajevo), 124 (Banja Luka), 134 (Bihać)
    Bicycle 54
    Bus 51-52 and 76 (general), 124-125, 133 and 143-145 (bus schedules for Banja Luka, Bihać and Tuzla respectively)
    Car 53-54 (general)
    Ferry 50
    Hiking 55
    Hitchhiking 54
    Train 51, 76, 76-77, 124, 125, 133, 143, 150
Gradačac 148-149
Gračanica 150

Health 56-57, (see also safety and spas)
Herbs 20, 69, **107-109**, 131, 133
Hiking 7, **55**, 57, 60, 78, 79, 80, 81, 93, 94, 113, 131, 141, 146, 154 (see also walking)
History 24, **30-45** (see also town sections and chapter introductions)
    Ancient **31**
    Austro-Hungarian rule 24, **37-38**
    Central Bosnia
    Illyrian period 24, **31-32**, 33
    Medieval Bosnia 24, 26, **33-35**
    Ottoman period 14, 21, 24, 26, 27, **35-37**
    Post-war period **44-45**
    Recent war 18, **43-44**
    Religious **24-25**
    Roman 20, 25, **32-33**, 69
    Slav 30, **33**, 34
    Tito 24, **40-41**, 42
    World War II **39-40**, 41
    Yugoslavia **38-43**
Hitchhiking 54
Holy sites 79, 84, 94
Hunting 18, 94, 125, 130, 131, 138, 149

Internet **63**, 97 (Jajce), 126 and 128 (Banja Luka), 165-167 (useful websites)

Jajce **95-97**, 99, 100, 101, 102, 104, 106, 109, 110

Kayaking 97, 106-107, 115, 128-129, 133, 134, 153

Kladanj 147
Kozora 121, 130, 131
Kozora National Park 131
Kraljeva Sutjeska 75, 76, 79, **80-83**, 84
Kreševo 75, 76, **83-84**
Krupa 136-137
Kupres 113, **116**

Lakes 16
    Bardaca's 130
    Blidinje 16, 113, 115
    Busko 16, 113, 114
    Eagle's 150
    Goransko 150
    Hazna 149
    Lončari 131
    Modrac 145, 146
    Orlovo 150
    Panonija 146
    Pliva 99, 100, 101, **102**, 104, 105, 106, 107
    Prokoško 85-86
    Vidara 149
Language **21-22**, 34
Legends 94-95, 136
Libraries 81, 82, 83, 92, 149
Literature **27-28**, 81, 82, 83, 84, 87, 90, 92, 129, 130, 149, 165 (list)
Livno 113, **113-114**
Lončari 131

Maglaj 152
Maps 55, **56**, 65
Media 60-61
Mills 78, 97, 98, 101, 106, 113, 127, 133, 136
Mines 54, 55, **57**, 65, 79, 84, 94, 115, 134, 139, 141, 146, 156, 159
Monasteries 26, 34-35, 36, 37, 41, 75, 76, 79, 80, 81-83, 83, 84, 92, 114, 115, 122, 129, 130, 139, 146, 148, 150, 151, 156
Money 63-64
Mosques 25, 76, 77, 80, 87, 91, 95, 122, 127-128, 136, 139, 142, 146, 147, 149, 150, 151, 152, 156
Mrkonjić Grad 98
Museums 78, 79, 81-83, 83, 84, 85, 90, 91, 114, 128, 136, 146, 147, 149, 151, 159
Mushrooms 107-108
Music **28-30**, 113

Nature Park Tajan 153-155

OHR 44
Olovo **79-80**, 153

People 20
    Interacting with people 71-73
Pits (see Caves and pits)
Pliva River Region 96-111

INDEX

Post 61
Prijedor 121, **130-131**
Public holidays 70

Rafting 128, 133, 134, 136, 137, 155
Railways 51, 76, 76-77, 124, 125, 133, 143, 150
Religion 24-25 (see also churches, mosques, monasteries and holy sites)
Restaurants (see eating)
Rivers 13, 14, 18
    Bistrica 113
    Blihi 139
    Borovnica 85
    Bosna 16, 78, 104, 149, 151-152, 152
    Buna 113
    Dabar 139
    Drina 34, 147, 155, 156
    Drinjača 147
    Fojnička 85
    Glinica 138
    Gostović 154, 155
    Gradišnica 148
    Grbarska 138
    Janj 97, 99, **101**, 109
    Josavka 102
    Kladušnica 138
    Klokot 134
    Kozica 85
    Krivaja 79, 153
    Krušnica 136-137
    Lašva 86
    Lubovica 97, **101**
    Pliva 95, 97, 98, **98-111**
    Sana 20, 122, 131, **133**
    Sanica 122
    Sanski Most's 139
    Sava 16, 119, 122, 130, 131, 141, 147, 148
    Skočnica 97, 109
    Spreča 150
    Suha 154
    Una 20, 65, 122, **131**, 135, 136, 136-137, 139
    Unac 122, 138, 139
    Usora 149, 151
    Volarica 101
    Vrbas 20, 86, 94, 99, 122, 127, 128, 129, 130, 131

Safety 54, 57-58, 58-59, 107, 111 (see also health and mines)
Sanski Most 139-140
Shopping 70-71, 94 (cheese), 148 (Arizona market), 150 (craft shops in Gračanica)
Sign language 22
Šipovo **97-98**, 99, 100, 101, 105, 109, 110, 111
Skiing 45, 78, 84, 92-94, 98, 114, 115, 116, 131, 155
Souvenirs (see shopping)
Spas 79, 85, 125, 130, 149, 151

Springs 13, 16, 68, 84, 101, 122, 137, 138, 142, 148, 150-151, 151, 155, 158, 159
Srebrenica 156-159
Srebrenik 149
Stećci / stecak 26, 33, 35, 115, 136, 147
Superstition 72-73
Swimming 80, 84, 97, 127, 130, 131, 136, 137, 138, 139, 145, 147-148, 150, 151 (see also spas, rivers, and lakes)

Tajan 153-155
Telephone 65-66
Tešanj 151-152
Teslić 150-151
Tomislavgrad 113, **114-115**
Tombstones (see stecci / stecak)
Tourist information office 55-56, 77 (Zenica), 88 (Travnik), 125 and 126 (Banja Luka), 134 (Bihać), 145 (Tuzla)
Trains 51, 76, 76-77, 124, 125, 133, 143, 150
Travnik 75, 76, **86-92**, 93

Vareš 79
Visas 46
Visoko 75, 82, **83**
Vlašić **92-94**, 99
Vranica 85-86

Walking 78, 79, 80, 81, 86, 90, 94, 113, 122, 127, 131, 133, 137, 147, 151, 152, 156, 159 (see also hiking)
Warnings (see health, mines, and safety)
Water 13, **14**, **16**, 56, 58, 68, 84, 138, 146, 151, 155, 159 (see also boating, drinking, fishing, kayaking, lakes, rafting, rivers, spas, springs, swimming and waterfalls)
Waterfalls 14, 85, 95, 99, 101, 122, 136, 139, 153, 155
What to take 59-60
When to visit 45

Yugoslavia 38-43, 76, 95-97, 138, 143, 150

Zavidovići 152-153 (see also Tajan)
Zenica 76-78
Zvornik 141, 142, **155-156**

INDEX